*Work Design
for the
Competent
Organization*

Work Design
for the
Competent
Organization

Felix Frei, Margrit Hugentobler, Susan Schurman, Werner Duell, and Andreas Alioth

Foreword by Ray Marshall

Quorum Books
Westport, Connecticut • London

Library of Congress Cataloging-in-Publication Data

Work design for the Competent Organization / Felix Frei . . .
[et al.] ; foreword by Ray Marshall.
    p.   cm.
   Includes bibliographical references and indexes.
   ISBN 0-89930-589-X (alk. paper)
   1. Work design.   I. Frei, Felix.
  T60.8.W67   1993
  658.5'42—dc20   92-34947

British Library Cataloguing in Publication Data is available.

Library of Congress Catalog Card Number: 92-34947
ISBN: 0-89930-589-X

First published in 1993

Quorum Books, 88 Post Road West, Westport, CT 06881
An imprint of Greenwood Publishing Group, Inc.

Printed in the United States of America

The paper used in this book complies with the
Permanent Paper Standard issued by the National
Information Standards Organization (Z39.48-1984).

10 9 8 7 6 5 4 3 2 1

Contents

Illustrations

FIGURES

TABLES

Foreword

Work Design for the Competent Organization is an important contribution to our understanding of high performance organizations, which in turn have become necessary for those societies and organizations that wish to improve the material and non-material welfare of their participants. It should be very clear to careful analysts everywhere that the traditional governance processes in the developed countries, especially the Unites States, are grossly inadequate in a more competitive, internationalized, knowledge-intensive world. Those mechanisms were designed mainly for mass production systems in countries that had substantial control of their national economies. In these conditions, enterprises and governments emphasized price stability and economies of scale through mass production processes with bifurcated work forces: elite managerial, technical, and professionals who needed thinking skills, and most workers who performed routine tasks requiring little skill. Because of economies of scale and supporting policies, especially the social safety nets, and Keynesian macroeconomic policies, democratic political institutions and collective bargaining, this system produced a long period of more equitably-shared prosperity in most industrial democracies. In the Unites States, abundant natural resources, a large and growing internal market and business-dominated national economic policies combined to cause "scientific management" to be more deeply entrenched in schools, governments, and industries than was true in other industrialized democracies.

The New Deal took some of the rough edges off of "scientific management" by encouraging collective bargaining and imposing some labor standards. But industrial democracy did not develop here anywhere near as much as it did in many Western European countries.

The major challenge for the United States and other industrial democracies is to restructure institutions to make them more compatible with the success criteria of a more competitive internationalized economic environment. Internationalization and technological innovations have combined to render inadequate both the macro and micro governance mechanisms that worked very well in the 1950s and '60s. (With internationalization, nations actually become more important at the very time traditional national policies have lost their effectiveness.) International markets reduce the power of national governments to control their economies by traditional means. New international policies and institutions are needed, but have not yet been created, mainly because the intellectual and political bases have not been established to replace the international economic system put in place after World War II.

The evidence suggests, however, that the economic future belongs to countries that develop high productivity economic strategies. Under modern conditions, individuals, companies, or countries compete either by reducing wages or improving productivity and quality. Successful public policies are therefore those that create incentives for companies to pursue high productivity strategies. Scientific management and free markets alone will cause competition to be mainly through wages, which implies lower and more unequal incomes. The low-wage strategy likewise greatly limits economic progress. With that strategy incomes can only be improved by using more labor, which clearly is self-limiting.

The high performance option, by contrast, offers almost unlimited growth potential for individuals, enterprises or countries. But this option requires public and private strategies to prevent low-wage competition and to focus management attention and resources on improving productivity and quality, or high performance. Basically, high performance organizations eliminate the rigidities and inefficiencies in traditional hierarchical management systems that no longer are compensated for by economies of scale. Technology and international competition combine to reduce the viability of large-scale producing units that achieve economies of scale by fragmenting work, maintaining large bureaucracies and detailed rules and regulations. Economic success now requires attention to quality, productivity, and flexibility through decentralized governance mechanisms that give frontline workers considerable discretion to improve technology and output. High performance organizations therefore substitute ideas, skills and knowledge for physical resources, which is what technological progress has always been about. Individual and group learning, or the development and use of ideas, skills and knowledge thus becomes the most important resource of personal, national and organizational success. Unlike the low-wage strategy, which uses more labor to produce the same output, the high productivity strategy has the potential for very steep learning and earning curves – limited only by intellectual abilities, not by the amount of physical labor.

High performance organizations require public strategies to improve all of our learning systems – families, communities, and most important, work. As has become very clear, U.S. learning systems are world class only in our best institutions of higher education. All other systems are geared to the learning requirements of the mass production system. If we want to be a high income country, we must develop public and private strategies to restructure all of our learning systems.

This book provides very important insights into how this can be done at work, but many of the lessons apply to schools and governments as well. It develops the European concept of *Qualifizierung,* an ongoing process to develop competence through the design of work, an area where the European experience is much more extensive and developed than it is in the United States. A good orienting hypotheses is that this process is most effective where workers have an independent source of power to protect and promote their interests, a condition that is met much better in Europe and Japan that in the United States, but better in Europe than in Japan. If this hypothesis is true, as I think it is, the Europeans are likely to surge ahead of the United States in the 21st century unless we restructure our learning systems.

These authors have an organic conception of work and learning that improves the quality of life at work and in other activities. By synthesizing diverse academic disciplines and experiences, they avoid the tunnel vision often brought to this subject in the United States. Thus, those who are interested in policies to strengthen the quality of life for all Americans will benefit from a careful study of this book.

Ray Marshall

Preface

This international collaboration was conceived in Zurich, Switzerland, in the summer of 1984. Margrit Hugentobler, a Swiss native then a graduate student at the University of Michigan, was back in Zurich for a year collecting data for her doctoral dissertation. She was aware of the similarities between the work of Susan Schurman and her colleagues at the University of Michigan Labor Studies Center on viewing the workplace as a setting for learning and development, and the work of Felix Frei and his colleagues at the Work and Organizational Psychology unit of the Swiss Federal Technical Institute on *Qualifizierung*, or designing work for competence development. She arranged a meeting when Schurman visited Zurich, and the initial seeds for this book were planted.

The original purpose of this volume was to introduce the European concept of *Qualifizierung* (the German word is pronounced qual-ee-fitz-earung) to American managers, trade unionists, employees, and others concerned with developing workforce quality and the quality of working life, and to show how it might be adapted for use in the American context. The plan was to translate the *Leitfaden für qualifizierende Arbeitsgestaltung*,[1] a practice-oriented guide for the implementation of work design processes aimed at competence development, into English. Co-authored by Werner Duell and Felix Frei in cooperation with Andreas Alioth, Christof Baitsch, and Eberhard Ulich, the original *Leitfaden* was developed in the context of a large-scale research program titled "humanization of worklife," initiated in the 1980s by the German ministry for research and technology.

The tenets of *Qualifizierung* are based on a synthesis of Western and Eastern European industrial and work psychology concepts. In contrast to the meaning of the term *qualification* in the American context, which usually refers to the completion of formal education or training curricula as evidenced by the attainment of degrees, licenses, certificates, or other credentials awarded by external agencies, the concept of *Qualifizierung* describes an ongoing process which we have translated as *competence development through the design of work activity*. This concept has been widely applied in a number of European countries where human skill is considered an important basis for economic competitiveness and the natio al standard of living. In Scandinavia, Germany, the Netherlands, and Switzerland, the notion of *Qualifizierung* (though not always referred to by this term) has been used as the underlying theory of work organization and human development to guide vocational education curricula and applied organizational change interventions in a wide variety of public and private sector enterprises. Given the present interest in the United States in strategies for workforce skill development and production reform, we decided to proceed with the project.

In our initial plan, Hugentobler would translate the original *Leitfaden* from German to English, and then she and Schurman would edit and "Americanize" the text. During the translation process in the summer of 1990, however, it became clear that the differences between the European and U.S. context precluded a simple translation. In particular, differences between U.S. and European employment and industrial relations policies and practices at both the national and enterprise levels created very different assumptions on which practitioners involved in assisting organizational change processes would base their approaches.

In a number of Western European countries the right of employees to an independent voice in decisions concerning their work and working life is built into the national industrial relations framework. In Sweden and Norway, for example, where over 90 percent of workers are represented by trade unions, national legislation mandates employee and union participation in virtually all decisions regarding work organization and the work environment, including plant closings. In Germany, where between 40 percent and 50 percent of the workforce is represented by unions, national legislation requires work councils with employee representatives in all but the smallest firms. These councils have codetermination rights on issues such as general working conditions, supervisory methods, and personnel policies connected with mergers, shutdowns, and adoption of new production methods. In addition, Germany's strong trade unions have the right to bargain over virtually every employer decision. The unions' institutional strength at the national and industry level in these countries has allowed them to permit greater flexibility in work rules and practices at the enterprise or facility level. By contrast, fewer than 17 percent of U.S. workers are represented by unions, and U.S. labor law permits employers to make unilateral decisions concerning matters *at the core entrepreneurial control*. Such lack of influence at strategic levels has been accompanied, in most American unions, by a preoccupation with creating protections at the job level. The result is an intricate system of classifications and rules designed to protect member employees' job security from unilateral managerial authority.

The effect of these differences on approaches to work redesign projects cannot be overstated. Hugentobler and Schurman, as labor and industrial relations practitioners in the U.S. context, were initially perplexed by the lack of attention in the original *Leitfaden* to securing employees' rights to a voice in work redesign efforts. It seemed to them to resemble either the naive "human relations" approach or the "employee involvement as substitute for unionization" approach common in the United States. However, the European members of the author team simply took the notion of employees' right to influence managerial decisions and working conditions for granted. They assumed that the most basic terms of employment would be settled in industrywide bargaining between unions and employer associations. Consequently they expected to find considerable latitude for initiating changes at the enterprise or worksite level. Their approaches were aimed more at "unfreezing" the entrenched bureaucratic power structures of both employers and employees. They were surprised to learn, during the writing process, of the relative lack of formal employee influence and protections in most U.S. workplaces.

As a result of these discussions, what began as a translation evolved into a new book, based on a genuine, if sometimes difficult, international and multidisciplinary collaboration. With backgrounds in psychology, philosophy, management sciences, organizational behavior, industrial relations, labor education, and sociology, we brought a variety of cultural and disciplinary perspectives to the task. Over the past decade, Frei, Duell, and Alioth have been teaching at universities in both Germany and Switzerland. They are members of various expert panels, and

Alioth has headed a national research program on questions of working life and technology. Since 1987 they have consulted with a wide variety of private and public sector firms and labor unions on projects focused on work design for competence development. Hugentobler and Schurman's perspective of the workplace as an educative environment based on their experience and work in labor education, joint labor/management programs, and action-research projects aimed at workplace development and change contributed to the expansion and transformation of the earlier *Leitfaden* into the present book. As the only American member of the author team, Schurman wrote the introduction and took the lead on a special chapter on union participation in order to lay out the challenges facing the American enterprise, since the American context is quite different from Europe.

What unites us is a jointly held conviction that work is or ought to be an opportunity for building a sense of personal dignity, efficacy, and competence while providing the material resources necessary for a decent standard of living. We further subscribe strongly to the idea that "one person's quality of work is the next person's quality of life," as our colleague Martin Morf is fond of saying. It is self-evident that there can be no competent society without individual competence. And work can be a powerful means of either promoting or inhibiting such competence. A great many of the daily hassles in our lives can be traced, upon reflection, to somebody somewhere not doing a good job – from that annoying car that refuses to start, to the airplane that takes off late, to the special occasion ruined by inexperienced, poorly trained restaurant staff. These experiences have their roots in our failure to link the quality of work experience with the quality of life and to view work-based competence as part and parcel of competence for life. We hope this volume contributes to the growth of such a view in North America.

ACKNOWLEDGMENTS

First, we would like to thank the many "invisible" contributors to this book: the employees, managers, and union leaders whom we've had the privilege to work with in many different work settings. They have, sometimes unbeknownst to them, been our most important teachers, letting us know when we moved in the wrong direction, forcing us to reflect on our interventions, and helping us develop many of the ideas and understandings presented here. It is through practice that the principle of participatory self-design becomes apparent: that each organization has to "invent" its own change process and that ignoring the involvement of the people affected is a good predictor of failure.

Thanks to the many colleagues spread across the globe with whom we have been engaged in debate and discourse on the topics of this book over the years and whose experiences and insights have become interwoven with our perspectives. Thanks to our Swiss-Canadian colleague Martin Morf of the University of Windsor for his early encouragement regarding the worth of this project and for his assistance in finding a publisher. A special thank you to Christof Baitsch and Eberhard Ulich, whose contribution to the original *Leitfaden* remains reflected in the present volume. We would also like to express our appreciation to Alcatel STR, Swissair, and Tetra Pak for permission to present and discuss their organizational change endeavors in the case study section.

We were especially fortunate to persuade Ken Mericle from the University of Wisconsin School for Workers to contribute a special chapter on the important topic of new compensation systems. Ken's contribution draws on his extensive experience helping unions plan and implement new manufacturing strategies and related changes in compensation practices.

We greatly appreciated comments on an earlier draft of this manuscript from our colleagues Edward Cohen-Rosenthal, Hyman Kornbluh, and Anthony Sarmiento. Thanks also to Eric Valentine, executive editor and manager at Quorum Books, for his input and valuable combination of prodding and patience, which helped this book see the light of day. Our thanks also go to Nita Romer, production editor.

Lynn Cooke volunteered her editing skills in reviewing some of the draft chapters. Our colleague Alec Meiklejohn at the University of Michigan Labor Studies Center contributed his time and Macintosh expertise to the authors' effort to produce this book directly on microcomputers.

Thanks also to Barbara Berger for her efforts and her competence in finalizing the desk top publishing version of the manuscript.

NOTE

1. Werner Duell and Felix Frei, *Leitfaden für qualifizierende Arbeitsgestaltung* (Cologne: TÜV-Rheinland, 1986). See also Werner Duell and Felix Frei, *Arbeit gestalten – Mitarbeiter beteiligen: Eine Heuristik qualifizierender Arbeitsgestaltung* (Frankfurt, Germany: Campus, 1986).

*Work Design
for the
Competent
Organization*

Introduction

It is no mere truism that the ultimate resource of an industrial economy is its people. One of the most disturbing ways in which the
United States has lately fallen behind other nations is in developing
and nurturing the skills of its people.

MIT Commission on Industrial Productivity
Made in America

The extent to which American enterprises are recrafting themselves
isn't clear, nor is it assured that a majority will even be able to do it.

Chicago Tribune
Recrafting America

THE CHALLENGE: DEVELOPING WORKFORCE QUALITY

The fate of American-made products in the international marketplace during the 1980s needs little elaboration. The list of
blueribbon commissions proposing strategies intended to reverse
the declining image of American products' quality and value
grows practically daily. And while there are perhaps disagree-

ments on the fine points, broad consensus has emerged on the vital importance of one factor: *the improved preparation and utilization of employee skill is the foundation on which a comprehensive strategy for recrafting American business and industry must rest.*[1] Judged against this standard, existing public and private policies to promote effective human resource development are almost universally regarded as in dire need of revision.

The widely cited report of the MIT Commission on Industrial Productivity, for example, places strong emphasis on the need for continuous education and training of workers as well as the need for alternative organizational practices for the deployment and maximum utilization of worker knowledge and skill.[2] Likewise, a massive report sponsored by the U.S. Department of Labor contains no fewer than forty-four specific policy recommendations aimed at both increasing and making better use of workforce qualifications. These recommendations include a range of issues, such as improving the foundation of workforce quality through school improvement; making lifetime education and training a reality; changing macro and micro employment policies to "put quality to work" through such measures as improved child care resources and increased worker participation in decision-making; and improved labor market research to better match people and jobs.[3]

Perhaps the most comprehensive blueprint for transforming American industry is contained in former Secretary of Labor Ray Marshall's eight-point plan for developing high performance work and learning systems (see list below).[4] The United States, Marshall argues, is seeking to restore economic competitiveness by pursuing a low-wage strategy. This can only lead to a downward spiral in the national standard of living as wages fall, unemployment rises, and tax bases deteriorate. Meanwhile, our most successful competitors in Europe and Japan are pursuing a high-wage strategy that preserves the general national standard of living while enhancing economic competitiveness. The centerpiece of a high-wage strategy is a national system of public and private cooperation to invest in human competence and skill.[5]

The Eight Components of "High Performance Workplaces"

1. Effective use of all company resources, especially the insights and experiences of front-line workers, in order to achieve continuous improvements in productivity.

2. Acute concern for the quality of products and services in order to satisfy the demands of a consumer-driven marketplace.

3. A participatory and non-authoritarian management style in which workers – both at the point of production and at the point of customer contact – are empowered to make significant decisions by (a) using their individual discretion, experience and creativity, and (b) cooperating with their peers in a mutually supportive atmosphere.

4. Internal and external flexibility in order to: (a) rapidly adjust internal production processes to produce a variety of goods and services; and (b) accurately comprehend the external environment and adjust to changing economic and social trends.

5. A positive incentive structure that includes: employment security; rewards for effectively working in groups; decent pay and working conditions; and policies that promote an appreciation for how the company functions as an integrated whole.

6. Leading-edge technology deployed in a manner that extends human capabilities and builds upon the skills, knowledge, and insights of personnel at all levels of the company.

7. A well-trained and well-educated workforce capable of: improving a company's work organization and production processes; adapting existing machine technology and selecting new equipment; developing new and improved products or services; and engaging in continuous learning, both on-the-job and in the classroom.

8. An independent source of power for workers – a labor union and collective bargaining agreement – that protects employee interests in the workplace; helps to equalize power relations with management; and provides mechanisms to resolve disagreements that arise because of the inherently adversarial nature of labor-management relations.

Despite widespread rhetorical consensus on the need to fundamentally redesign the American workplace to promote continuous employee learning and skill development, several recent studies suggest that the handful of well-publicized success stories represent exceptions.[6]   In practice such new forms of work organization as "employee involvement," "quality circles," "teamwork," "self-managed work teams," and other types of high-involvement techniques have been greeted with skepticism by both managers and employees and, when initiated, have proved difficult to sustain.   Despite more than forty years of accumulating evidence that designing work activities according to principles that give employees greater responsibility and authority for doing good work can produce important gains for all organizational stakeholders, the practice has not spread rapidly.   According to one recent study, only about 5 percent of American firms have initiated work redesign efforts that significantly alter the work activities of front-line workers.[7]   And those that have seem to have adopted them piecemeal, as Band-Aids for particular symptoms rather than systematically as new production systems.[8] Few cases on record involve more than 25 percent of the workforce actually participating, and most programs are relatively narrow in the range and scope of decisions that employees are allowed to make.[9] Not surprisingly, this relatively low level of intensity of effort has produced lots of initial euphoria and few long-term transformations.

The slow pace of change recently led W. Edwards Demming, the American statistician whose "fourteen steps to quality production" are a cornerstone of the Japanese production system, to express great skepticism concerning American management's ability to redesign their organizations in order to promote continuous improvement. "I am not encouraged," he says, "Management in this country still doesn't seem to understand that idea and is still not taking ultimate responsibility for the performance of their company."[10]

The Supply Problem

Some critics argue that the difficulties U.S. companies face in redesigning their production systems stem from the fact that this country lacks the kind of *work-based learning and training infrastructure* that exists in Germany or Japan. In these countries, strategies for reorganizing work to promote continuous product and process improvements through continuous job-based learning are closely linked to systems of formal education and training. In the United States, however, the average American workplace lacks any systematic mechanism for tapping or developing employees' ideas and problem-solving capacities, despite the fact that learning on the job accounted for more than half the productivity increases between 1929 and 1989 – twice as important as either technology or formal education.[11]

Part of the problem can be accounted for by differing patterns of investment in human capital development. While the United States appears to spend vast sums from both private and public coffers on developing a skilled workforce, on average it invests less of its gross domestic product on K-12 education than virtually every other major industrialized democracy.[12] Investment in active labor market training and placement programs designed to reduce the unemployment time of dislocated workers and facilitate the transition back into jobs with comparable pay is also lower than in most other Western industrialized countries.[13] In addition, U.S. investment in human resource development also varies greatly among different socioeconomic and occupational categories.[14] The bulk of U.S. resources, for example, are concentrated on developing the white-collar workforce – ironically the segment of the workforce experiencing the greatest shrinkage during the eighties.[15]   And two-thirds of corporate spending on education and training is spent on professional, technical, and supervisory employees. Only about one in twelve front-line workers has received any formal job-related training beyond new employee orientation or safety training.[16] In one recent study only 35 percent of the U.S. workforce say they received any formal retraining after they went to work, and the vast majority – 90 percent – never get any formal training provided and paid for by the employer. Training, furthermore, is very unevenly distributed across economic sectors: most training goes on in major firms representing as little as one-half of 1 percent of this nation's 3.8 million companies.[17] In comparison to this two-tiered system, countries like Germany, Japan, Sweden, and Switzerland have invested in broader workforce qualification through combinations of formal and workplace-based education and training.[18]

"There seems to be a systematic undervaluation in this country of how much difference it can make when people are well educated and when their skills are continuously developed and challenged," the MIT Commission on Industrial Productivity argues.[19] This is evidenced by the fact that many managers contend, on one hand, that employees with the right education and skills are hard to find and, on the other, that *they* have no training problem. More recently the educational system has been identified as the culprit. Sixty-four percent of major U.S. companies are not happy with the reading, writing, and reasoning skills of their entering workforce, according to a survey of the National Alliance of Business.[20] The deficiencies of the American educational system and the absence of well-organized, publicly funded vocational training structures typical for most European countries are rapidly becoming widely discussed concerns.[21]

The Demand Problem

Yet even a successful education reform movement aimed at increasing the *supply* of skilled and competent new workers entering U.S. labor markets will do little to solve the present problem. Most people who will be in the workforce for the next two to three decades have already completed their formal education. And the vast majority of these workers now occupy jobs that neither demand nor permit the full use of their present level of competence. The job design principles associated with the American mass production paradigm intentionally restrict the opportunities for nonmanagerial workers (as well as many managers) to contribute their knowledge and skill to improving products and services.[22] In the absence of such opportunities, workers are unlikely to see the wisdom of investing in their own further skill development. The present volume assumes that a comprehensive strategy for upgrading workforce qualifications requires, in addition to increased investment in education and training, a radical change in the existing principles of work design. Workplaces must become major centers for continuous learning and competence development. How to bring about such change is among the most compelling problems presently facing Americans.

THE PARADOXICAL NATURE OF ORGANIZATIONAL CHANGE

The fragmented manner in which American companies are attempting to respond to the pressures for change reflects the paradoxical nature of the change process pointed out by one of the great "change masters" of this century, Kurt Lewin. Lewin was one of the founding members of the modern human resource development movement. Writing about the need for a new science of human development, Lewin, comparing it to the construction of a new highway system across an uncharted continent, wisely observed: "There is a peculiar paradox in the conquering of a new continent and even more so in that of a new scientific field. To make the proper tests, some machinery has to be transported, and such transportation presupposes more or less the same road, the construction of which is contingent upon the outcome of the test. In other words, to find out what one would like to know one should, in some way or other, already know it."[23]

We believe that American companies, unions, employees, and other stakeholders in American economic performance are faced with precisely this same paradox. Implementing the kinds of change implied by the policy analysts presupposes having already developed the maps and mechanisms for doing so. Clearly, if this were true, then the problems the changes are meant to correct would not have developed in the first place. How are we to overcome this paradox? Given the constraints imposed by the present organizational paradigm, how are we to design the activities, structures, and processes of the "new American workplace?" The present volume is an effort to contribute to the process of map-making that can lead to successful change.

QUALIFIZIERUNG: A THEORY OF CHANGE

In 1978 Ivar Berg and his colleagues at Columbia University's Conservation of Human Resources Project surveyed what they termed the limited success of work reform experiments conducted in the 1970s. In contrast to the faith shared by many Americans that workplace reforms would reduce workers' complaints while increasing their output, Berg et al. found little evidence to support that faith.[24] They pointed to an underlying theoretical problem facing proponents of such reforms. Most work reform experiments, they argued, were rooted in the traditions of the human relations approach to work design and human resource development. These traditions emphasized introducing work reforms in the micro settings of work groups, departments, or workplaces but ignored the imbalance of power between managers and workers as well as factors in the larger macro contexts of the corporation, the industry, or the nation that also strongly influenced managerial and worker strategies. Many of these macro factors were outside the control of any of the parties to work reform experiment. At the same time, the industrial relations perspective on work reform tended to focus in a deterministic way on macro factors and largely discounted the micro behavior of workers and managers in the workplace. Berg and his colleagues recommended that a useful theoretical apparatus would have to incorporate both of these perspectives as well as incorporating a historical (or developmental) perspective. In practice, as the past decade in the United States has made clear, for work reform efforts to have any chance at success, the approach to intervention must attend to both micro and macro factors.

The theoretical underpinnings of this book represent an attempt to develop a practical synthesis of micro and macro factors. This synthesis is embodied in the concept of *Qualifizierung*. There is no single English term that captures the meaning of

Qualifizierung. In German, the term refers broadly to a systemic process of developing human potential, or "personality," by *designing* important human activities and experiences in such a way as to promote lifelong learning, growth, and competence development. As such the concept applies not only to the workplace but also to the educational system and other important areas of social and political life. It also recognizes the ecological relationship between the immediate micro context of work and family life and the larger social, economic, and political environment, which is typically outside the direct influence of individuals.

The choice to focus on work redesign as a strategy for promoting competence development is based on the fact that, on workdays, most adults spend more than half of their waking hours at work. Work activity therefore plays a central role in human development. Applied to the workplace, the process of *Qualifizierung* implies that work activities should be designed in such a manner as to promote the ongoing development of increased competences or "higher qualifications." Thus, work design for competence development refers to more than the attainment of a degree or certain credentials. Instead, it encompasses a person's *general competence,* or the accumulation of knowledge, skills, and abilities, along with attitudes, needs, values, and goals, acquired through experiences in various work-related activities. The sum total of this accumulated competence is available not only for use in immediate task performance, but also for general problem-solving and idea contribution. Such "surplus competence," that is, competence beyond what may be immediately required on the job, not only represents a potent force for creativity and development within the enterprise, but also spills over into important life-roles such as spouse, parent, and citizen, contributing to the development of communities, and ultimately societies, that are better able to function economically, politically, and socially.

This view of human potential is profoundly optimistic as well as realistic in its vision of the possibilities for growth and development. No claim is made that every person is a potential Einstein – the theory recognizes that people have different natural endowments and proclivities. Indeed, it is premised on the notion that equal opportunities are needed precisely because people are different. As people develop their own unique capabilities in an environment that provides opportunities to learn and practice, both personal and group or organizational competence grows.

WORK DESIGN

If people develop their competences primarily through learning as a result of experiences, often in concert with other people, then attention must be paid to the design of work experiences or activities in ways that provide opportunities for such learning. Competence development through learning at work can either be enhanced or actively inhibited depending on the specific features of a person's work activity. Thus *Qualifizierung* also refers to organizing work activities into an ensemble of technical, interpersonal, and cognitive tasks – at both individual and group levels – that promote new learning and development as an intrinsic requirement of effective performance. In this respect an employee's capacity for learning is as valued as his or her level of technical skill. For this learning capacity both fosters further development of qualifications and contributes new ideas and better methods of work.

Organizing work activities in ways that enable employees steadily to expand the range and scope of their problem-solving, decision-making, and technical and social skills creates a "demand" factor. This encourages and rewards individuals for putting their efforts into competence development. In addition, opportunities to participate in appropriate education and training programs linked to job demands help to ensure that employees will be able to master new demands and reduce the anxiety that can accompany changing job content. In an era when, according to some forecasts, the content of the same job may change seven to ten times during an employee's career due to technology and other factors the importance of fostering continuous learning cannot be overemphasized.

Viewed as a single developmental strategy, the two-pronged – or *dialectical* – process of *Qualifizierung* represents a highly practical approach to developing individuals who are not only competent workers but also competent human beings able to deal effectively with problems both at the workplace and in their families, communities, and society. In this sense the process of *Qualifizierung* can play an important role in developing the five basic competences identified in the SCANS report:

Workplace Know-How

Competences – effective workers can productively use:

- Resources – allocating time, money, materials, space, and staff;

- Interpersonal Skills – working on teams, teaching others, serving customers, leading, negotiating, and working well with people from culturally diverse backgrounds;

- Information – acquiring and evaluating data, organizing and maintaining files, interpreting and communicating, and using computers to process information;

- Systems – understanding social, organizational, and technological systems, monitoring and correcting performance, and designing or improving systems;

- Technology – selecting equipment and tools, applying technology to specific tasks, and maintaining and troubleshooting technologies.[25]

THE CENTRAL ROLE OF PARTICIPATION

Qualifizierung is based on the premise that competence development requires the *active participation* of the developing person in shaping and reflecting upon his or her experience. Without such active involvement there can be little development. While a certain amount of learning can, of course, take place vicariously or passively (by reading, observing others, attending classes, or listening to presentations, for example), such learning can only be translated into new behavioral competences through practice. Participation, in this sense, can be thought of as a pedagogical method to foster teaching and learning interactions that simultaneously build more effective work processes and more competent employees.[26] This means that everyone in the organization must be afforded the opportunity or, as they say in Sweden, *activated* to participate directly in developmental experiences.

While at first glance similar in many of its concrete practices to the famous Japanese management system, *Qualifizierung* is radically different in its underlying philosophical and theoretical premises. These differences, we believe, translate into an alternative vision of the healthy, productive workplace more compatible with American cultural values of personal autonomy, democratic decision-making, and individual development. The concept of *Qualifizierung* is also highly consistent with the historic goals and core values of U.S. trade unions: economic security, a high standard of living for all Americans, and safe, productive, and democratic workplaces in which individuals can develop their full potential as adult human beings and have a voice in their own destiny.[27]

It would be naive, to say the least, to suppose that the kinds of changes in the design of work proposed in this volume will come easily in the American context. They have not come easily nor are they yet widespread in the European context, where employees have a much stronger voice in the management of their work. Nevertheless, we believe that there is now substantial evidence that principles of participatory design embodied in this book can lead to successful long-term change in the organization of work activities in a manner that promotes ongoing learning and competence development.

WHO SHOULD READ THIS BOOK

This book is aimed at multiple audiences. It is intended both as a conceptual guide and as a practical tool for planning and implementing participatory processes for competence development in the design and organization of work activities. It is addressed to organizational decision-makers, planners, managers, and consultants who understand that meaningful employee participation is more than a suggestion program or a weekly employee input meeting, and who are interested in creating organizations that benefit all organizational stakeholders by focusing on the central relationship between the quality of working life and the quality of product or service. It is also directed at union leaders who recognize that the negotiation of working conditions must include the design of work activities aimed at ongoing skill and competence development as the central base for long-term job security and workers' influence over their own destiny. And finally, the book, we hope, will be read and used by employees in many different occupations and workplaces to stimulate involvement and to provide a basis for assessing the value or limitations of proposed participation schemes. In short, this is not a book for people interested in quick fixes or cookbook recipes to workplace change. It is for readers who are willing to learn and contribute to their own competence development through the process of understanding and engaging in collective change.

Our hope to reach this broad an audience is not founded on the assumption that different stakeholders in the employment relationship have the same goals. We are not suggesting a solution to the many conflicting interests of distributive nature that are still best addressed through collective bargaining and political action. We believe, however, that the model of competence development and participation proposed here can contribute to the future economic and psychological well-being of the American workforce while simultaneously strengthening the effectiveness and competitiveness of the organizations in which most of us spend a large part of our lives.

The book is divided into five parts. Part I places the conceptual model of competence development through work activity in historical perspective and discusses how this approach may assist today's enterprises in meeting the challenges of an increasingly global economy. Chapter 1 starts with a description of the conceptual model of work design for competence development, its theoretical underpinnings and practical implications. It is intended for the reader interested in the theoretical foundation of the approach proposed in this book. The practitioner less concerned with theory may wish to skip to Chapter 2, which presents a brief historical review of different work design concepts that took shape in the changing economic, social, and political contexts over the course of this century. This is followed, in Chapter 3, by a discussion of the challenges faced by today's organizations in responding to new market demands, rapid technological innovations and changing workforce demographics and values. Chapter 4 describes three examples of currently emerging production systems in the auto manufacturing sector and their implications for work design alternatives.

In Part II we focus on various aspects of the organizational change process. Chapter 5 presents a conceptual model of the change process itself and highlights a number of basic principles central to the successful planning and implementation of competence development projects. Chapter 6 provides more concrete suggestions for how to approach the planning and implementation of a participatory organizational change process aimed at competence development. In Chapter 7 we discuss the key requirements and structural characteristics that foster the joint optimization of technical and social systems and provide the background for group-based self-regulation and competent problem-solving.

Part III presents three case studies that illustrate the practical application of the concept of work design for competence development in the service and manufacturing sector. These examples show that while the same underlying principles guide each of these projects, the concept of participatory self-design leads to different processes and structures created to achieve the desired outcomes based on each organization's unique history, character-istics, and objectives.

Part IV contains a variety of practical tools that can be used to initiate and implement the competence development process. Chapter 11 shows how an analysis of ongoing organizational and technological innovations can be utilized to identify meaningful opportunities for employee participation and influence in the de-sign of work activities. The exercises and workshop guidelines presented in Chapter 12 provide the reader with a hands-on tool box for how to approach participatory work activity redesign pro-jects.

Finally, in Part V we address some specific issue areas that require attention if competence development processes are to be initiated successfully. Chapter 13 discusses the issue of unions and employee participation and labor-management cooperation in the context of the U.S. industrial relations system. The parame-ters of a proactive union role in skill formation and competence development that protects employee interests while simultane-ously contributing to employer effectiveness are outlined. Group-based work organization aimed at increasing employee competence and decision latitude requires a simultaneous re-design of the traditional supervisor role. Chapter 14 points to the importance of actively involving supervisors in the change pro-cess and suggests implications for a new supervisory role with broader, more rewarding responsibilities. Organizational re-design aimed at improving quality and flexibility by means of supporting employee creativity and problem-solving skills also necessitates a rethinking of traditional compensation systems. Chapter 15 presents a discussion of new compensation systems that support group-based work organization and bring pay sys-tems rooted in Taylorist work structures and focused on individ-ual production standard in line with the requirements of the new manufacturing environment.

NOTES

1. The term *recrafting* is from a *Chicago Tribune* series, "Recrafting America" (November 3-8, 1991), describing the process of American manu-facturers entering the "post mass-production age."

2. Michael L. Dertouzos, Richard K. Lester, and Robert M. Solow (MIT Commission on Industrial Productivity), *Made in America: Regaining the Productive Edge* (Cambridge, Mass.: MIT Press, 1989).

3. U.S. Department of Labor: Commission on Workforce Quality and Labor Market Efficiency, *Investing in People: A Strategy to Address America's Workforce Crises*, Vols. 1 and 2 (Washington, D.C.: 1989).

4. Ray Marshall was Secretary of Labor during the Carter administration. His eight-point blueprint was delivered at a conference on "High Performance Work and Learning Systems," Washington, D.C., September 26-27, 1991.

5. Ibid.

6. Commonly cited successful transformations include Motorola, Xerox, and Harley-Davidson.

7. U.S. Department of Labor: Commission on the Skills of the American Workforce, *America's Choice: High Skills or Low Wages!* (Rochester, N.Y.: National Center on Education and the Economy, 1990).

8. See T. Juravich, H. Harris, and A. Brooks, "Mutual Gains? Labor and Management Evaluate Their Employee Involvement Programs," *Journal of Labor Research.* 14,2 (Spring 1993): 501-521, for a review of the sketchy evidence on this subject.

9. Ibid.

10. W. Edwards Demming, quoted in *Chicago Tribune* (November 6, 1991).

11. E. Denison, *Accounting for United States Economic Growth 1929-1989* (Washington, D.C.: Brookings Institution, 1990).

12. L. Mishel and D. Frankel, *The State of Working America* (Washington, D.C.: Economic Policy Institute, 1990-1991), p. 247.

13. Ibid., p. 269.

14. Ibid., p. 247.

15. Anthony P. Carnevale, *Put Quality to Work: Train America's Workforce* (Alexandria, Va.: American Society for Training and Development, 1990).

16. Ibid.

17. Ibid., p. 12.

18. Dertouzos, Lester, and Solow, *Made in America.*

19. Ibid., p. 82.

20. Tamara Henry, "Firms Dissatisfied with Workers' Skills," *Ann Arbor News* (July 18, 1990).

21. See, for example, U.S. Department of Labor, Secretary's Commission on Achieving Necessary Skills, *What Work Requires of Schools: A SCANS Report for America 2000* (Washington, D.C.: June 1991).

22. W.J. Abernathy, K.B. Clark, and A.M. Kantrow, *Industrial Renaissance: Producing a Competitive Future for America* (New York: Basic Books, 1983).

23. Kurt Lewin, *Field Theory in Social Science* (New York: Harper and Row, 1951), p. 3.

24.   Ivar Berg, Marcia Freedman, and Michael Freedman, *Managers and Work Reform: A Limited Engagement* (New York: Free Press, 1978).

25.   U.S. Department of Labor: *What Work Requires of Schools,* p. vii.

26.   Edward Cohen-Rosenthal, "Participation as Pedagogy: Quality of Working Life and Adult Education," *Convergence.* 15,1 (1982): 5-16.

27.   The similarities of the *Qualifizierung* concept and John Dewey's educational theories can be appreciated by reading R. Westbrook, *John Dewey and American Democracy* (Ithaca, N.Y.: Cornell University Press, 1991), or S.J. Schurman, "Reconstructing Work for Competence Development: A Collective Resources Approach", Ph.D. dissertation, University of Michigan, 1992. This is not surprising since Dewey drew many of his ideas from German neo-Hegelian philosophy, which is also evident in the *Qualifizierung* concept.

PART I

WORK ACTIVITY IN A
CHANGING ENVIRONMENT

1. The Process of Developing Competence Through Work Activity

WHAT DO WE MEAN BY COMPETENCE DEVELOPMENT?

Until quite recently the common wisdom held that the process of human learning and development occurs between birth and late adolescence. When viewed this way, a person's potential to develop one's talents and contribute important achievements is governed primarily by basic biological factors such as one's intelligence quotient (I.Q.). Once a person enters adulthood, not much additional development or change in basic personality or general abilities takes place.[1]

The authors share a different image of human potential. In our view, human development is a *lifelong process* in which people continue to change their beliefs and values, adding to their store of knowledge and skills as long as they continue to encounter new experiences in pursuit of their various life goals and interests. Barring injury or organic illness, we believe that this process continues throughout life as people respond to the challenges and opportunities presented by new experiences.

Our image of human development leads us to pay attention to the nature of the environments people inhabit and the kinds of experiences that they encounter in these environments. The environments people occupy vary greatly in terms of the kinds of activities that go on there and the opportunities, resources, and rewards provided to people for maintaining and developing their potential.[2]

Basic everyday activities in the various environments in which people work, play, and raise their families present them with problems and opportunities that challenge and stimulate them to learn new things and develop new competences. Competence thus refers to one's capabilities for organizing and effectively using cognitive, social, and behavioral skills in order to achieve one's purposes and goals.[3]

Competence, as we mean it, is not therefore something that a person either has or does not have, such as specific knowledge, skills, or abilities. Goals, interests, values, and attitudes also influence the manner in which one organizes one's personal resources for mastering the problems and challenges encountered in life. Every person has a level of competence that has been developed in different ways and to varying degrees. In principle, a person has the potential for further developing his or her competence at any point during life. *Development* is defined as a "lasting change in the way a person [or group] perceives and deals with the environment."[4]

Our concept of lifelong competence development also assumes that human beings are capable of responsible self-governed action as well as creative and spontaneous expression. We term this assumption *the autonomy principle*.[5] The autonomy principle is important because it means that, while the environment plays an important role in competence development, people are not simply the products of their environments. Rather, people have the potential for managing and changing the course of their lives. At the same time it is clear that the roles we play in the different environments in which we act – our workplaces, unions, schools, churches, families, civic organizations, and so forth – exert strong influences on our actions. Our behavior, in other words, is shaped in part by our own goals, values, and skills, and in part by the opportunities afforded us to perform particular tasks, roles, and functions in our different life settings. The feedback or messages we get concerning how well our actions are meeting our goals – in our own eyes and in the eyes of other people whose opinions we judge to be important – also play a role in influencing our behavior. We develop greater competence as a result of the experience we acquire through ongoing activities in our environments.

If we wish to enhance opportunities for competence development, we need a *model* or *theory* concerning how the process of competence development works. Such a model has to include some ideas about the developing person, group, or organization as well as about the features of the different environments in which the developing person lives.

In this book our focus is on the workplace environment, since work represents such a central activity for most adults. This does not mean that other life settings are unimportant – quite the contrary. For many people, especially those whose worklife is frustrating or unrewarding, and for those unable to find meaningful employment, activity in other life settings such as family and community offers much greater opportunity for contributing their talents and developing new ones. However, for adults in the paid labor force, work activity often affects how much time, energy, and other resources they are able to devote to activities in other contexts. Not only do an increasing number of people spend more and more of their waking hours in the *process* of working, but the *outcomes* of work also exert profound effects on life outside of work. Work schedules affect patterns of family life and opportunities for community involvement. Compensation for working influences everything from what neighborhood we can buy houses in to what schools we can send our children to or what we can afford to spend on life's necessities.

Beyond these obvious factors, the design of work activity has been shown to influence how we spend our leisure time, whom we and our families socialize with, and what values and beliefs we rely on to raise our families.[6] And, even more important, there is increasing evidence that the design of our work activity profoundly affects our physical and mental health and well-being.[7] Alternative work design principles have been shown to correlate with very different patterns of such basic health and lifestyle outcomes as levels of depression, risk of coronary heart disease, style of child-rearing, and so forth. Two features of work design in particular – opportunities for ongoing learning and development and opportunities for self-governed action – are consistently associated with better physical and mental health. Not surprisingly, these two design features are also consistently associated with higher productivity, quality and other measures of effective enterprise performance. Exploring our model of the process of competence development will help us understand why this is so.

THE PROCESS OF COMPETENCE DEVELOPMENT

Figure 1.1 shows the ongoing process of competence development as a consequence of the interplay of various factors influencing how people seek to master the challenges presented by their environments.[8]

Figure 1.1   Competence as the Interplay of Various Factors Influencing the Mastery of Human Life

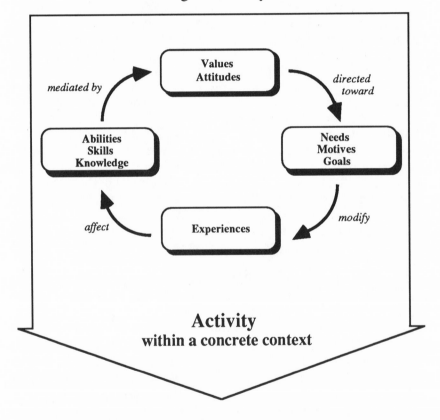

Goals and needs motivate activities that produce experiences. Through experience, people build up their store of knowledge, skill, and ability. Experiences also produce values and attitudes, which are used to help determine goals and interests. This learning and development process is ongoing throughout a person's life but is not just a kind of maturation process that happens automatically. Instead, the development process depends on two kinds of preconditions, which might be termed the *possibility* and the *receptivity* for competence development.[9]

The Possibility of Competence Development

First we must try to understand the potential resources human beings have – as members of a particular species, culture, community, family, and so forth. Figure 1.2 shows that human behavior, like that of animals, is based on biological characteristics as well as individually acquired experiences.[10] The former are *genetically* based, the latter involve *learning processes*. However, in contrast to all other animals, humans have access to a third resource to help them master their lives: *the acquisition of cultural meanings.*

The acquisition of cultural meanings refers to the process by which individuals can acquire the storehouse of "things" that a society has produced over the course of its history. These "things" include knowledge, skills, and abilities as well as ideas, values, norms, and beliefs. The cultural storehouse, significantly, also includes the tools and technologies that a culture has developed to improve the quality of life.

A child, for example, first has to be able to grasp something *literally* in order to be able to grasp it *mentally*, in other words to develop an understanding of what it is. As adults, we don't always need the sensing experience of touching or grasping something in order to comprehend its meaning. But direct experience remains an important element in learning throughout our lives, and we can do without it only if our level of competence development has reached a degree of elaboration that permits a purely cognitive acquisition of new meanings.

What are the implications of these processes for the possibility of competence development? Quite simply, they suggest that in order to develop competences we need more than the ability to learn; we need arenas in which we can acquire and master the important meanings of our culture.

That is, we need
- access to technologies and to the knowledge society has produced;
- the permission and freedom to explore them;

- the experience of culture that embodies the values and norms of society; and
- the opportunity and challenge to contribute to the development of new knowledge, technology, and culture.

In short, we need the stimulation or purpose to motivate us to develop our competences as well as the freedom to learn and grow and access to the support and resources to help us succeed. The ability to learn is ours as a matter of birthright. The opportunity to acquire cultural meanings is a matter of how access to the cultural storehouse is distributed among members of the culture. Occupation is one major way in which access to cultural meanings is distributed in most societies. Since work activities occupy the biggest part of the time available to us, and since work is of great social relevance, it is important whether or not our *work activity itself* provides us with this type of freedom and stimulation.

Figure 1.2   Acquisition – The Uniquely Human Approach to Mastering Life

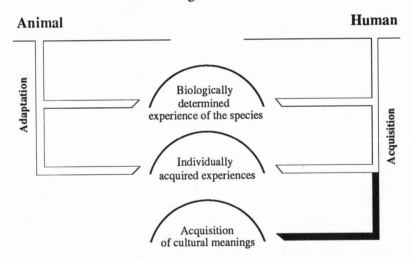

The Dialectics of Possibility and Receptivity

While freedom and stimulation are necessary, they are by no means sufficient preconditions for the development of competences. Another important prerequisite is the individual's receptivity to opportunities for competence development, discussed below. Before addressing this issue, however, we need to consider the *dialectic* of the relationship between the *possibility for competence development* and *competence development* itself, which tends to be characterized by what we have called the *Matthew principle:* "Them that gots are them that gets" or, literally quoted: "For whosoever hath, to him shall be given, and he shall have more abundance."[11] In other words, the more one has been able to develop one's competence, the more likely that possibilities to develop it even further will become available. This point is critical to understanding, why a particular person or group of people will or will not be receptive to new opportunities for competence development. If people have experienced limited opportunities for competence development during most of their working lives, the sudden provision of new demands, challenges, and expectations may very well exceed their evaluations of their capacities to respond successfully. New demands may also threaten to disrupt the existing ecology of power and influence relationships that have determined who has access to what kinds of knowledge, skill, and rewards. We will return to the issue of conflict later. For now it is important to remember the Matthew principle and the dialectic of possibility and receptivity.

Receptivity for Competence Development

If the purpose of competence development is, as we argue it should be, to strengthen people's capacity for responsible self-governed action, then it cannot be externally stimulated or demanded. It has to be valued and desired by the individual. However, as Figure 1.3 shows, the growth of a person's subjective receptivity toward further competence development depends heavily on the level of competence development already reached.[12]

Although Figure 1.3 refers to *receptivity* in a singular sense, this is an oversimplification. It would be wrong to assume that there is such a thing as *one* general receptivity for competence development inherent in a person. Rather, individuals are likely to develop very different receptivities to different opportunities based on their earlier life experiences in different contexts. Thus a person might be receptive to new opportunities for taking responsibility in his or her union or church based on successful experiences in the past, but be unreceptive to new opportunities presented on job based on a past experience where nothing positive occurred as a result of attending a training program, for example.

Figure 1.3   Receptivity for Competence Development

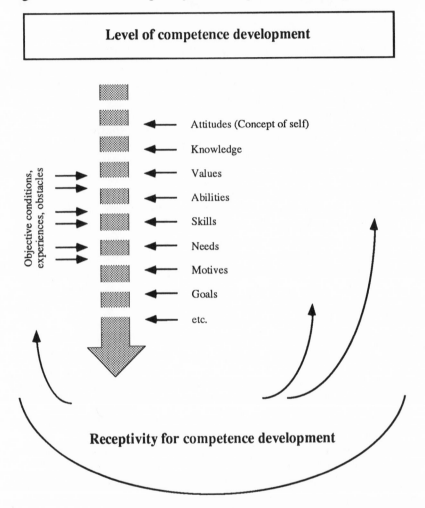

Furthermore, all the important factors for mastering life discussed at the beginning of this chapter will influence people's decisions about participating in new activities that might lead to enhanced competence development. Depending on their unique perspective – their level of self-esteem, knowledge, skills, and abilities, and particularly values, needs, motivations, and goals – different individuals might consider development of their competences as more or less possible and/or important.

Applied to the question of how to design work for competence development, the dialectical relationship between possibility, receptivity, and the present level of competence development has the following implications: To be receptive toward competence development, individuals must already have reached a certain level of competence development. To reach this level, they must be able to experience latitude (freedom) and stimulation in an area of immediate interest to them. That, in most cases, is the area of their own immediate work activities. That is why participation in an expanding range of work activities is a necessary prerequisite for further competence development in the workplace.

What has been said about the possibility of competence development also illustrates that the process of competence acquisition (in contrast to learning processes) is not limited to the individual alone. It assumes that the design of one's own life sphere can be influenced, which again requires participation. It is also clear that individual competence development is facilitated or constrained by the features of the larger environments in which the individual is embedded (work groups, departments, divisions, and so forth). These larger environments are also engaged in a process of change and development.

The Double Helix

We can now show how the process of competence development unfolds. The analogy of the *double helix* can help to clarify the concept. The double helix describes a process of competence development in which individual and social or systemic changes are inevitably intertwined. Changes in a person's mind alone are an insufficient prerequisite for competence development; these "mental learnings" have to be accompanied by changes in the social system in which the person acts in order to allow for the actual performance of new competences. Otherwise, new ideas, knowledge, skills, beliefs, and so forth remain purely intellectual and are never acted upon. Mastering new competences requires more than education and training. It requires corresponding changes in tasks and social relationships, communication, cooperation, and influence patterns of the workplace.

The difficulty in understanding the link between individual and social change is based in part on a bias we have inherited from the Western cultural storehouse: the tendency to distinguish clearly between individual persons and their environments. While such a separation is necessary for analytical purposes, in reality the understanding of one aspect is possible only in relation to the other, just as a figure can only be seen as such when set off against its background. For analytical purposes, however, we make a distinction between *individual learning processes* and *social learning processes* and explore their interrelationship in the process of competence development.

Individual Learning Processes

Learning is not solely a matter of a quantitative change in the amount of competence we have based on the acquisition of new knowledge or the utilization of skills and abilities. Rather it also consists of a qualitative change in our basic "mental architecture" – our capacity and flexibility to use multiple reasoning and problem-solving approaches to respond to problems and opportunities. In general, this occurs in a three-stage process, defined as growth, differentiation, and integration. Somewhat simplified, we can define these processes as follows:

- Growth
  - Becoming involved in new experiences
  - Being confronted with new situations
  - Taking on new activities or tasks
  - Experiencing different conditions

- Differentiation
  - Seeing known things in a new light
  - Noticing subtle differences
  - Discovering new characteristics in a person or a thing
  - Reassessing known things differently

- Integration
  - Recognizing relationships/connections
  - Discovering underlying similarities among people, events, or conditions that appear different on the surface
  - Considering multiple aspects of a problem or situation simultaneously
  - Thinking holistically

GDI Loops

Though these processes always occur as a result of our direct involvement in specific social and physical environments, they physically happen in the mind, and the learning acquired is stored in the mind without necessarily having any immediate effects on our behavior.

Figure 1.4   The Internal Helix: Individual Learning Processes

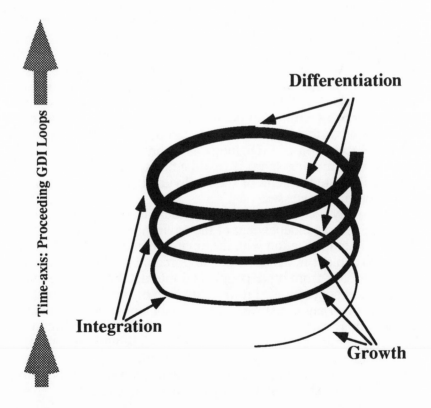

The processes of growth, differentiation, and integration (abbreviated as GDI) tell us nothing about what an individual learns, whether the learning is in his or her interest, or whether or

not it contributes to positive personality development. GDI processes are not always conscious processes. They occur almost
continuously as we deal with problems, things, or people – in
short, as we interact with our environment in the course of daily
living. Sometimes we become aware (or somebody else makes
us aware) of some of them, and then we realize that we have
learned something.

The above description should not be interpreted to mean that a
person is either in a G, a D, or an I phase at any given point in
time. In relationship to different areas of learning and activity,
the human mind can be in different phases at the same time since
it is capable of simultaneously processing a variety of things.
And there is increasing evidence that much learning is *domain
specific:* that is, people can use new knowledge or skill in relation to a specific task or activity but not necessarily transfer it to
other life domains unless the learning process explicitly incorporates application in different settings.[13] Depending on the specific
area of learning, a person can be at different levels of progress in
each area. We can assume, however, that learning processes in
general follow the sequence of G, D, and I phases, where normally many such GDI loops occur in succession. As these
learning loops continue to occur and, as we propose here, continue to lead us to a higher level, we can picture this process of an
endless succession of GDI loops as a three-dimensional spiral.
This upward-moving spiral is called a helix in Greek. Figure 1.4
tries to illustrate the helix of such individual or, we might say, internal learning processes.

As already mentioned, these individual learning processes are
not to be seen as independent of the environment; rather they can
occur *only* in interaction with the environment. The social part of
our environment is of particular importance here, as we can receive feedback from other people and interact through communication and cooperation. From least some of these people (those
who are important to us) we need a certain amount of acceptance.
Without this acceptance it would become difficult to maintain the
"result" of our learning processes and to behave accordingly
(though there is obviously variation depending on the individual
and the area of learning and behavior in question). We thus have
to understand social systems and how they change.

Social Change Processes

When we speak of a "social system" we always refer to more
than one individual. While the above described GDI loops occur

more or less continuously in the minds of all these individuals, in order to understand social systems we need to know more than the sum of all these individual learning "events." What is of importance is the interaction of the learning loops of individual members of the system.

To understand this we can refer to the most famous model of change in our cultural storehouse, Kurt Lewin's social change model of unfreeze, move, and freeze. This model will be described in more detail in Chapter 5. For now the following overview of the change processes in relation to the discussion of individual learning processes is enough to help illustrate the concept of the double helix.

- During the *unfreeze* or *open* phase, some event or stimulus creates a sense of dissatisfaction with the existing patterns of doing things in the system and creates an impetus to change. When this happens it stimulates movement in the GDI loops of individual members of the system. They may begin to look at things differently; they may start to question why things "have always been done this way," and imagine something different than what is "normal" in their social system. They may begin to recognize in themselves and in others some initial motivation to change. However, at this point people only begin to *think* differently, while they still behave as usual. In addition, nothing guarantees that they will arrive at similar conclusions about either what should be changed or how to do it. They may in fact have very different opinions, and a great deal of conflict may develop as people search for new patterns of system behavior. The process involves a lot of uncertainty, for how is one to know if others interpret a new idea the same way? Whether the initial impetus to change will result in a new level of improved system performance or a process of disintegration and frustration depends heavily on the patterns of communication, influence, and access to resources of the system.

The *move* phase is characterized by behavioral change in a social system. Behavioral change is to be interpreted in its most general sense: In work systems – the area of interest here – it means that certain measures are taken; for example, new ways of organizing work tasks are tried, the range and scope of activities are expanded, new leadership structures are experimented with, new technologies are introduced, and so forth. Again, this requires that a variety of GDI loops occur in the individuals involved. Only then it is possible to coordinate the required individual learning processes and to enable individuals to change their behavior in similar directions. At this point the change itself is still an experiment, and errors are likely to occur. To reduce mistakes and to limit the risk of the experiment, somebody might deliberately focus on the coordination of these individual learning processes. In this case we may speak of a "planned change process." But even if the change processes are not deliberately planned or guided, the three phases are likely to occur. In this case, individuals themselves will strive to regulate and mutually correct the GDI loops and adapt them to each other during the move phase. Much of this is likely to occur in a conscious process, as interpersonal communication necessitates conscious reflection. This is the period of most intense learning as people participate in new activities.

In the *freeze* or *consolidation* phase the degree of conscious reflection on one's own behavior and learning processes in relationship to this particular behavior is likely to decrease again within the social system. The new behavior loses its novel character; it becomes the new state of "normal" or routine. One starts to identify the positive aspects of the "new situation" and to enjoy it. We can assume that fewer demands are placed on individual GDI loops during this phase. The behavior required to achieve the goals of the social system becomes well coordinated and commonplace, and the occurring GDI loops relate either to other content areas or to the coordination and long-term stabilization of new communication and cooperation patterns (requiring, by the way, a lot of individual learning processes). This seemingly undisturbed balance, defined by Lewin as "quasi-stationary" equilibrium, lasts until a change in conditions within or outside the system initiates a new unfreeze or open process.

The relative inertia of social systems implies that the succession of the three-phase open/move/consolidate process occurs over much longer periods of time than do individual learning processes. Whether it is a matter of weeks, months, or years in any individual case is not very important. What is certain, however, is that systemic change processes tend to lag behind individual learning processes. Figuratively, the former encompass the latter.

Returning to the image of the spiral or helix, the flow of systemic change processes can be illustrated as shown in Figure 1.5.

Figure 1.5   The External Helix: Systemic Change
                    Processes

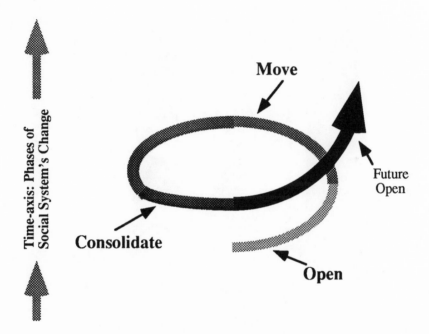

The Double Helix: The Process of Competence Development

Taking the individual as the focus of analysis, we can now explore what distinguishes the process of competence development qualitatively from the process of individual learning processes. It is the interplay or interaction of the internal and the external helix in a largely congruent direction perceived as in the interest of the individual. This interaction between individual learning processes (internal helix) and systemic change processes (external helix) is what we call the *double helix of competence development*. Figure 1.6 illustrates this interaction.

Figure 1.6   The Double Helix: The Process of Competence Development

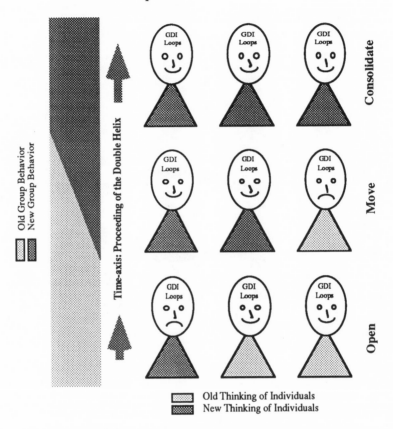

Old Thinking of Individuals
New Thinking of Individuals

The double helix model implies that for new behavior to occur (be it in relation to work activities, cooperation, leadership, or political behavior) change processes cannot be directed only toward individuals or only toward the structures and processes of the social systems of which the individuals are a part. Competence development requires simultaneous change at *both* levels. Then and only then can new behavior last over time.

Participation Is the Means

This discussion of simultaneous change illustrates why the concept of participation is of central importance in redesigning work activity to promote ongoing learning and competence development. *Direct participation* in the redesign process is the primary means through which people can acquire the level of competence required for them to be receptive to further possibilities. Direct participation also allows people to acquire influence over the possible outcomes of the redesign process which, in turn, enables them to trust that the changes will not be against their basic interests.

Figure 1.7 illustrates the role and outcomes of direct participation in the redesign process. Opportunities to participate in the redesign of one's own work activity create both understanding of and influence over the demands of the new activities. Through participating in the redesign of their own work, people gain insight into the nature of technical and organizational interdependencies between their work and the work of others. In formulating their own goals and interests in interaction with their coworkers they come to understand the goals and interests of others in different positions or areas. The experience of implementing successful modifications to one's immediate work situation leads to a positive expectation that change is possible and things can be improved. This experience in turn leads to a willingness to examine further what changes or improvements could result in even better outcomes. In the process workers may become more interested in and receptive to participating in new training and education opportunities, especially if they believe that there will be opportunities to apply the results of their learning to further improvements in the workplace.

As former U.S. Secretary of Labor Ray Marshall has argued, in addition to opportunities to learn through direct participation in work redesign, workers also need an independent source of power and influence to represent their collective interests in the employment relationship. Thus the participation of unions and other types of employee organizations in the process of designing work for competence development is an important issue, one that will be discussed further in Chapter 13.

The next chapter traces the development and change of alternative work design concepts in several important historical periods.

Figure 1.7   The Outcomes of Participation in the Process of Competence Development

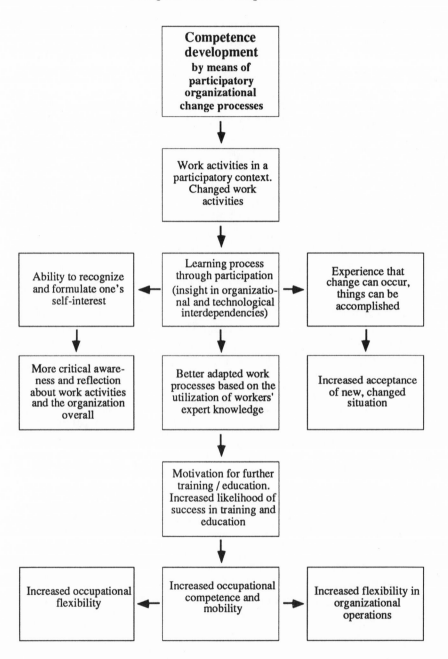

NOTES

1. A good overview of different perspectives on human potential can be found in M. Perlmutter and E. Hall, *Adult Development and Aging* (New York: Wiley, 1985).

2. Ibid.

3. This definition is adapted from Albert Bandura, cited in R.J. Sternberg and J. Kolligian, Jr., *Competence Considered* (New Haven, Conn.: Yale University Press, 1990).

4. U. Bronfenbrenner, *The Ecology of Human Development* (Cambridge, Mass.: Harvard University Press, 1979), p. 3.

5. The discussion of autonomy is based on several related views of human development. See Howard Goldstein, *Social Learning and Change* (New York: Tavistock, 1984), and T. Tomaszewsky, *Tätigkeit und Bewusstsein* (Weinheim, Germany: Beltz, 1978).

6. For longitudinal research on the relationship between job characteristics and personality and intellectual flexibility, see M. Kohn and C. Schooler, "Job Conditions and Personality," *American Journal of Sociology* 87 (1982): 1257-1286; and M. Kohn and C. Schooler, "The Reciprocal Effects of the Substantive Complexity of Work and Intellectual Flexibility: A Longitudinal Assessment," *American Journal of Sociology* 84 (1978): 24-52. See also Robert Karasek and Toeres Theorell, *Healthy Work: Stress, Productivity, and the Reconstruction of Working Life* (New York: Basic Books, 1990).

7. Karasek and Theorell, *Healthy Work.*

8. More rigorous theoretical descriptions of the model of competence development presented here may be found in Felix Frei, Werner Duell, and Christof Baitsch, *Arbeit und Kompetenzentwicklung* (Bern, Switzerland: Huber, 1984).

9. Ibid., p. 31.

10. Ibid., p. 42.

11. Matthew 13:12.

12. Frei, Duell, and Baitsch, *Arbeit und Kompetenzentwicklung*, p. 98.

13. B. Rogoff and J. Lave, eds., *Everyday Cognition* (Cambridge, Mass.: Harvard University Press, 1984); M.K. Singley and J.R. Anderson, *The Transfer of Cognitive Skill* (Cambridge, Mass.: Harvard University Press, 1989).

2. Design Concepts in Their Historical Context

Designing work for competence development implies nothing less than a *fundamental rethinking* of the concepts of organization, coordination, and control that characterized early factory life from the dawn of industrialization through its most elaborate representation in the form of Frederick Taylor's scientific management principles.

This chapter provides a brief historical overview of the major organizational and work design concepts preceding and influencing the characteristics of today's workplace. Economic, political, social, and technological developments changed the design principles characterizing the management, coordination, and production processes of the emerging modern enterprise, as did evolving images of human nature. The different design eras are shown in Table 2.1 and described in more detail below. While these design concepts are discussed in chronological order, one did not simply replace the next over time.

Thus, if Taylorism is no longer a distinct school of thought today, it is because its principles have become synonymous with the concept of work organization, extending from the production of goods and services to the education of children and the training of adults in twentieth-century America. Indeed, these principles are often referred to as the "American mass production paradigm." [1]

Table 2.1   Overview: Design Concepts in Their Historical Context

ECONOMIC, POLITICAL, SOCIAL CONTEXT	DESIGN CONCEPT	DESIGN PRINCIPLES	IMAGES OF HUMAN NATURE	HUMAN ROLE / MANAGEMENT FOCUS
American Revolution / Early factories	"Driving Method"	Focus on technology; production, output increase	People as self-interested individuals resisting control	Human effort auxiliary to technical system / Management by threat and intimidation
Mass distribution (railroads) / Early mass production	Taylorism Scientific Management Fordism	Scientific task analysis; separation of planning and execution functions; minimizing job content	People as economic beings	Human effort auxiliary to technical system / Focus on system coordination control
Post Depression	Human Relations	Unchanged work organization; introduction of personnel management function to address psychological needs	People as social beings	Human effort auxiliary to technical system / Focus on social "climate" to improve motivation
Market expansion / Worker dissatis-faction	Job Enrichment	Delegation; management by objectives; expanding job content	People as intending self-actualization	Self-motivation through responsibility for task execution / Theory Y
Global economy / Quality focus / Changing values	Sociotechnical Systems	Joint optimization of social and technical system, autonomous work groups	People as active learners, seeking perso-nal and competence development	Work group self-regulation / Boundary regulation, team coaching

HARNESSING LABOR'S POWER IN THE EARLY INDUSTRIAL AGE

Throughout the eighteenth and nineteenth centuries, early European industrial entrepreneurs struggled to achieve a measure of labor discipline that would allow them to accomplish the intensification of production for which the early factories had been established. Traditional work patterns such as those of agricultural workers or cottage weavers vacillated between periods of intense effort and leisure. Achieving sustained work activity meant battling the industrial laborer's prevailing subsistence mentality. In an effort to protect themselves from the harsh demands that early industrial labor imposed on their bodies, workers alternated between intense spurts of activity and rebellion against confinement and discipline. A combination of elaborate fines, threats, and punishments was utilized to overcome the ambivalence of the workers and the multitude of ways they used to limit output and exhaustion. Numerous historical accounts present a vivid picture of the difficulties faced by the industrial entrepreneurs and their managers in instilling work habits that would allow them to utilize more efficiently the capital invested in new machinery.[2]

> The ship's carpenter in one New York shipyard describes the typical workday: cakes and pastries in the early morning and again in the late afternoon, a trip to the grog shop by eleven for whiskey, a big lunch at half past three, a visit from the candyman at five, and supper, ending the workday at sundown.
>
> Or, as Josiah Tucker described domestic weavers transplanted to factory life: "They think it no crime to get as much wages and to do as little for it as they possibly can, to lie and cheat and do any other bad thing, provided it is only against their master whom they look upon as their common enemy, with whom no faith is to be kept... Their only happiness is to get drunk and make life pass away with as little thought as possible."[3]

American industrialists faced an even greater problem than their European counterparts. The early American working class was formed just prior to and after the American Revolution. Central to the cultural beliefs and values of Revolutionary America was a view of human nature as inherently self-interested and seeking to acquire power over other people. Samuel Adams, speaking for the Boston Town Meeting, summarized the prevailing view, "that ambition and lust of power above the law are predominant passions in the breasts of most men."[4]   From the beginning, American "democratic republicanism" linked economic independence with political freedom.[5]

The well-known statements of the Founding Fathers, such as Thomas Jefferson's famous "dependence begets subservience and suffocates the germ of virtue," or Alexander Hamilton's "give a man power over my subsistence and he has a right to my whole moral body," were used by workers first to obtain political enfranchisement and then to oppose the economic inequalities and injustices associated with the growth of nineteenth-century industrial capitalism and wage labor. American workers identified wage labor with the loss of political independence and personal freedom and resisted in many ways.

Despite the widespread application of what was known as the "driving method" – a combination of supervisory authoritarian combativeness and physical intimidation – the work ethic in early twentieth-century America remained a major problem for entrepreneurs. One survey suggested that between 1905 and 1917, the majority of industrial workers changed jobs at least once every three years. For example, turnover reached 232 percent in New York City garment shops in 1912, 252 percent in a sample of Detroit factories in 1916, and 370 percent at the Ford Motor Company in 1913.[6]

Controlling skilled workers presented a different problem for entrepreneurs. The knowledge embodied in the activities of the craftsmen distinguished their work from that of the laborers. Thus, while they looked down on the frolicking, drinking, and escapism common to many of the laborers, craftsworkers used their "functional autonomy"[7] and management's dependence on their know-how to limit or withhold compliance with prescribed standards of output and discipline.

THE EMERGENCE OF THE MODERN BUSINESS ENTERPRISE

Understanding the development of predominant forms of work organization requires a brief history of the emergence of the modern business enterprise.[8] Characterized by multiple distinct operating units and managed by a hierarchy of salaried executives, this mode of organizing industrial activity is a relatively recent phenomenon dating back to the late nineteenth century. As the traditional family and financier controlled enterprises typical of the last century grew in size and diversity, ownership and management of firms became increasingly divorced. The growing dominance of career managers who came to determine the structures and policies of the modern firm shifted the emphasis from maximizing current profits to long-term stability and growth. The continued existence of the enterprise became essential for the lifetime careers of professional managers. By the middle of this century, the transformation from family and finance capitalism to managerial capitalism was complete as the salaried managers of a relatively small number of large enterprises coordinated the flow of goods and services and allocated the resources in major sectors of the American economy.

Technological innovation, rapid population growth, and expanding markets were central to increasing the complexity and speed of the process of production and distribution. Mass distribution preceded mass production. The first modern enterprises were the expanding railroad and telegraph companies in the 1850s and 1860s. The coordination of the traffic flow and the safety of passengers required elaborate administrative procedures and organizational innovation. The revolution in mass production came more slowly, as it required new technologies and processes. Thus, while mass distribution was largely based on organizational innovation and improvements, breakthroughs in mass production relied on the development and utilization of more efficient machinery and higher quality raw materials along with the intensified application of energy. The adoption of continuous process machines that turned out products automatically greatly increased output per worker. In the early 1880s, these new processes became widespread in the tobacco and the refining and distilling industries. The metalworking industries faced a bigger challenge. They relied on a greater variety of raw materials and needed to coordinate multiple subunits for the production of castings and moldings and the assembly of complex products such as stoves, firearms, sewing machines, and typewriters. The initial focus was largely on refining the technology. But the prolonged depression of the 1870s meant a continuing drop in demand and an increase in unused capacity. As a result interest shifted to organizational innovation to improve efficiency and productivity.

The pioneers of modern management in the railroad companies had all been trained civil engineers experienced in railroad and bridge construction before moving into the management of these enterprises. Similarly, major organizational and management innovation in the mass production sector originated in the

American Society of Mechanical Engineers (ASME). A number of the papers presented at its 1886 meeting shifted the focus of interest from technology to cost and other capital accounting methods and to problems of managerial coordination and control.

While rather complex systems of internal cost accounting and controls were proposed and implemented in many firms, the basic weakness in these recordkeeping systems – the foremen's or workers' lack of interest in filling out the requested forms – was quickly recognized. In response, a number of metalworking firms developed what they termed gainsharing plans, which offered workers and their foremen higher pay for increased output. At the 1889 annual meeting of ASME, Henry Towne, the senior executive of a metalworking manufacturer, described a scheme in which any reduction in unit costs achieved through improved equipment and plant design, more effective scheduling, and fuller use of the machines and materials would be shared equally between the company and the workers. This and similar widely adopted systems were criticized by Frederick W. Taylor from the Midvale Steel Company. Taylor pointed out that the costs and the resulting savings should not, as was generally done, be based on past experience; rather, standard time and output should be determined "scientifically" through detailed job analyses and time and motion studies of the tasks involved. Applying the carrot as well as the stick, he argued for a differential piece rate; workers who did not meet the standard set would receive lower pay, while those who exceeded the rate would receive higher pay.[9] Taylor soon became the nation's best known expert on factory management with his principles of "scientific management."

But Frederick Taylor applied himself to more than the determination of output standards. He was convinced that the function of the general foreman, the key figure in traditional factory organization, could not be competently performed by one individual. Instead, these tasks should be "scientifically" subdivided and moved to a planning department. The factory as a whole should be administered through a number of highly specialized functions. While Taylor's proposal for extreme specialization proved unacceptable to many manufacturers and was criticized for its focus on task analysis, which neglected the synthesis of the organization as a whole, many of Taylor's concepts were integrated into the organization of the modern American firm.

increasing the amount of pig iron workers handled from 12.5 ns to 47.5 tons per worker per day, without increasing workers' xhaustion level. In addition, Taylor claimed, the workers were ow more satisfied, since their wage increased significantly. While this new way of organizing work tasks decreased the cenrality of worker experience, skill, and knowledge in the production process, it gave management new control over the work process. The effect was maximum interchangeability of workers and minimum dependence on workers' abilities and motivation.

Five key design principles essentially characterize Taylorism:

1. *Shift all responsibility for the organization of work from the worker to the manager;* managers should do all the thinking relating to the planning and design of work, leaving the workers with the task of implementation.
2. *Use scientific methods* to determine the most efficient way of doing work; design the worker's task accordingly, specifying the *precise* way in which the work is to be done.
3. *Select* the best person to perform the job thus designed.
4. *Train* the worker to do the work efficiently.
5. *Monitor* worker performance to ensure that appropriate work procedures are followed and that appropriate results are achieved.[12]

With the application of these five principles, a structure of work was created narrow enough to eliminate the individual worker's discretion and independent judgment, presumably leaving the worker no choice other than to follow the prescribed "right" way to do the job. However, it was the development of corresponding logistic principles incorporated in Henry Ford's moving assembly line that actually signaled the broader transformation of previous craft production structures to the modern mode of mass production. Inspired by the assembly line concept during a 1913 visit to Chicago slaughterhouses, Ford's highly mechanized conveyor belt technology gave birth to what has become known as Fordism: combining mechanized and highly fragmented tasks with management control over the work pace and production output. The function carried out by the worker became subordinate to the function of the machine. Direction and guidance were built into the technological design and the resultant work system. This is best expressed in Ford's famous dictum that "any improvement the worker makes on the process will be fatal."

Though Taylor's methods were aimed at establishing managerial control and coordination over the work process on the as-

TAYLORISM

Though known as the father of scientific manag
did not invent something radically new. As histo:
gued, Taylor set out "to synthesize and present as
coherent whole ideas which had been germinating ;
force in Great Britain and the United States through
teenth century. He gave to a disconnected series
and experiments a philosophy and a title."[10]

The driving force behind Taylor's early experim
obsession with efficiency and his hatred of wasted ef.
tute observer and skilled craftsman himself, Taylc
aware that each worker approached his or her task in
cratic manner, doing things slightly differently and fi.
to make the task easier. His conclusion was that th
different ways of doing things were not all optimally e
equally efficient. Also, reliance on workers' skills
knowledge, particularly that of the skilled craftsworke
management's control over the efficiency of production
lor noted:

> The managers recognize frankly that the workmen, include:
> twenty or thirty trades, who are under them, possess this r
> traditional knowledge, a large part of which is not in the pos:
> of management. The management, of course, includes forem
> superintendents, who themselves have been first class worl
> their trades. And yet these foremen and superintendents kno\
> ter than any one else, that their own knowledge and personal
> fall far short of the combined knowledge and dexterity of a
> workmen under them.[11]

Taylor concluded that the implicit knowledge of the
could be carefully studied in action and explicated in o:
yield its secrets. Work tasks had to be observed, analyze
measured in meticulous ways in order to discover "the on
way" for doing a specific task. Taylor translated his finding
step-by-step detailed instructions for workers that went as
prescribing when a worker had to sit down and relax in or
preserve the body's capability to work over an extended peri
time.

In one of his first major experiments, Taylor described th
troduction of his system in the pig iron handling process at E
lehem Steel. By dictating the exact timing of each operation
the result to be achieved by the end of the day, Taylor succee

sumption that this would improve efficiency and quality, he believed, along with many of his engineering colleagues, that workers' attempts to restrain their efforts was perfectly rational and in line with their own interests. Thus he proposed that the productivity increases to be gained from more efficient task organization should be shared in the form of the differential piece rate system. But, contrary to Taylor's proposal, management frequently intensified the pace of effort by changing piece rates as workers learned to meet the standards. In general, workers showed little enthusiasm for the new system of machine-paced labor, though the application of Taylorist methods improved on the strenuous ways of accomplishing tasks in many cases. Workers' resistance to this new form of work organization was reflected in absenteeism rates at Ford's famous Highland Park factory: to maintain a workforce of 14,000, Ford had to hire 52,000 workers in 1913. In order to tackle his almost unmanageable turnover problem, Ford took drastic action and doubled the daily wage to an unheard of five dollars in early 1914.

Fordism flourished in an economic environment in which the output quantity/price ratio was the key to market leadership. As Henry Ford proved beyond doubt, success in supplier-dominated markets depended on the ability to increase output at relatively low price based on largely standardized products and a far-reaching mechanization of the manufacturing process. The price of the Model T came down from $780 in 1910-11 to $360 just before World War I.[13]

The growth and economic payoffs of Fordist mass production, modeled after Taylor's principles over the following decades, firmly established this approach to industrial production in the American workplace. It continues to be the dominant form of work organization today, although its limitations are becoming increasingly obvious in the rapidly changing economic and social environment (see list below).

Taylorism works well if

- tasks are simple and clearly defined;
- market demands are stable and the service or good produced is likely to be accepted by the market;
- the goal is to produce the exact same product or service for as long as possible;
- manual precision is important;
- the human "parts" are obedient and behave exactly as prescribed.

The limitations of Taylorism emerge if an organization

- has great difficulty in adapting to changing circumstances;
- is inclined to develop a disproportionate and unquestioned bureaucracy;
- has little scope for flexibility if organization members start deviating from organizational goals and policies and focusing on their own interest;
- the lowest hierarchical level is characterized by a large number of monotonous and taxing jobs.[14]

THE HUMAN RELATIONS MOVEMENT

Despite the widespread adoption of Taylor's principles, many doubted and resisted Taylorism from its inception. American unions, for example, convinced Congress to prohibit the use of stop watches, the key instrument of Taylorist time and motion studies, in the public sector. Doubts about the all-encompassing utility of Taylorism emerged in the scientific community in the twenties and thirties as scientists, following traditional Taylorist principles in their study design, set out to explore the relationship between working conditions and productivity.

One study involving the Hawthorne utility company became particularly famous. The study's goal was to assess the impact of lighting changes on workers' output. As the researchers improved the lighting, output of the women workers in the plant increased. The lighting was further improved, leading to additional performance gains. After this happened repeatedly, the scientists decided to reverse the experiment. They reduced the lighting, but the women's productivity increased further, negating the researchers' original hypothesis. Elton Mayo, the leading scientist in the experiment, and his colleagues concluded that it was not the change in lighting, but the public attention and the researchers' interest in the women's work that had led them to intensify their efforts. Known as the Hawthorne effect, this insight represented the beginning of a movement that viewed people as *socially rather than purely economically motivated.*

These changing assumptions about human nature did not challenge the Taylorist structure of work. Rather, the focus shifted to the work environment and worker management. The growing industrialization, in part a result of the integration of Taylorist principles with Fordist production methods, had increased the standard of living such that people started to focus on more than material subsistence. In other words, workers could "afford" to be social beings, reflecting needs other than mere material concerns.

The human relations movement contributed to the strengthening of managerial authority, which had been badly shaken by the Great Depression. Mayo agreed with the necessity of unity of purpose and central authority. Yet managerial authority was not to be based on coercion but rather on scientific training that would allow managers to set their own emotions aside and, through careful training, acquire the knowledge and technical skills needed to systematize operations and organize cooperation.[15] While scientific management had systematized and expropriated workers' knowledge and skill, the manager was now to be trained to understand the workers' "psycho-logic in ways that workers themselves could not."[16] Through such rational and logical communication, managers would thus enhance the possibility of unified command by better listening to workers' perspectives and, in turn, provide them with more facts about the enterprise.[17] However, scientific management principles continued to dominate the process of production, with workers having little or no influence over the content of their work. If anything, the view of management as "the guardian of special knowledge," able to understand information and its implications for coordination, administration, and profitability, carried with it the responsibility to protect the rights of ownership, while workers could not be trusted to act in ways that supported the well-being of the firm.[18]

Central to the human relations approach was the improvement of the organizational climate, stemming from the assumption that motivation increases if workers feel good, and that workers feel good in a pleasant environment with supportive social relationships. The work environment thus was not to be organized so as to narrowly channel work efforts and prevent deviation, but rather to create the conditions conducive to performance. Personnel departments now aimed toward sustaining work output by fostering communication, often through superficial improvements of the work environment. As cynics have suggested, the worker continued to screw in the same two bolts all day long, but the drudgery was now sweetened by a radio playing in the background, flowers on the table, and an occasional friendly word.

JOB ENRICHMENT

The post-World War II economy in the United States was characterized by the absence of international competition as well as expanding markets, product diversification, and a steadily improving standard of living for the majority of American workers. The sixties heralded a gradual disintegration of supplier markets as consumer preferences gained in importance and the ability to meet them became a key competitive element. At the same time, employee skill and knowledge gained in importance; operator mistakes on the capital-intensive, technologically advanced production equipment became increasingly costly. In the context of a booming economy, a tighter labor market, social unrest, and the emergence of postmaterialist values, many workers became unwilling to follow the detailed instructions and orders inherent in Taylorist work organization. Absenteeism and turnover were rampant in the auto industry – the epitome of Fordism – and the blue-collar worker blues became a much discussed topic.

It was against this background that American psychologist Frederick Herzberg launched a major study asking employees to describe a recent work situation in which they had either felt particularly unhappy or particularly satisfied.[19] The results of his study led Herzberg to propose the so-called *two factor theory of job satisfaction* suggesting that ameliorating the factors that led to job dissatisfaction would not necessarily increase workers' job satisfaction. Where factors such as wages, external working conditions, the behavior of supervisors, and the organizational climate are judged negatively, they contribute to job dissatisfaction. By contrast, the ingredients of real job satisfaction, according to Herzberg, stem from different sources. The workers surveyed described those situations as particularly satisfying where they felt challenged by a task, where they could apply their skills and talents, and where they had a sense of accomplishment.

Herzberg viewed his findings as confirming the theory of another American psychologist, Abraham Maslow. Maslow had proposed the existence of five basic human needs: elementary physiological needs for food, the need for shelter and security, social needs for acceptance and being loved, so-called ego needs for respect and appreciation, and finally the desire to develop and grow, called the desire for self-actualization. Of relevance, though not a uniformly accepted premise, was Maslow's contention that these needs are hierarchically ordered. In other words, only if the primary needs are sufficiently met will the higher-level needs develop in ascending order. These ideas fit with Herzberg's theory. Suggesting that the need for food and shelter had been satisfied for most people in industrialized countries, along with elementary ego needs in the form of basic social respect, people were now ready to express the need for self-realization and motivation through the work content itself.

Based on these notions, the design principles of job rotation, job enlargement, and job enrichment emerged. Herzberg focused on job enrichment since, as he pointed out, zero plus zero still equals zero, as in the case of simply rotating different monotonous and unsatisfying jobs, for example. He emphasized that jobs had to be enriched so as to include planning, preparation, and control tasks in addition to mere execution functions. Conceptually, this indicated a radical departure from Taylorist principles of strict separation of planning/control and executing functions. According to the proponents of job enrichment, work motivation was no longer to be regulated through technology and/or external motivation systems. Instead workers were to be encouraged to "regulate" themselves, to take on responsibilities and become interested in their work.

These changes demanded a form of managerial coordination and control relying on workers' willingness to cooperate in achieving company goals. But what would encourage workers to cooperate given management's image of them as incapable of taking responsibility? The solution was supplied by Douglas McGregor's "Theory Y" style of management, which he contrasted with "Theory X," the prevailing approach fostered by scientific management.[20] McGregor recognized that the assumptions about human nature and the corresponding Taylorist work design principles were no longer functional in the emerging economic environment, in part because skilled work is hard to supervise, and because the Theory X style promotes conflict between employer and employees. The task of management was to create a sense of overlapping interests between the employee and the organization. If people believed that by furthering the company's interests they would also be furthering their own, then they would be motivated to perform without excessive external supervision. Theory Y represented an alternative set of assumptions that would lead to the development of common goals.

Comparing Theory X with Theory Y, McGregor illustrated the self-fulfilling prophecy of assumptions about human behavior (Figure 2.1). Assuming, for example, that people are basically lazy and try to avoid responsibility (Theory X image), managers will tend to force or cajole people into doing the task, using various mechanisms to control and supervise them. Workers are not supposed to make any decisions, and must be motivated through the use of threats or financial incentives, bonuses, and so on. The likely outcome is that people will not be interested in their work, will focus on money only, and will try to find ways to circumvent the controls. In other words, they will behave according to expectations. As this will confirm the original assumption, the manager will probably increase instructions and controls. By contrast, Theory Y assumes that people can be trusted to take on responsibilities. Treated accordingly, they are likely to confirm the positive expectations.

Figure 2.1   Images of Human Nature and Their Effects

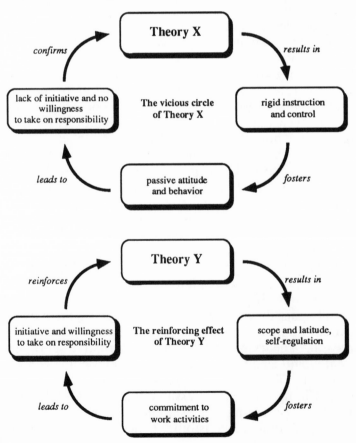

While the Herzberg approach redefined the role of the person in the workplace, raising serious questions about traditional management theory, it was essentially individualistic and psychology-based and assigned the design of "enriched jobs" to experts brought in by management. The appropriateness of existing organizational structures and production processes was not seriously questioned and remained largely unchallenged.

SOCIOTECHNICAL SYSTEMS

Even before the emergence of the American job enrichment movement, another approach radically departing from Taylorism and human relations developed in Europe. In the British coal mining industry, which provided the central source of energy at the time of postwar reconstruction, stagnant productivity, labor disputes, and high worker turnover prompted to a number of research projects conducted by scientists of the Tavistock Institute. The focus was on improved labor-management relations and the diffusion of innovative work practices and organizational arrangements, in an effort to increase productivity without major capital investments. In this context, the almost accidental discovery of a novel approach to organizing work in a coal mine in South Yorkshire led to the formulation of a set of principles that became the foundation of the sociotechnical systems approach.

> Work organization in the new Haighmoor seam consisted of a set of relatively autonomous groups interchanging roles and shifts and regulating their affairs with a minimum of supervision. Cooperation between task groups was evident: personal commitment was obvious, absenteeism low, accidents infrequent, productivity high. The men had evolved a form of work organization based on practices common in unmechanized days, when small groups, who took responsibility for the entire cycle, had worked autonomously. These practices had disappeared as the pits became progressively more mechanized in relation to the introduction of "longwall" working. This had enlarged the scale of operations and led to aggregates of men of considerable size having their jobs broken down into one-man-one-task roles, while coordination and control had been externalized in supervision, which had become coercive. Now they had found a way at a higher level of mechanization of recovering the group cohesion and self-regulation they had lost and of advancing their power to participate in decisions concerning their work arrangements.[21]

Eric Trist, along with his colleagues Fred Emery, Philip Herbst, and later Einar Thorsrud, became the key proponents of this new way of conceptualizing organizations as open systems engaged in an exchange process with their environment. In this perspective, organizations were viewed as consisting of both a social and a technical system, each of which functions according to different rules and thus has to be regulated and organized according to different principles. Finally, the concept of sociotechnical systems design implied that the system as a whole cannot be optimized through independent optimization of solely the social or the technical system; the integrated or joint optimization of both systems leads to the optimal functioning of the organization as a whole.

In contrast to the American focus on the enrichment of individual work activities, the sociotechnical systems approach proposed the concept of semi-autonomous work groups based on the underlying assumption that learning and the development of social and occupational competences largely occur in cooperation and communication with others. In addition, industrial production does not lend itself well to the improved design of individual jobs, since most tasks are highly interdependent. The group thus is often the "natural" work unit. Optimal functioning of open, continuously changing systems is seen as predicated on the degree to which the resources and competences for controlling the work of different organizational units are returned to the members of that unit. The principle of motivation through task orientation rather than external control is enhanced in relatively independent organizational units that allow increased scope for self-regulation of work groups. Acknowledging that individuals are guided by varying goals and motivations, work has to be organized in a manner that allows different individuals to satisfy varying needs and to develop new goals and aspirations. And rather than enriching jobs in consultation with external experts, employees themselves are to plan and regulate their work activities by means of direct participation based on the principle of self-design.

This conceptualization of human nature and work leads to forms of work organization aimed at the development of competences by giving work groups the scope and latitude to complete tasks based on their own planning and guided only by specified deadlines and standards. There is no longer a "one best way" for doing things; rather there is discretion and decision latitude rooted in the recognition that different paths might equally well achieve the same goals. The metaphor is that of an organism where different organs fulfill different functions but are dependent on each other, and can function appropriately only in interaction with all other parts of the organism. (For an in-depth discussion of sociotechnical design principles, see Chapter 7.)

Scattered experiments with sociotechnical systems design occurred throughout the fifties and sixties in Britain, India, and Australia as well as in the United States.[22] Though often highly successful in terms of productivity increases, workplace safety, and worker commitment, various factors prevented the widespread adoption of this approach. In particular, work rules rooted in traditionally adversarial labor-management relations, management's reluctance to share control over work organization, and the expanding economy in many industrialized countries during the sixties provided little impetus for change. A breakthrough came with the Norwegian Industrial Democracy project. A lag in industry modernization had slowed Norway's economic growth compared to other Scandinavian countries. These economic difficulties, combined with surging union demands for worker participation and control, led to a number of sustained sociotechnical field experiments.[23] A more widespread diffusion occurred in Sweden at the end of the decade. A younger generation of well-educated and affluent workers signaled their refusal to be confined to boring and menial jobs through a high level of absenteeism and turnover. By 1973, between 500 and 1,000 work improvement projects of various size and scope had been initiated in many sectors of the Swedish economy.

Yet the diffusion of sociotechnical systems experiments in Norway declined as workers lost interest in designs focused on changes in job distribution and wage systems rather than on workers' concerns. Similarly, in implementing projects developed jointly by union and management in Sweden, conflicts between union and management goals became evident. Largely management-dominated designs led unions to shift their focus to a collective resource approach, involving researchers, workers, and union representatives in the design of technologies linked to opportunities for skill development and expanded influence on the organization of work.[24]

Once again, a combination of economic forces and changing values gave rise to a new way of conceptualizing work and work organization and experimentation with new organizational choices. In the United States, these forces have only recently come into focus. Rapid technological change, quality instead of quantity of output as the key competitive element in an increasingly global economy, the shift from a producer- to a consumer-oriented market, and the changing expectations of an increasingly educated segment of the workforce have created an environment in which companies are forced to search for new ways to assure organizational success and survival. The next chapter takes a closer look at the implications of this changing context and the opportunities and threats that it presents.

The overview of the different conceptualizations of work and work organization throughout this century can be summarized as follows: Depending on the approach taken, the design of work activities and work organization may create a more broadly or more narrowly defined structure that may either deliberately stifle and limit, or enhance the developmental potential of human beings in the context of work activities. These structures and processes have a powerful influence on the characteristics and behavior of the organizational members. People in rigid and bureaucratic organizations tend to develop rigid and bureaucratic personalities; if the organization does not change, people are not likely to change either. Organizations that are flexible and dynamic tend to "reproduce" similar characteristics in their employees. While characteristics of work and organizational design reflect the changes in the economic, political, and social environment, rather than replacing each other, different elements of the design approaches discussed here tend to coexist in various combinations in today's organizations or in different industrial contexts.

NOTES

1. W.J. Abernathy, K.B. Clark and A.M. Kantrow, Industrial Renaissance: Producing a Competitive Future for America (New York: Basic Books, 1983).

2. E.P. Thompson, The Making of the English Working Class (London: Gollancz, 1963); Shoshana Zuboff, In the Age of the Smart Machine: The Future of Work and Power (New York: Basic Books, 1988).

3. Alfred P. Wadsworth and Julia Mann, The Cotton Trade and Industrial Lancashire 1600-1780 (Manchester: Manchester University Press, 1931), p. 16.

4. Quoted in B. Bailyn, *The Ideological Origins of the American Revolution* (Cambridge, Mass.: Harvard University Press, 1967), p. 60.

5. Merrill has distinguished between the "democratic republicanism" of revolutionary Americans from the "middling classes" and the classical republicanism subscribed to by more well-to-do property owners. See Michael Merrill, "The Anticapitalist Origins of the United States". *Review* 13, 4 (Fall 1990): 465-497.

6. Daniel Rodgers, *The Work Ethic in Industrial America, 1850-1920* (Chicago: University of Chicago Press, 1978).

7. David Montgomery, *Workers' Control in America; Studies in the History of Work, Technology and Labor Struggles* (Cambridge, Eng.: Cambridge University Press, 1979).

8. The summary in this section draws largely on the excellent historical analysis of the evolution of the modern business enterprise by Alfred Chandler, *The Visible Hand: The Managerial Revolution in American Business* (Cambridge, Mass.: Harvard University Press, 1977).

9. Ibid., p. 275.

10. Lyndall Urwick and E.F.L. Brech, *The Making of Scientific Management*, 3 vols. (London: Management Publication Trust, 1945, 1946, 1948), vol. 1, p. 17.

11. Frederick W. Taylor, *Scientific Management* (New York: Harper, 1911), p. 32.

12. Gareth Morgan, *Images of Organization* (Beverly Hills, Calif.: Sage, 1986), p. 30.

13. David Halberstam, *The Reckoning* (New York: William Morrow, 1986).

14. Adapted from Morgan, *Images of Organization*, p. 34.

15. Elton Mayo, *The Social Problems of an Industrial Civilization* (Boston: Harvard University Graduate School of Business Administration, 1945), pp. 120-122.

16. Zuboff, *Age of the Smart Machine*, p. 234.

17. Reinhard Bendix, *Work and Authority in Industry* (Berkeley: University of California Press, 1974).

18. Zuboff, *Age of the Smart Machine*, p. 235.

19. Frederick Herzberg, Bernard Mausner, and Barbara Block-Snyderman, *The Motivation to Work* (New York: John Wiley and Sons, 1959).

20. Douglas McGregor, *The Human Side of Enterprise* (New York: McGraw-Hill, 1960).

21. Eric Trist, "The Evolution of Socio-technical Systems," Ontario Quality of Working Life Centre: *Issues in the Quality of Working Life*, No. 2. (June 1981): 8.

22. For a useful summary of the early sociotechnical systems experiments, see ibid., pp. 18-28.

23. Frederick Emery and Einar Thorsrud, *Democracy at Work* (Leiden: Martinus Nijhoff, 1976).

24.   For a critique of the sociotechnical systems experiments in Sweden and a description of the newly emerging collective resources approach, see Pelle Ehn, *Work-Oriented Design of Computer Artefacts* (Falköping, Sweden: Gummesons, 1989).

3. Key Factors for Change and Strategic Response

The economic, social, and political context in which organizations operate is changing rapidly. A number of factors are forcing both public and private enterprises to abandon their old ways of doing business and to search for new avenues to future effectiveness. As suggested in Chapter 2, many of the difficulties faced by a growing number of companies are the result of trying to meet the challenges posed by the late twentieth century with nineteenth-century methods. The engineering approach to organization design associated with the American Society of Mechanical Engineers, eventually culminating in Fordist work organization, adequately supported mass production in a producer's market. But most experts agree that producer-controlled markets are a relic of the past, though some companies have been slow to veer from Henry Ford's legendary pronouncement, "You can buy our car in any color – as long as it's black."

In its heyday in the 1950s and 1960s, the mechanistic approach to organizing production enabled the United States and other countries to experience the largest productivity increase in history, associated with the greatest increase in the general standard of living ever recorded. Many of these design principles are still advocated by organization theorists for companies that operate in stable environments with highly rationalized methods. However, in the turbulent and uncertain economic and social environment of the late twentieth century, fewer and fewer such companies exist. In this chapter we review key factors of environmental change that demand corresponding internal organizational changes.

THREE KEY ENVIRONMENTAL CHANGE FACTORS

The major factors contributing to the need for change are changing market demands in a global economy, technological developments, and changing workforce demographics and values (see Figure 3.1).

Figure 3.1   Three Key Environmental Change Factors

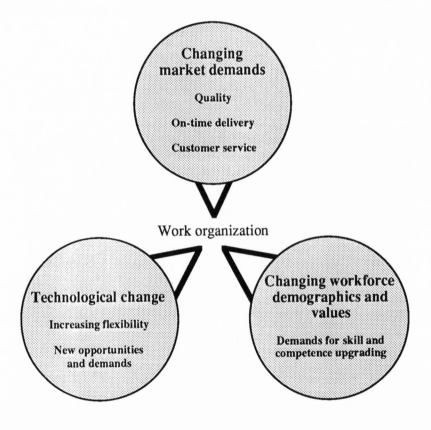

Changing Market Demands

Today's market is increasingly consumer-driven and segmented. New technologies have made it possible to achieve profits at lower volumes in "niche markets." Thus, the goal of high-volume production at low price has given way to new differentiation criteria such as quality, flexibility, on-time delivery, customer service, and custom-designed production. Within saturated markets and growing technology-based flexibility, competitiveness is no longer a function of price alone (see Figure 3.2).

Figure 3.2   Changing Market Demands

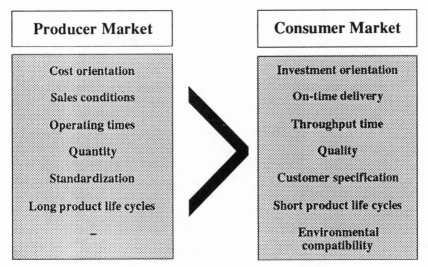

In general, this change in market demands is related to technological developments as both product and process innovations make it possible to meet diverse demands at a relatively acceptable price level. While price is no longer the only criterion, it is of course still important. Low value-added production processes are often shifted to developing countries with low wage levels and limited government regulations about workplace health and safety and environmental protection standards. Though beneficial to the corporate bottom line and the shareholders, at least in the short term, the expansion and profitability of major corporations have become increasingly independent from the nation's economic well-being and the prosperity of its workforce. The economic future of industrialized countries such as the United States, it has been argued, depends on the degree to which the nation's workforce will be able to perform the sophisticated tasks involved in complex production that justify higher wage levels and support a decent standard of living.[1] This challenge cannot be met with outdated management philosophies and organizational strategies designed for mass production and the producer markets of the past.

Competition is also intensified by the increasing globalization of economic exchange relationships and markets. Resulting changes in the size and variety of markets require quick responses and adaptation to new demands. Delayed or inadequate reactions to changing demands are likely to decrease competitiveness in the global economy. The ability to respond adequately to these challenges and to develop proactive strategies requires flexible forms of production and organization.

Implications

High value-added production processes in adaptable and flexible organizations place new demands on employees' skills, competence, and commitment to organizational goals. Hardly a day passes without newspaper headlines calling for greater investment in basic literacy and numeracy skills of the future U.S. workforce, or lamenting the inadequacy of the scientific and technical skills of the existing workforce. Yet these skills are unlikely to be developed through formal education and training programs alone. Both Germany and Japan have achieved leadership in workforce skill development through a combination of on-the-job training and the design of jobs that promote skill development. Economic success in an integrated world economy is likely to be contingent upon the design of work activities and organizational structures that promote the development of employee competence and problem-solving skills.

Technological Change

The primary technological advance that directly impacts work organization is the application of microelectronics, with its potential to save labor *and* capital (see Figure 3.3).[2] CAD/CAM (computer-aided design / computer-aided manufacturing), CNC (computerized numerical control), industrial robots, and computer-based information and material handling systems are radically altering production processes.

Figure 3.3   Technological Change

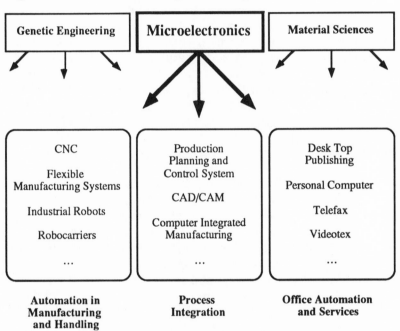

More and more areas in the manufacturing and service sector rely on microelectronic-based technology. Yet, as dramatic as they seem, the recent developments have only begun to tap the vast potential of this new technology. Improvements in the linking of applications – as in computer integrated manufacturing (CIM), for example – are likely to further rationalize production processes. Historically, rationalization gains contributed to improved quality and reliability of the production process, and simultaneously increased productivity and flexibility. Over time these gains translated into shorter working hours and a higher standard of living. The distribution of future rationalization gains, however, will in part be a question of the fit between workforce skills and competences and the demands of new production processes.

What distinguishes microelectronic-based information technology from earlier generations of machine technology is its ability to not only reproduce, extend, or improve on the accomplishment of human tasks, but to provide feedback about the process. It thus not only *utilizes* information in the form of programmed instruction, but also *produces* information. It has the potential to *automate* as well as to *informate*.[3] As the need for physical labor input decreases, the nature of skill is redefined. The traditional view of labor as a variable cost factor becomes contradictory to the training and ongoing competence development required for these different, often mental inputs. Employees' abilities, in concert with the application of new technology, become a source of creativity, problem-solving, and improved decision-making in support of productivity, quality, and flexibility.

The question of whether new technology is an opportunity or a threat is really the question of how new technology is designed and applied in work systems. Properly implemented, with a view toward enhancing human performance and creativity, the *adequate application* of new technologies offers new opportunities for improvements in workplace design and work organization. Microelectronic-based technologies offer *potential* for increasing competence (new skills and knowledge), integrated (holistic) job design, and less physical and mental strain.

Whether these opportunities are utilized, however, depends on the way in which these technologies are designed and implemented. Are they aimed at increased centralization, performance and output control, and increasing demands, or is their utilization directed toward increased decentralization, decreased division of labor and task fragmentation, and expanded decision latitude and scope of activities?

While the latter positive outcomes are by no means an "automatic" by-product of the introduction of new technologies, many organizations are starting to search for ways in which the utilization of new technologies can support the following:

- quality and quantity of production
- flexible responses to market demands
- employee motivation, interest, and commitment
- utilization of employees' knowledge and skills
- development of a competent workforce

- other cost-saving strategies (e.g., cell manufacturing, just-in-time production systems)

Why Current Applications Often Miss These Opportunities

Quite rarely does the current application of microelectronic systems lead to the desired outcomes described above. The reason is inappropriate work design; or, put differently, work design is not planned at all. The focus is on the design of technology. The starting point frequently is some specific problem in the production process. Technical experts are called upon to improve the existing technology or develop new systems. Sometimes new technology is acquired because it promises increased productivity, because "everybody" is using it, or because it's fashionable to be technologically innovative.

The result: technology is the starting point. Work activity and job design are afterthoughts. People then have to make up for the flaws in the technology by supervising, maintaining, and fixing the equipment. Thus human capacity is underutilized and undervalued, based on the assumption that the functioning of the whole system is dependent on how well the technology works. We will illustrate in Chapter 7 that production systems can be optimized only if both the technical and the social systems are jointly optimized. Only then can technology be viewed as the product of design choices rather as a fait accompli.

Technology Is Not a Fait Accompli

Technology frequently becomes a driving force if it is developed and implemented without consideration of the social system, which is usually "adjusted" after technology has been introduced. Yet, technology does not have to be a fixed factor; it offers choices and options. While this is no revolutionary insight, in the context of presently emerging technologies the choices made have far-reaching consequences. Key choices encompass the three areas of person/machine interaction illustrated in Figure 3.4:

The concept of *person/machine coupling* describes the extent to which the employee is dependent on the equipment in order to complete his or her task. *The less dependence exists, the greater the discretion and scope of activity for employees.*

Product distance refers to the psychological distance between the employee and the product produced. This distance is considerable if what a person does all day is tighten a bolt; the distance is small if a person produces a complete product or a major part of a product. *The smaller this distance, the greater the likelihood for motivation through task orientation and the possibility of self-regulation.*

Process integration describes the extent to which individual processes or operations are linked to the total production process. *The less centralized the process, the more freedom exists for regulation of work processes.*[4]

Figure 3.4   Technology and Organization: Options and Choices

Relationship between person/machine coupling and the discretion/decision latitude of workers and supervisors

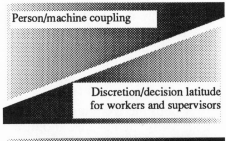

Relationship between product distance and task orientation and self-regulation

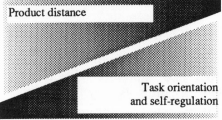

Relationship between process integration and degrees of freedom regarding the regulation of work processes

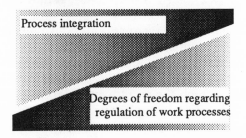

New forms of work organization take these options into consideration. For example:

- Abandoning assembly-style production lines, many companies have developed new forms of group-based production and assembly processes, sometimes called cell manufacturing. Technically, this involves breaking down previously connected assembly lines into parallel groups which, while still retaining features of the assembly line principle, gain increased independence through the addition of buffer zones and stock areas. This requires new transportation and material handling systems, such as robocarriers, etc.
- Another concept, also developed for assembly purposes but mostly utilized in electronics manufacturing, links assembly cells in a star-shaped structure. The modules of each aggregate product are assembled at the "points" of the star and brought together in the center. Especially in component manufacturing various models of group technology have been developed. This involves machine configurations that link operations of different types. More recent applications combine CNC and conventional technology in flexible manufacturing cells. Technologically advanced forms such as fully automated flexible manufacturing systems tend to limit the potential for employee or work group self-regulation.
- Overall, particularly in office and clerical work settings, the opportunities inherent in information technology lead to a variety of new forms of work organization that combine the core activities necessary for the production and administration on a product-focused basis. The extensive use of computer-based data management systems suggests that technological options are found mostly in the area of software development, often implying decisions about centralized or decentralized organization of work activities.

The design concept for such forms of work organization is presented in more detail in chapters 4 and 7.

Implications

The optimal utilization of the potential of microelectronic-based technology requires an approach to equipment and process design with a focus on their implications for work activities. If the desired outcomes of quality, flexibility, and continuous competence development are to be achieved, work design has to be an integral part of the total design process. Continuous improvement means continuous learning. In the informated workplace, learning is no longer a classroom activity; rather, the organization itself becomes a learning environment. As it becomes more difficult to anticipate future knowledge and skill requirements, work itself must be organized so as to allow for continuous learning and development.

Workforce Competence, Changing Demographics, and Values

Workforce demographics are changing. The baby boomer surplus of the seventies is giving way to a shrinking pool of future employees, many of whom are without the benefit of a sound education and the opportunity to acquire the knowledge and skills needed to maintain an adequate standard of living and to assure the long-term competitiveness of American firms. The U.S. Department of Labor estimates that two-thirds of all new workers entering the workforce in the 1990s will be women; 29 percent will be members of minority populations. The percentage of women in the full-time paid workforce has increased from 28 percent in 1940 to 42 percent in 1990. It is estimated that by the end of the century, 80 percent of women between the ages of twenty-five and fifty-four – about the same percentage as men – will be working outside the home.

Women with young children constituted the largest increase in the labor force in the past decade. What prompted many of these mothers to entrust their children to expensive and often inadequate child care facilities was the decline of real wages over the last decade. Family incomes have remained relatively stable over this period of time only because more family members have joined the workforce or because more hours are worked.[5] Yet the resulting actual increase in usable family income amounts to no more than between $ 1,000-1,500 annually, after taxes and added work expenses.[6] Money alone, especially if women remain stuck in low-income brackets, earning no more than sixty cents for every dollar earned by men, may be insufficient to keep these women in the labor market. In addition, falling real wages and the marginal increase in family incomes for the majority of American families produce little economic stimulation and growth, as spending money is tight and consumption remains limited, a major factor cited for the slow recovery from the current recession.

One current attempt to ease current and predicted labor shortages involves changing immigration laws to encourage the influx of foreigners with skills required in understaffed occupations such as nursing. Yet this appears to be a short-term solution at best. It does little to ease the struggle of many young families trying to make a living or to address the challenge of integrating the growing number of unemployed or underemployed Americans who for reasons of ethnic origin, gender, and family background lack the educational prerequisites to compete for increasingly demanding jobs.

Finally, workforce values are changing. While making money is still important, for those with some options it is not all that matters. Many people look for interesting, challenging tasks. Contrary to the futurist predictions of the sixties about the coming leisure society, work still appears to be a central value in human life. This is particularly true in circumstances where occupational activity is one of the most important determinants of social identity. As a growing percentage of the workforce is better educated than previous generations, employees look for opportunities not only to apply existing skills but to further develop their competences in the workplace. The importance of job content is reflected in the results of a recent study of working women, which found that a majority of the women surveyed considered the quality and challenge inherent in their job to be more important in retaining them than the child care arrangements offered by their employer.

Implications

Efforts to improve the U.S. educational and vocational training system need to be complemented by strategies of work redesign that allow for on the job skill and competence development of the existing workforce. The economic well-being of the nation – increasingly unrelated to the profits of its multinational corporations – will depend on a rising standard of living tied to growing rather than falling real wages. The baby boomers and the succeeding generation are more critical and more demanding than their parents. Rather than bemoaning the loss of the work ethic of the past, employers need to harness the potential inherent in these changing, postindustrial values, especially the increasing receptivity for challenge and continuous learning. Rhetoric in the form of organizational "beliefs and values" statements, accompanied by narrow "participation" programs, is not enough. Required are a managerial philosophy and organizational strategies that view people as adult, mature, self-reliant individuals, willing to learn and to cooperate. Chapter 8 provides an example of a work redesign project that successfully integrated efforts to achieve organizational production and quality goals with a process of skill and competence development in a challenging context of cultural diversity.

THREE STRATEGIC AREAS FOR INTERVENTION

The three key factors of change discussed above pose a challenge to every organization. The continuously changing environment requires reassessment of the adequacy of organizational goals, structures, and processes.

Figure 3.5   Three Strategic Areas for Intervention

Changing market demands

Mission

Visions and plans for future innovations

Structure

First and second order integrative rationalization

Work organization in the context of three strategic areas

Technological change

Changing workforce demographics and values

Process

Participation, training, and job design related to competence development

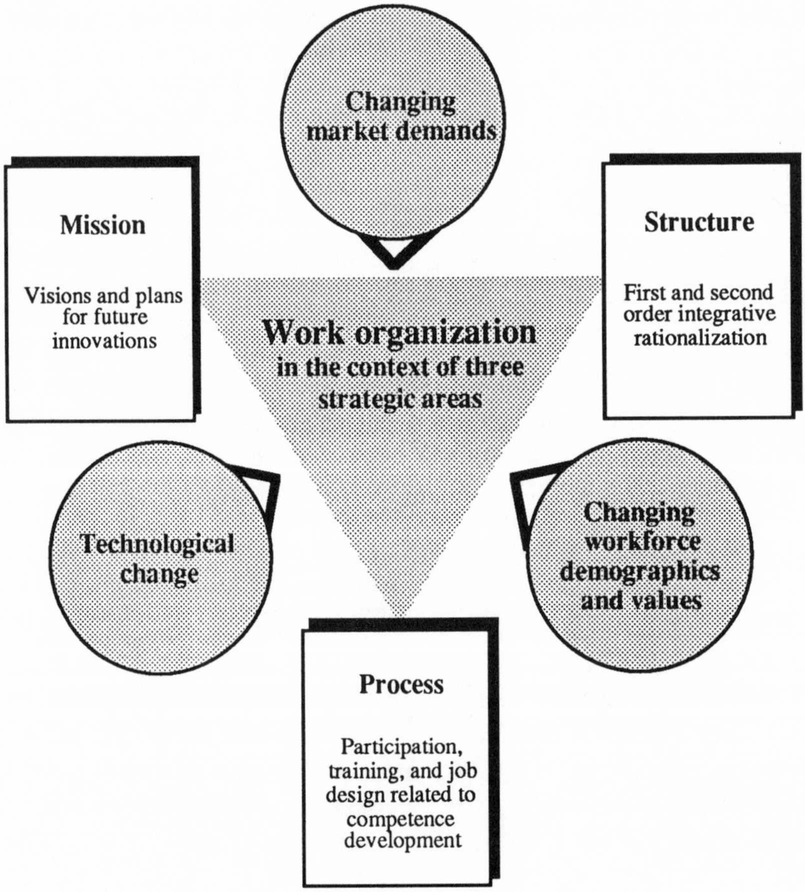

New market demands, technological innovations, and changing workforce demographics and values cannot be directly influenced. The task thus becomes to develop an economically sound and flexible business philosophy capable of responding quickly to ongoing environmental changes. To be successful, this philosophy will have to be reflected in organizational structures and processes aimed at work organization designs that make optimal use of employee skills and problem-solving capabilities.

In this section we propose some key concepts for organizational redesign that link mission, structure, and process in ways that increase the organization's ability to address the problems and uncertainties of a turbulent environment (see Figure 3.5).

Mission

Strategic interventions have to be guided by a clear understanding of the organization's mission and purpose. Such a mission statement, based on explicit values, provides the basis for analyzing organizational strengths and weaknesses in light of environmental threats and opportunities. The analysis of these opportunities and threats as related to each of the three areas of change, needs to be more specific than the above general discussion of trends. By carefully assessing these factors, one can formulate specific strategic as well as tactical objectives and identify the *innovations* required to achieve these goals. Innovation here is defined as any kind of future-oriented and mission-based strategic change, including product, process, and structural organizational change.

More specifically, this involves the *linking* of product, process, and organizational innovations (Figure 3.6). Manufacturing-oriented product design is increasingly coupled with process innovations aimed at reducing of long lead times and freeing capital tied up in large in-process inventories. Group technology concepts such as cell manufacturing linked with JIT (just-in-time) systems are transforming job shops into continuous process systems. The focus on product and process design only means that implications for organizational innovation are often neglected and considered last. Linking product and process innovations with organizational redesign aimed at integration and self-regulation is crucial, particularly in the service industry (see Chapter 9 for an example).

Implications

The potential benefits of mission-based process and product innovations will be reaped only in conjunction with adequate organizational innovations. But organizational innovations are social interventions that often require changes in work organization aimed at increased employee skill and competence development. The skills and abilities of a person hired today may not be adequate tomorrow. A person's developmental potential and willingness to learn and change will be of increasing importance. Both these aspects can be powerfully affected by work activities that promote and reward such potential.

Figure 3.6   Linking Product, Process and Organizational
                  Innovation

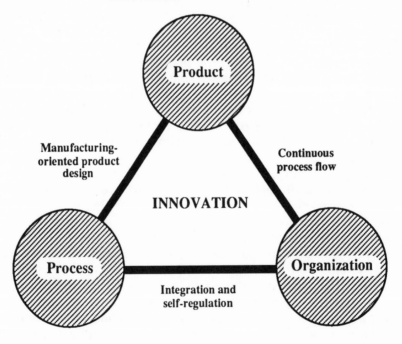

Structure

Taylorist-style division of labor and the separation of planning and execution are incompatible with a flexible systems approach. The goal is to reintegrate planning, execution, maintenance, and control functions (see Figure 3.7).[7] Holistic tasks have to be created for individuals as well as groups. This is called *first-order integrative rationalization.*

Figure 3.7   First-Order Integrative Rationalization

"Classical" task fragmentation of work ...

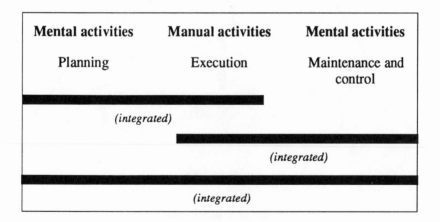

... is replaced by reintegration of mental and manual activities

First-order integrative rationalization must be complemented by *second-order integrative rationalization* (Figure 3.8), which refers to the reintegration of technical and staff functions back into line functions.[8] The goal is to solve as many problems as possible where they occur. In contrast to traditional hierarchies, designed to maximize managerial control at all levels, integrative organizations promote ongoing learning, synthesize members' interests, and promote a two-way flow of information and knowledge. The past division of labor is replaced by a division of learning, predicated on the flattening of existing organizational hierarchies. Both aspects of integrative rationalization are aimed at supporting and maximizing self-regulation, thus increasing overall organizational flexibility and adaptability.

Figure 3.8   Second-Order Integrative Rationalization

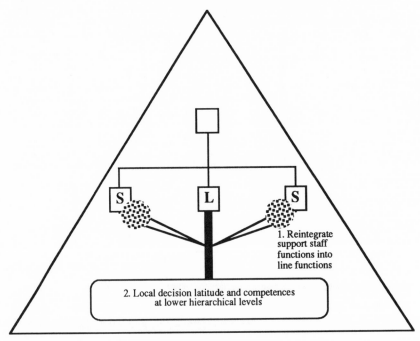

L = Line functions
S = Support staff functions

Functional specialization
versus
Organizational integration

Implications

In the context of the continuously evolving requirements of occupational competence development, successful organizations will share rationalization and productivity gains with employees in a win-win situation. For example, time at work may involve fewer hours spent on task completion and more hours allocated to continuing education and learning.

Process

Unfortunately, the design of the *organizational process* itself is mostly undervalued and insufficiently understood. Training and competence development are often treated as issues of secondary importance. As a result, training and development budgets are often the first to be cut when cash flow problems arise. Successful integrative rationalization and innovation will depend on the degree to which employee competence is being developed on a timely, adequate, and continuing basis. Integrative rationalization and organizational innovations are likely to fail in static organizations and structures that inhibit workforce skill utilization and further development after an initial training period.

Figure 3.9   Four Levels of Competence Development

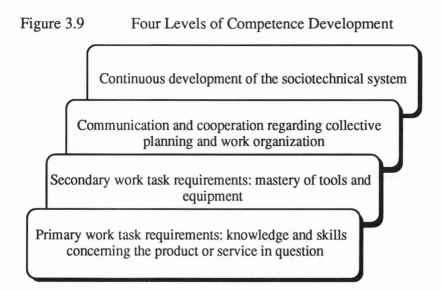

We distinguish between four levels of competence development (Figure 3.9): The first level encompasses the primary work task, involving an understanding of the organization's product or service and one's contribution to it (e.g., knowledge about customers, materials, the product in general). The next level, the secondary function, includes mastery of the tools or equipment used in the process. This may encompass setup, maintenance, or programming functions. The third level, social competence, involves communication and cooperation with others, including the ability to collectively plan and organize work activities. The fourth level, related to ongoing organizational redesign, focuses on the continuous adjustment of the technical and organizational system. This process is based on the knowledge and experience embodied within the first three levels.

Implications

The development of a "competent" organization involves much more than narrow skill training of the existing workforce or the recruitment of new employees able to meet these competence requirements. Much of the knowledge and many of the skills required at the four levels outlined above are best acquired within the organization. A complementary human resource policy would determine medium- and long-range competence development profiles, and assess employees' qualification potential in light of these requirements. Personnel recruitment then becomes an internal as well as an external function. Employees already part of the organization are "recruited" and encouraged to take on new tasks, with training, education, and work design matching the goals of continuous competence development. This requires an organizational philosophy with a developmental and learning orientation that is convincingly communicated externally as well as internally.

The next chapter presents an overview of how some major manufacturing companies have tried to respond to the challenges described in this chapter. We will focus on emerging production systems and their implications for work organization and competence development. Three examples from the automotive industry, involving a Japanese, a European, and an American approach, will be compared as to their potential for meeting organizational needs for quality production and flexibility as well as for creating work organization structures and processes that foster ongoing learning and competence development.

NOTES

1. Robert B. Reich, "Corporation and Nation," *Atlantic Monthly* (May 1988), pp. 76-81.

2. Developments in genetic engineering and the material sciences are not discussed here. It is to be expected, however, that technological advances in these areas are likely to be as dramatic in the nineties as was the advent of microelectronics in the seventies and eighties.

3. Zuboff, *Age of the Smart Machine.*

4. Andreas Alioth, "Technik – kein Sachzwang," in Duell and Frei, *Arbeit gestalten*, pp. 155-202.

5. Mishel and Frankel, *State of Working America.*

6. Spencer Rich, "Purchasing Power Little Better than Ten Years Ago," *Washington Post,* reprinted in *Ann Arbor News* (July 5, 1990).

7. Eberhard Ulich, "Psychologie der Arbeit," *Management Enzyklopädie,* vol. 7, (Landsberg, Germany: Moderne Industrie, 1984), pp. 914-929.

8. Andreas Alioth, "Flexibilität und Innovation durch Neustrukturierung der Arbeit," *Fides Mitteilungen* 46, 3 (1985): 44-47.

4. Emerging Production Systems and Work Design Alternatives

American business has responded to the challenges discussed in Chapter 3 in diverse ways. One broad strategy involves experimentation with various forms of *worker participation programs* such as employee involvement groups, quality circles, and team concepts. In some cases, these efforts have been accompanied by work organization changes aimed at rotating jobs or creating work teams to improve communication and problem-solving capacities or to allow for increased flexibility in job assignments. A second strategy might be called the *high-tech* approach, focusing on the utilization of computer-based technologies expected to improve quality and production flexibility while simultaneously reducing labor costs. Obviously, these are not mutually exclusive choices since, as discussed in the previous chapter, the successful application of sophisticated computer-based equipment frequently requires organizational changes.

In conjunction with introducing new technologies and different types of employee involvement programs, many American firms have searched for other ways to reduce labor costs and increase or preserve managerial flexibility and control. The number of manufacturing companies shifting production offshore or building new facilities in the less unionized southern and southwestern regions of the United States is growing rapidly. More direct attempts to circumvent union demands for decent wages and working conditions have involved efforts to decertify existing unions or to aggressively prevent unionization drives.[1] This approach was encouraged by the Reagan administration's response to the air controller (Patco) strike in 1980 and an increasingly business-oriented National Labor Relations Board (NLRB). The assault on unions, particularly in the private sector, is evidenced in the number of unfair labor practice complaints filed with the NLRB in recent years.[2]

In the traditional union stronghold sectors of the automotive, steel, and communications industries, management and unions have engaged in a wide variety of collaborative training, education, and employee involvement efforts to increase competitiveness through improving quality and productivity.[3] At the same time, however, many firms pursued outsourcing, subcontracting, and offshore production strategies in order to take advantage of lower wages in less regulated foreign labor markets.

More recently, the production concepts underlying the sweeping success of the Japanese manufacturing industry, both at home and in the growing number of Japanese production facilities abroad, have caught the attention of American as well as European managers. Heralded as the model for the manufacturing process of the future, Japanese automotive and electronics manufacturers, who in the fifties and sixties sent their executives to the United States to learn about making cars and TVs, have become the destination of a reverse pilgrimage. Thousands of American managers, sometimes accompanied by union leaders, have visited the new economic powerhouse, determined to discover and, it is hoped, to adopt the Japanese secret for success.

FINAL CAR ASSEMBLY: EXPERIMENTAL GROUND FOR NEW PRODUCTION CONCEPTS

Historically, the automobile industry has played a central role in the way we organize the production of goods and services and design work activities. Just as Henry Ford, by combining assembly line technology with scientific management principles, made this industry the birthplace of mass production, so is Toyota (by implementing the production principles of its earlier vice president, Taiichi Ohno, has become the cradle of what is known as *Toyotism* or *lean production*. In *The Machine that Changed the World*, proponents of lean production declare it to be a radical departure from the mass production system still dominating large parts of the American and European industry.[4] The authors argue that lean production will fundamentally change the way we produce goods and services, and that it will "supplant both mass production and the remaining outposts of craft production in all areas of industrial endeavor to become the standard global production system of the twenty-first century. That world will be a very different and a much better place."[5]

Lean Production

What are the features of this revolutionary new approach to manufacturing? Lean production is based on the notion that lean means using less of everything – less human effort, less manufacturing space, less investment in tools and engineering hours for product development, less inventory on site – to manufacture a growing variety of products with fewer defects, while achieving higher quality and productivity.[6] This overall reduction is to be achieved through the application of a number of specific principles, summarized below based on the description of Womack and his colleagues:

The Elements of Lean Production

• Production

At the assembly line, for example, workers are grouped into teams and told to work together on deciding how best to perform the necessary operations. In addition, teams are encouraged to continuously suggest ways to improve the production process by eliminating any form of waste. Such efforts, known in Japanese as the *kaizen* concept, also underlie the introduction of "quality circles" in the West. In contrast to traditional mass production facilities where quality inspectors try to discover problems in the final product, requiring considerable time and effort for rework, each worker has the task of searching for quality problems and stopping the line if necessary. More important, rather than simply "fixing" individual problems and hoping that they do not recur, a process of systematically tracing the ultimate cause of the problem is established.

• Inventory and Supply

Parts suppliers in traditional mass production work to the blueprint of their customer, which results in little incentive to improve quality. Lean production manufacturers, by contrast, organize their suppliers into tiers. The suppliers are given performance specifications and are encouraged to communicate with suppliers responsible for other components. The establishment of long-term relationships with suppliers and the elimination of fierce competition among suppliers responsible for various components create incentives for supplier cooperation and efforts to improve the quality of their particular components. Through cross-ownership and joint development, suppliers become closely involved with the assembly plant. In addition, the flow of parts in the supply system is coordinated on a daily basis, using the famous just-in-time or *kanban* system, in which only the parts immediately needed at each stage of the production process are available.

• Product Design

The Taylorist system of product development and engineering characterizing traditional mass production companies assigns different tasks to the design and manufacturing engineering experts responsible for parts of the product. Weak communication links and a step-by-step process from design to manufacturing rather than a simultaneous approach lead to lengthy product development times and a high number of engineering hours spent per new product. Lean design, it is argued, is different in terms of leadership, teamwork, communication, and simultaneous development. It is based on a strong team leader rather than a loose coordination model. The team leader works with a tightly knit team involving experts in market assessment, product planning, styling, advanced and detail engineering, production engineering, and factory operations. Communication is open, and conflicts are voiced and resolved at the beginning of the process.

Finally, simultaneous development means, for example, that die production starts at the same time as body design, which is possible because of the close interaction among die and body designers. Lean design is aimed at essentially cutting the engineering effort in half and saving one-third in development time. This allows for a fast-paced increase in product range and product adaptation to changing consumer demands.

• Distributors and Customers

The lean producer views the buyer as part of the production process. Data collected on owner preferences for new vehicles are fed back into the design process. Fewer dealers work with a limited three-week supply of finished units, most of which have already been ordered. Dealership service is considered of great importance, so as not to lose any customers once they have bought a company product.

At first glance it would seem hard to argue with the merits of the lean production concept. And no one would suggest that there is not much to be learned from the Japanese system, such as their recognition of the importance of employee input at all levels, their often superior customer service, or their innovations in the product design and development process. Yet, while the economic success of Japan's manufacturing industry in the past two decades is truly impressive, it is by no means solely a result of the application of lean production principles.

The social, cultural, political, and economic context characterizing postwar Japan also played a key role. The close cooperation between government and industry and a capital financing system that decreases dependence on short-term profit-oriented shareholders reduce the pressures for quick profits in favor of long-term product development and marketing strategies. Furthermore, a more homogeneous, almost universally literate population, close ties between the education system and the employment system, and an employment relationship in which the destiny of the worker is closely linked to that of the employer (lifetime employment, seniority-based wage rates) engender a mutual commitment and incentive to invest in worker training and skill development.

Critics of lean production have argued that to ignore all these important factors or to subsume them under the concept of lean production reduces its utility for companies operating under different economic and cultural conditions.[7] It has also been suggested that the lean production argument as made by Womack and his colleagues at MIT boils down to "if it is efficient and it works, it must be lean production; if it's inefficient and it doesn't work, it's mass production."[8] Sean McAlinden notes that Ford's accomplishments (which the MIT authors attribute to its moving toward lean production) over the last six or seven years and General Motors' improvements in quality and cost reduction might be a result of paying greater attention to the consumer, better cooperation with labor, and careful use of capacity that could be summarized simply as *sound management.*

A case in point is the new Ford Engine plant in Romeo, a suburb of Detroit. Based on a sociotechnical system design and manufacturing approach, a product launch team of about 30 people was in charge of the design, purchase and installation of equipment. This team included managers of production, quality, finance, and personnel, the training coordinator, key process engineers and a small number of hourly skilled trades and production employees, as well as members of the union leadership. All major decisions were made by consensus. The organizational structure has only three levels. Major decisions for each product area including changes in equipment, quality and safety issues, scheduling and policy changes are jointly made in work team meetings involving hourly workers, a union representative, engineers, the area manager and a financial analyst.

When the engine was launched in the fall of 1990, there were only 37 defects per 1000 engines compared to a range of 135 to 190 defects characterizing other Ford engine plant launches during the eighties. And launch costs stayed within the projected budget, historically a rare event in the U.S. auto industry. Nine months into production the defect rate at Romeo has been reduced to 10 per 1000. Without being based on many of the principles of the Japanese model, this V8 luxury car engine has been praised for meeting world class quality standards by auto industry experts.[9]

Work Design and Lean (or Mean?) Production

Because this book focuses on how designing work to foster ongoing competence development and decision latitude, we need to explore the characteristics and implications of lean production for *work design* and *work organization*. Here again, the proponents of lean production are very optimistic, contending that the key feature of a lean production process is the transfer of a maximum number of tasks and responsibilities to workers, with the dynamic work team being the heart of its success; "while the mass production plant is often filled with mind-numbing stress, as workers struggle to assemble unmanufacturable products and have no ways to improve their working environment, lean production offers a creative tension in which workers have many ways to address such challenges."[10] Unfortunately, the MIT group's analysis of the virtues of lean production does not include an empirically based description of working conditions, work organization, and the physical and mental strain that accompany this approach to production.

Many experts interested in questions of work design and work organization have concluded that lean production relies on an intensified management structure while retaining a basically Taylorist system of work organization aimed at the optimal utilization of assembly lines with short work cycles and highly standardized and predefined tasks.[11] A glimpse at Satoshi Kamata's account of life as a temporary employee at Toyota conjures up images of U.S. factory life in the preunion days of the twenties. A Japanese freelance journalist, Kamata took a job with Toyota in 1970 in order to experience at first hand what supposedly is to become the production system of the future.

> Almost as soon as I begin, I'm dripping with sweat. Somehow I learn the order of the work motion, but I'm totally unable to keep up with the speed of the line. I do my best, but I can barely finish one gear box out of three within the fixed length of time. I'm thirsty as hell, but workers can neither smoke nor drink water. Going to the toilet is out of the question. After standing five hours, my legs are numb and stiff. My new safety shoes are so heavy that I feel I can barely move.
>
> ...
>
> Some call this labor but we don't actually create anything. A single car can be disassembled into five or six thousand different parts, and it's the parts that now determine the organization of labor. Work is separated according to the function of the parts, then reorganized, framed and fixed. A car is the integrated sum of all its parts, like a plastic model assembled in a fixed order, and we workers who assemble the parts are, in fact, controlled by the parts. Slowing the conveyor speed by five seconds might make the work easier for a while, but once we got used to this new speed, we'd again be trapped in the same narrow routine.
>
> ...
>
> In Kudo's workshop, a seasonal worker on the other shift had a finger crushed, and in my workshop, too, a worker on the other shift lost a finger. The strange thing is that no news about these accidents ever gets published. Even when a worker dies, management simply announces that there has been a "serious accident." There's never a word of apology or condolence for fingers cut off, arms chopped off, or legs crushed.[12]

As this account dates back twenty years, the question is, In what ways has Toyotism changed over time? More important, as the economic success of lean production both in Japan and in Japanese manufacturing facilities abroad has led many American firms to experiment with at least parts of this concept, we need to explore what can be learned from attempts to implement the Japanese production model in other social, political, and economic contexts.

Pressures for export restraints of Japanese vehicles to the United States and the uncertainty created by fluctuating exchange rates have spurred the development of Japanese manufacturing plants in the United States and other countries in recent years. The number of wholly or partially Japanese-owned, plants known as transplants operating in the United States in 1990 is estimated at 640, with more than 100 additional new plants expected to start operation by 1991. According to Japan's Ministry of International Trade and Industry (MITI), about 840,000 Americans are expected to work for Japanese companies by the end of the decade.[13]

The influence of the Japanese manufacturing system on efforts to improve competitiveness and to adapt traditional mass production to changing technologies, markets, and customer demands has been considerable in the United States and, increasingly, in Europe. Yet, other experiments have emerged in the manufacturing sector that must be contrasted with the lean production approach, as they appear much more promising from the perspective of participatory work design and competence development.

THREE APPROACHES TO CAR ASSEMBLY

Below we will compare the Mazda assembly plant in Michigan, an example of the transfer of the Japanese system to the United States, with General Motors' Saturn project, the attempt of a traditional automaker to redesign small car production for the highly competitive North American market. These two projects, both containing elements of lean production but based on very different management philosophies and labor-management relations, are contrasted with Volvo's experiment in the radical transformation of the car assembly process in its Uddevalla plant in Sweden.

Mazda: Everlasting Effort for Everlasting Competition

The typical strategy of Japanese car manufacturers like Honda, Nissan, and Toyota has been to pick "greenfield" sites in rural areas (Tennessee and Kentucky, for example) as the preferred locations for their factories in the United States. Thus removed from the industrial heartland, they relied on local labor markets to recruit an eager, young, and pliable workforce inexperienced in traditional manufacturing and with little knowledge about unions or interest in unionization. In addition to paying lower wages than those typical for the U.S. auto industry, and making unionization drives more difficult, this allowed the new employers to "socialize" their workforce to the values of the Japanese production philosophy.

By contrast, Mazda picked the town of Flat Rock, near Detroit, in the industrial heartland of the country.[14] Mazda, capital-
izing on the heavy unemployment in the Detroit area, was able to
select 3,500 employees from of a pool 96,500 job applicants.
The workers that were eventually hired had passed an extensive
screening process, involving up to five trips to the plant and sixteen hours of basic testing, interviewing, and problem-solving
exercises.[15] The result was a very young workforce, largely inexperienced in factory work and "untainted" by previous union
membership – considered a source of "bad attitudes" by many
Japanese managers. However, as Mazda was engaged in a cooperative venture with Ford Motor Company, its American business
partner,[16] it consented to enter into a bargaining relationship with
the United Auto Workers, the union that also represents Ford's
hourly employees.

Flexibility in Exchange for Input and Job Security

In the first collective bargaining agreement, management
stressed the need for flexibility reflected in demands to rotate
workers on different shifts. Contract language also allowed
lower level salaried employees to help with the jobs of hourly
workers when production problems arose. In contrast to the
twenty-five skilled trades job classifications typical for many
American automakers, Mazda split its skilled workers into three
groups: tool and die, mechanical, and electrical. The company
also asked for a temporary "wage discount" that started Mazda
workers at substantially lower pay than their Big Three (General
Motors, Ford, and Chrysler) counterparts. In exchange, Mazda
committed itself not to lay off employees unless the long-term financial viability of the facility was threatened due to severe economic conditions and financial circumstances, and to provide
"meaningful joint employee involvement programs."[17]

The promise of a work system different from traditional car
assembly jobs, known for short work cycles, monotony, and little
if any employee input on decisions affecting the quality of working life or the product, seemed to become reality for Mazda
workers, at least in the initial orientation and training phase.

> A three-week orientation for all the newly hired employees focused
> on interpersonal relations exercises, stressing direct communication
> and the building of trust and cooperation between team members.
> Consensus decision-making was practiced in the context of group
> problem-solving exercises and production project simulations.

These sessions were followed by what the company considered to be the most important part of the training program: an introduction to the purpose of *kanban*, the Japanese term for the just-in-time inventory system, and *kaizen*, the process of constant improvement introduced with the slogan "Everlasting Effort for Everlasting Competition." Three days were spent applying the kaizen approach in a series of flashlight assembly exercises, reminiscent of Frederick Taylor's time and motion studies done some 80 years ago. Workers learned to do their own time study, and to compare the time it took them to accomplish each step of a work activity to a set time standard. This, they were told, would be important to make the Flat Rock operation efficient by finding all possible areas for improvement.

...

The extent of on the job technical training varied from 80 hours for some workers in the body shop to less than 10 hours for employees assigned to the final trim and assembly area. Skilled trades workers received six weeks of cross-training to increase their flexibility and utilization given the reduced number of skilled trades. Production was to be organized into teams of six to ten workers, led by a team leader. These team leaders, themselves UAW members, were to coordinate work schedules, assist in the design of jobs, oversee the team's supply of tools and spare parts and the rotation of team members into different job assignments.[18]

Production Reality and Worker Dissatisfaction

However, only two years after production start-up, the promised "Mazda family" looked much like a traditional assembly plant, with increasingly disgruntled workers and a variety of quality and health and safety problems. A growing number of workers, 40 percent more than Mazda had anticipated, left the new factory. In so-called exit interviews, Mazda tried to explore the reasons for this unexpected departure. Team leaders who left complained that they lacked the legitimacy and authority to coordinate team activities meaningfully. Caught between worker and management demands, they found that many of their tasks were being taken over by management unit leaders. The number of maintenance unit leaders had grown from four to twenty over two years. These lower level managers assumed an increasingly high profile, and workers no longer talked about belonging to a team but to a larger unit. Team meetings were replaced by larger, less personal unit meetings that were now run by management.

Team members themselves grew increasingly frustrated. Despite earlier promises, they were given no real voice in designing jobs. Once on the job, they quickly learned that each step of every job had been precisely spelled out on programmed worksheets prepared by Mazda engineers. Improvement suggestions to be made at consensus meetings were first submitted to American managers but had to be authorized by Japanese advisors and could be rejected without explanation. Rather than providing the expected opportunity for input and problem-solving, team meetings became a way for management to communicate new orders and work assignments. As job assignments for absent workers were divided among those who were present, Mazda established a self-regulating attendance system based on peer pressure. Not surprisingly, along with an increasingly stressful work pace and growing frustration, workers' commitment declined and quality problems increased. In 1988 Mazda's defect rate for cars coming off the assembly line exceeded the company's projection by 60 percent.[19]

Health and Safety Headaches

Developments in the area of health and safety reflect a similar process of transformation; despite initial promises and hopes, the situation became worse than in many traditional assembly plants.

At the outset, Mazda's approach to health and safety was to be based not only on respect for *human life*, but on respect for *human beings*, a distinction which, in the mind of the plant's director for health and safety Don Kricho, "... was not just concerned with life or the physical body – but with the way a person thinks – everything. Kricho's vision of a fit and healthy workforce that would change unhealthy habits accordingly, also included worker awareness, and the touted goal of a 'zero-accident' safety process. Every accident, even minor ones, would be viewed as a disaster and would be thoroughly investigated so it would never happen again."

The reality looked quite different. Workdays lost due to occupational injury or illness during the plant's first year of two-shift operation was higher than that of the Big Three auto plants in Detroit: 42.6 days lost for every 100 workers at Mazda compared with 33.9 days lost for all Michigan motor vehicle and assembly plants. The most common complaint of Mazda workers were cumulative trauma injuries [CTI], mostly carpal tunnel syndrome, a painful inflammation in the hand and wrist resulting from excessive repetitive motions. Mazda Flat Rock CTI incidents were almost twice as high as those at the Chrysler Sterling Heights assembly plant, even though it had longer hours of operation and a much larger workforce. The occurrence of these problems was largely attributed to the plant's just-in-time production pace. Not only did Mazda workers have to perform their repetitive tasks faster and more often, they had to do so over long stretches of time without rest, because almost all idle moments had been kaizened out of their work routines. Though Mazda's production set-up actually contains some not yet widespread ergonomically advantageous features that allow for tilting of car bodies and engines while they are being worked on, these advantages are counteracted by the fast workpace and the long working hours frequently imposed.[20]

A membership survey conducted by the union in 1990 to determine bargaining priorities and member attitudes reflected employees' concern about health and safety. Seventy-three percent agreed with the following statement: "If the present level of work intensity continues, I will likely be injured or worn out before I retire."[21]

A Critical Union

In 1989 an unhappy workforce voted a new union leadership team into office. The newly elected leaders had a highly critical perspective on Mazda's way of running the business. During the subsequent bargaining process in connection with the expiring initial labor contract, more than 90 percent of the voting union membership authorized the new leaders to call a strike if negotiations stalled. The new contract signed in spring 1991 achieved wage parity with workers at the Big Three American auto manufacturers. Other contract gains were advance notice regarding the introduction of new technologies; more union influence in company decisions about the outsourcing of work historically performed by bargaining unit employees; and the establishment of a structure for joint union/management deliberations over policies affecting union members in areas such as quality, equal opportunity employment, training, and health and safety. In view of the health and safety problems in the plant, the new agreement also strengthened the union's position in this area through the addition of one more fulltime union health and safety representative and one full-time ergonomics representative in conjunction with a planned jointly developed ergonomics training program. As in other Big Three plants, there is now a written health and safety grievance procedure, and the union has access to more information.

Is Mazda Different from Other Transplants?

Some of the problems found at Mazda in Flat Rock are unique to that plant. Yet unfulfilled promises regarding employee input in job design and the decision-making process, the tendency to revert to Taylorized, short work cycles with limited job rotation or multiskilling, understaffing, and frequent orders to work over-time on short notice are themes reiterated by employees at the Diamondstar plant in Normal, Illinois, a joint venture between Chrysler and Mitsubishi operated according to similar principles.

A recent report by a group of Swedish researchers who visited eight Japanese auto transplants in the United States and Canada (including Mazda and Mitsubishi) concluded that lean production is characterized by a great contrast between the quality of the product and the quality of working life that transplants offer.[22] On the positive side, many of these plants make a commitment to job security, assign high priority to product quality, take worker suggestions in this area seriously, and instill a sense of pride in the plant's achievements. On the down side, the work pace is fast and intense, and the amount of overtime work is high and frequently occurs on short notice. Though considerable emphasis is placed on safety, and the production process is often designed for efficient and high-quality manufacturing, the intense pace, short work cycles, and long working hours nevertheless lead to significant health and safety risks, particularly for cumulative trauma disorders.[23] Along with stringent management policies about the mandatory wearing of uniforms, as well as detailed codes of behavior and discipline, running counter to the cherished American values of individualism and personal freedom, this new "model for the workplace of the future" holds little promise for restoring human dignity at work or for the proposition that work activity should allow for continuous learning and competence development.

GM Saturn: The Union as a Partner in Business

Saturn's development has to be understood in the context of General Motors' struggle to regain competitiveness in the eight-ies. Saturn was the brainchild of GM's former chairman, Roger Smith, whose tenure as General Motors' leader saw the U.S. market share of the world's largest automaker drop from 45 per-cent in the late seventies to 35 percent in the late eighties. General Motors was beset by quality problems and declining sales of its look-alike models. The automaker had cloned its basic models in divisional reorganizations, which resulted in the loss of the traditional name plate identity for Chevrolets, Buicks, or Oldsmobiles.

Described by his former speech writer as the man who "transformed the industry leader [GM] into a fallen giant,"[24] Smith believed that the way to get GM out of trouble was to implement his high-technology dream. By 1986 Smith had spent $ 40-50 billion to build eight new assembly plants and extensive modernize nineteen existing facilities. Yet the first two of these high-tech assembly facilities, the BOC Orion and Hamtramck plants, equipped with state-of-the-art robots, had tremendously costly start-up problems. A *Wall Street Journal* article described the Hamtramck plant as "more of a basket case than the showcase it was meant to be."[25]

In addition to experimenting with the latest (but often untested) technology available, General Motors pursued an assortment of *seemingly unrelated strategies*. One was to build component plants along the Mexican border, where nonunionized workers could be hired for less than two dollars an hour, a small fraction of the hourly wage cost of a UAW worker in the United States.

At the same time, Smith initiated an unusual joint venture with one of GM's main competitors, Toyota, in the NUMMI (New United Motors Manufacturing Inc.) project in Fremont, California. This fifty-fifty joint investment was to replace the former Fremont assembly plant, one of GM's nightmares, plagued by a 20 percent absenteeism rate and hundreds of unresolved union grievances when it closed in 1981. Under Toyota management, but working with essentially the same workforce, NUMMI soon turned into GM's most productive assembly plant. Using relatively traditional technology, NUMMI produced 25 percent more cars an hour than any other GM facility, with absenteeism down to 2 to 3 percent. NUMMI management eliminated executive perks such as assigned parking spaces and separate cafeterias and pursued a comprehensive quality philosophy. Small work teams of four to seven members were created, guided by hourly team leaders who were sent to Japan for training. Team leaders acted as facilitators, eliciting employees' ideas on how to improve production, and allowing workers to pull a cord and stop the line if a quality problem was discovered. NUMMI also used the *kanban* (just-in-time) system typical of the Japanese approach. Though NUMMI's success was a little embarrassing to Roger Smith in light of the problems his high-tech plants were struggling with, it became a training ground for thousands of GM managers who spent time there learning the new system.[26]

Soon the NUMMI team concept became a fad in GM and was introduced in many of its other plants. However, leaving much of its traditional management system and incentive structure intact (e.g., supervisors are responsible for "getting the job done"; workers have no real influence on quality decisions, and have no cord to pull when quality problems occur), "team concept" came to mean a lot of different things at General Motors. The models ranged from workers learning five to eight jobs, but still ending up doing mostly the same one, to meeting for a discussion about production problems once a week, to approaches that resembled the NUMMI system more closely.[27]

Yet even at NUMMI, original worker enthusiasm faded as production pressures increased and with them the speed of the assembly line. Teamwork began to suffer as most workers were struggling just to finish their own job with little time to help out others. Meetings became less frequent, and workers were discouraged from pulling the cord to stop the assembly line when quality flaws were detected.[28] While things improved again, many workers had lost trust in the new system, and though most of them say that they do not want to go back to the old way of building cars, they admit that working for the Japanese is more demanding. As one worker aid, "You don't know hard work until you've been at NUMMI."[29]

Saturn: A New Company – A New Concept

At the same time all this happened, the Saturn concept was taking shape – one step removed from other events at General Motors. Named after the ambitious NASA rocket program, Saturn was established as a wholly owned new GM subsidiary. It was to embody Roger Smith's vision for redesigning the auto business as Americans had known it and was to be proof that the Japanese could be beaten in the entry level small car market. And Saturn was to be high-tech, incorporating the most advanced technology that could be found. Every aspect of how to build a car would be rethought, and no existing machinery or processes were be used. Smith committed 350 of GM's best people to apply their ideas to the project. They were to develop their entrepreneurial spirit equipped with a generous $ 5 billion budget. Yet, Smith had a rather specific vision of what Saturn would be like, a concept that could be pieced together from his speeches and interviews on the subject:

> The buyer – arriving at the Saturn dealership – would sit down with a salesman at the computer terminal. He would say "I don't smoke and I don't want others to smoke in my car," so the salesman would punch in "no ashtrays." He'd say "I like the car to feel firm in curves and yet give a soft ride on the open highway." The salesman would punch in a tailor-made suspension system. ... The salesman would show the prospect a wide range of interior and exterior colors on the display screen to choose from. While all this was going on, the computer would be checking the buyer's credit and ordering him insurance on the vehicle. When he pressed the "execute" key, every one of the fifteen thousand parts that would go into his car would be automatically ordered from the right suppliers and computer-directed to arrive at the factory at precisely the right time for assembly. A robot would meet the shipments at the dock and deliver them to the high-tech assembly line. ... All of this would be accomplished – from buyer's first choice to delivery – in just two weeks, without a single piece of paper changing hands along the way. Orders, supplier invoices, billings, and even the monthly payments would be handled electronically."[30]

The Union: An Acknowledged and Empowered Stakeholder

Soon it became clear, however, that Saturn would not resemble Roger Smith's fantasy very much. Yet, while Saturn never turned into the ultra high-tech fiction, it does represent *a radically new and different approach* to planning and building a car in the U.S. history of labor-management relations. UAW advisors were involved as full partners from the very beginning of the planning process. An unprecedented agreement, based on a consensus decision-making model, allows both parties to veto any decision and to suggest alternatives. While developing and incorporating a number of technological innovations, Saturn's uniqueness turned out to be in its approach to managing and involving people. Many of the Saturn engineers had spent time at NUMMI and had come to rethink what matters in car production. As Guy Briggs, a Saturn vice president, suggested in describing the Saturn approach:

> Let's face it, none of the technology – the robots, the computers, the machine intelligence – none of the processes – none of it is going to make much difference without the right people. Saturn, more than anything else, is an experiment in people management – not in the

> management of brains and worker brawn, but in total participation, contribution, and commitment of every person involved. ... The union is our partner. The UAW is a stakeholder in Saturn and participates in decisions. Our Saturn-UAW agreement ... is a genuine living document. We're a team, and we're going to work every challenge through with group consensus.[31]

Roger Smith was disappointed at the demise of his high-tech concept, but reluctantly agreed to let the planning team follow its course.[32] Employees rather than computers would pick up the parts at the loading docks. Some existing parts from other car lines would be used, and the envisioned paperless production and ordering system was dropped. At the same time, the first Saturn models were slightly more expensive than originally planned, and production projections had to be delayed.

In 1985, when the future Saturn site was still a large green meadow in Springhill, Tennessee, a team of ninety-five people, including management members, UAW representatives, and a group of future employees (recruited from existing GM plants), set out to plan the 4.5 million square foot facility. The team was gradually expanded as different groups tackled various aspects of the plant design and layout. Physical simulation and modeling techniques were used to determine appropriate locations for team centers and to simulate various work processes. Effects of changing patterns of night and day and the impact of artificial lighting were simulated. Another group studied the impact of garment type and color on safety and comfort, productivity, and personal satisfaction. The findings of the "team center project group" radically changed the originally envisioned plant layout, and the report submitted by the "lighting group" led to the cancellation of an already signed contract with a major supplier.[33]

Integration of People, Technology, and Business Systems

The Saturn mission, stated in its memorandum of agreement (a binding document jointly agreed upon by union and management), is to market vehicles that are world leaders in quality, cost, and customer satisfaction through the integration of people, technology, and business systems. The explicit Saturn philosophy is based on the belief that people want to be involved in decisions that affect them, that they care about their jobs, and that they take pride in themselves and in their contribution. To achieve this mission, a structure and a decision-making process were created based on the following principles:

- Recognition of stakes and equities of everyone in the organization being represented
- Full participation by the representatives of the union
- Use of a consensus decision-making process
- Placement of authority and decision-making in the appropriate part of the organization with emphasis on the work unit
- Free flow of information
- Clear definition of the decision-making process

From the start, the consensus decision-making process was aimed at the efforts of both parties (union and management) to negotiate the "best" solution. This process allows any of the parties to block a potential decision. However, the party opposing the decision must search for alternatives. This decision-making process is used at all organizational levels. At the core of the production process is the self-directed work unit that understands and can accomplish the tasks within its area of responsibility without direction. Team leadership is rotating. The unit makes its own work assignments, resolves its own conflicts, plans its work, designs its jobs, controls its own scrap and its materials and inventory, performs equipment maintenance, organizes communication within and outside the group, keeps its own records, selects new members for the unit, seeks continuous improvement, does its own budgeting, and schedules vacations, absences, and so forth. Saturn's organizational structure is illustrated in Figure 4.1. It shows the union representation at each organizational level and the responsibilities of the different organizational units.

Assembly Line and Semi-Autonomous Work Teams

Although the work team responsibilities at Saturn are similar to those at Uddevalla (see below), the actual assembly process is more conventional. The plant is highly integrated, with injection molding, stamping, body assembly, painting, and engine and transmission production occurring in different parts of the production complex. New aluminum casting technology is used, and the degree of automation is high in the body assembly shop, while final assembly is still largely manual. Wood-covered conveyors carry the cars down the assembly line, allowing workers to remain stationary, with work cycles of up to ten minutes in some sections. Hydraulic skillets allow for an adjustment of the car to a comfortable working height.[34]

Figure 4.1   Saturn Corporation Organizational Structure

Organizational Unit	UAW Input	Responsibilities
Strategic Advisory Committee **SAC** Company planning, dealer relations, etc. Membership determined with "appropriate input from Saturn and the UAW"	**UAW SAC Advisor**	Long-term viability, responsiveness to the marketplace
Manufacturing Advisory Committee **MAC** All concerns of the entire manufacturing and assembly complex Composed of business unit advisors	**UAW MAC Advisor** Consensus decision-making body Highest local administrator	Responsible for implementing Saturn philosophy • Provides resources to Business Unit: timely and effectively • Appraises performance • Represents and protects the interests, stakes and equities of Business Unit members
Business Unit Integrated group work units and work unit modukes Stamping, powertrain, etc.	**UAW Business Unit Advisor** Administrator of Agreement	Short and near term advance planning • Determines resources needed by work units
Work Unit Module Integrated group of work units technical, product, etc.	**Common Work Unit Module Advisor**	Consensus decision-making • Resonsibilities: Producing to schedule, maintaining product quality, performing to budget, safety and health, maintenance, housekeeping, job assignments, inventory control, repairs, scrap control, absenteeism, record keeping • Selects new group members • Communications
Work Unit 6-15 members self-directed	**UAW Work Unit Coordinator** Working member of work unit	

The Saturn production concept incorporates many lean production principles: rapid material flow; an efficient supplier structure (with only about 200 direct suppliers, compared to over 400 typical for conventional assembly plants); flexible work rules; few job categories; a commitment to eliminating the cause of quality defects; and an emphasis on attendance and consensus.

Yet in important ways Saturn differs from the Japanese approach to lean production: union participation and influence are extensive at all levels of decision-making; strong emphasis is placed on ergonomically sound working postures and tools and on expanded cycle time for individual jobs. And finally, self-directed work teams with broad decision-making responsibilities resemble the concept of semi-autonomous work groups[35] much more closely than the team structure in Japanese plants, where workers have little autonomy and virtually no decision latitude as to how to accomplish a particular task.

An Island of Success Surrounded by Problems?

General Motors' announcement in late 1991 that it will reduce its U.S. workforce by about 75,000 employees and close twenty-one plants over the next five years increases the pressure on Saturn to become a success story. While it is still early to make any final judgment, initial consumer response has been very encouraging. GM's goal of breaking into the Japanese-dominated small car market in the United States appears to be in reach as the sporty small coupes and sedans draw praise from buyers, many of whom say they would otherwise have bought Japanese cars. After a slow production start, GM had to replace close to 2,000 cars because of quality defects. Other problems – perhaps not surprising, given the challenge of dealing with so many innovations at the same time – were addressed before the cars were shipped. Yet in spite of the slow start-up, Saturn's first-year gains are impressive, according to the news media: sales are brisk, and Saturn's customer satisfaction level is high; Saturn won the best "basic small" honors in a study by the prestigious J.D. Powers customer satisfaction research firm. Saturn's dealership network has grown from 29 outlets in ten states in 1990 to 130 in thirty-eight states by September 1991.[36] In October 1991, when most American auto dealers were suffering from the slowest new car sales since the last recession, 90 percent of Saturn dealers were profitable.[37]

The new relationship with the union and the hourly workers appears to have a positive impact on quality. In the summer of

1991, tension between union and management rose briefly as workers were alarmed about the rising number of defects. They complained of increasing delays by engineers who fixed machines. As a silent expression of their frustration, the workforce, worried that quality was being sacrificed for greater output, donned armbands when the new GM chairman, Robert C. Stempel, toured the plant in October. "They are very hard on their leaders," said Mike Bennett, president of the local union. "They always want to know why things aren't fixed yet."[38] And although production per hour has greatly increased, the work pace is still described as comfortable and the ergonomics of the assembly line are considered "superb."[39]

Volvo at Uddevalla: The Assembly Line Transformed

Volvo's leadership in pioneering new approaches to car assembly has in part been attributed to a different management philosophy and a labor relations system in a legislative framework of joint consultation that gives unions and workers the right to participate in workplace decisions. In the 1960s, the Swedish labor unions broadened their concerns beyond fair wages and benefits and proposed a more encompassing conception of quality of working life. The expanded agenda included questions of psychosocial aspects of well-being at work, such as group cooperation, union input in the design and implementation of new technologies, worker participation structures, multiskilling, and the development of competences beyond immediate production tasks. The particular characteristics of Volvo's various experiments in redesigning car assembly thus represent a compromise between union goals of enhancing worker autonomy and collective competence development and management's objectives of increasing quality, flexibility, and productivity.

Labor Market Constraints Breed Innovation

The impetus for the first major wave of automobile production reforms at Volvo, the leading Swedish car manufacturer, was the extreme worker recruitment difficulties the Swedish car industry faced in the economic boom of the early 1970s. In a tight labor market, the young, well-educated Swedish workforce had alternative options, and many were no longer willing to spend their working day in monotonous assembly line jobs. High absenteeism and turnover rates as high as 100 percent resulted in a continuously changing workforce with little production experience and low motivation, seriously threatening the quality standards expected of Volvo's costly upscale cars. Initial experiments with changes in work organization and production techniques were aimed at reducing absenteeism and turnover rates while at the same time improving the company's attractiveness in the labor market. Such early efforts at a variety of Volvo and Saab component plants indicated that workforce stability could be improved provided the changes were far-reaching enough.[40]

The moving assembly line, the symbol of car production since its establishment by Henry Ford in 1912, was first abolished in Volvo's Kalmar plant in 1974. The design of the production facility itself was to reflect and support the emphasis on work groups or teams. At Kalmar, a computer-guided platform moves the car body through its different phases of assembly. On each platform two workers move with the car past six work stations, involving work cycles that vary between sixteen and forty minutes. Work groups are responsible for the twenty-five different assembly areas. The assignment of work tasks at Kalmar remained relatively traditional, however, with most groups being in charge of different assembly areas, and fewer working on quality control and repair of defects. Though group meetings occur, they vary in frequency and duration, since opportunities for input in work organization remain very limited. A brochure published by Volvo on the occasion of Kalmar's tenth anniversary hailed the success of the project: assembly costs at Kalmar were 25 percent lower than at its more traditional Torslanda facility, and quality costs had been reduced by 40 percent. While economic benefits were thus considerable, this system provided only limited possibility for more worker autonomy, competence development, or control over the work pace. Seventy-five percent of the members of surveyed assembly groups felt that they had no influence over how to do their job, and 80 percent suggested that they had no control over the work pace or opportunities for new learning on the job.[41]

In 1985, when planning for the new Uddevalla project started, Kalmar was still considered the "best practice" factory among Volvo's plants in Sweden, characterized by high efficiency and reliable production. Yet work intensity was high, and while work cycle time was longer than in traditional car assembly, self-regulation and decision latitude of individual work teams remained very limited. This led Volvo chairman Pehr Gyllenhammar to comment: "Volvo Kalmar is no ideal workplace. It is a first step in that direction. But in terms of work design much remains to be done. I can imagine a work situation that allows for much more freedom and self-reliance."[42] Meanwhile Volvo had gained further experience in the late seventies, experimenting with various forms of work group assembly in its Vara plant, which produced small marine diesel engines, and in its Tuve truck assembly plant.

In 1985 Volvo decided to locate a new assembly plant for its upscale Volvo 740 models in Uddevalla, a coastal town hard hit by industrial depression and the closing of the shipyard there in 1984. Planning for the new factory started in a period characterized by a 2 percent unemployment rate, economic growth, and high profits at Volvo. The company's successes and failures in its earlier work reorganization experiments led to a critical re-evaluation of past experiences. At the same time, Volvo's chairman reiterated his great interest in organizational and production innovation, including the humanization of factory work and his commitment to placing strong value on long-term cooperation with the Swedish metalworkers' union. The union in turn made a strong push for group-based work organization with maximum self-regulation and decentralization.

A Developmental Design Process Leads to a Bold New Concept

A special project group was created to start the planning process. This group encompassed Volvo managers and engineers as well as trade union representatives, who were involved on a full-time basis from the outset, participating for the most part on the same terms as the other group members. The project group's goal was to develop a factory characterized by high productivity, great flexibility, and good jobs for employees. The criteria for a good job were defined as follows: it should be ergonomically sound and provide enhanced work content; it should be oriented toward problem-solving and lead to personal development. These goals were associated with the notion of "complete cars – complete products," which would allow workers to determine the assembly pace.

The final assembly concept at Uddevalla emerged from a five-year planning and experimentation process described by Ellegard, Engström, and Nilsson, and summarized below.[43] The original pilot study proposal submitted to the project group in the spring of 1985 showed little variation from the Kalmar concept. Automated guided vehicles would carry the car body through the shop during assembly. Work cycles were one to two minutes, and about 700 people would be involved in the assembly of a single car. The project group considered this proposal unacceptable and was assigned the task of developing an alternative design. Over the next three years, the group developed an alternative plan that underwent a series of revisions, moving further and further away from more traditional assembly concepts toward a "crafts" model of car assembly.

The group's first proposal, called "Uddevalla Ultra," entailed eight organizationally independent product shops that were to be serially connected, so that each car would pass through all of them. The work content at each station was to encompass fifteen to twenty minutes of assembly per person, with about 100 people participating in the assembly of a single car. In addition to exceeding the predetermined budget, this proposal failed to provide the job quality characteristics sought by union representatives. Subsequent work on the concept moved further in the direction of producing a complete car in one product shop with four serially linked ten-member team zones, each assembling one-quarter of the car. This proposal formed the basis for determining the total investment volume and decisions about facility design and layout. Further analysis indicated, however, that this team zone design would not achieve the stipulated production quota of 40,000 cars per year in one shift. Further revisions resulted in the final concept of each team assembling a complete car, which saved space and reduced the time and expense of moving the car from team to team. In this design, ten workers were in charge of building a complete car, with each person acquiring the competence of building one-quarter of the car. Figure 4.2 illustrates the various phases in the development of the production concept over time.

The developmental process for designing the final Uddevalla manufacturing concept received much impetus from the "Red Shed," an experimental workshop inside the old shipyard. Under the leadership of an unconventional industrial engineer assigned to the Uddevalla project, the components of a completely disassembled Volvo were laid out on the floor to experiment with new ways of assembling the car. This different perspective on the car, broken down into its components, supported the notion of an assembly sequence in four functional groups allowing each worker to assemble one-quarter of a car.

Figure 4.2   Development of the Uddevalla Production Concept

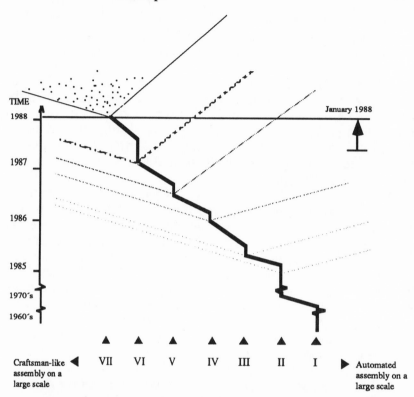

(I) Assembly line. (II) Automated guided vehicles. (III) Automated guided vehicles easily converted to parallel assembly. Approximately 700 people build a car. (IV) Eight series-linked product shops each with parallel-linked stations. Approximately 100 people build a car. (V) Six parallel-linked product shops each with four series-linked team zones – *Complete car in product shop.* (VI) Six parallel-linked product shops each with four parallellinked team zones – *Complete car in team zone.* Approximately 20 people build a car. (VII) Six parallel-linked product shops each with eight parallel-linked teams – *Complete car in team.* Approximately 10 people build a car.

Illustration of the position of the project in January 1988. Strong arguments were made during work on the project for allowing a team to build complete cars. Since a team would consist of 10 people, no more than approximately 10 people would therefore be involved in the assembly of each complete car. This meant that 6 parallel-linked product shops each came to contain 8 parallel-linked teams, each of which assembled complete cars.[44]

The first education workshop started in April 1986. It was aimed at creating competence in the new profession of car builder that was to characterize work at the Uddevalla plant. Based on a craftsperson-apprentice model, competent "teachers" worked with incoming employees, getting the premises ready for material handling and assembly, ordering equipment and tools, and setting up administrative structures. The principle underlying this approach was "learning through work activity."

The work in the education workshop was a testing ground for the project group's unconventional vision for the design of a new production process. Experiences in the workshop proved an assumption held by many of the planners – that a twenty-minute work cycle was the maximum that could be expected from an individual worker – to be incorrect.

The new workers similarly had expected various forms of courses and training programs and wondered initially how participation in production could be education in car building. Yet interviews with employees indicated that they considered their jobs to be good, though not well organized. White-collar employees' assessment fell into two categories: those who experienced the possibilities for development and change as positive were more satisfied than those who missed clarity in organization and decisions.

Ellegard and her colleagues suggest that the following factors were key to the developmental process described above:

- Both the company and the union were looking for decisive changes in working conditions in the car industry.
- Openness of the project leadership to suggestions involving extra efforts to get approval of the parties involved.
- Agreement about the direction of the project among the company and the union.
- The role of the union team member as "suggestion maker" rather than "demander," leading to a new way of active cooperation and the reevaluation of management attitudes toward union involvement in the project.
- A delay due to protracted negotiations for a wastewater treatment permit and the above-budget cost estimate of the original Uddevalla Ultra allowed for an extension of the project development time.
- Experimentation with functional assembly in the "Red Shed" supported new principles of education and competence development.[45]

The plant consists of an L-shaped building in which car components (e.g., transmission, brake system, front and rear axles) are preassembled in work groups of ten workers who rotate the different tasks. Their work involves planning of parts needed, transport, problem-solving, assembly, and quality control. The component blocks assembled at Uddevalla, together with the painted body (shipped from the Torslanda stamping plant) then are transported on electric carriers to the assembly areas at either end of the L. There is space for eight teams of eight to ten people in each assembly area, with work stations in which groups of two to three workers accomplish 25-50 percent of the assembly of each car. This allows for adaptation to the existing qualification structure of the workers depending on individual training and skill level achieved. The key to this production concept is communication. Nobody has to walk more than thirty yards to talk with co-workers. Cars don't move, and workers have the time necessary to solve problems and to plan ahead.

The following principles guide the process:

- Competence development occurs through task involvement.
- Learning processes are as important as production processes.
- Competence development is a social and communicative process.
- Work tasks are seen as embedded in functional contexts.
- Lively discussion about working conditions and goals takes place.
- The assembly of component groups with task cycles of 120 minutes (in self-determined order) allows workers and the group to develop individual and collective assembly strategies, and to plan and develop their activities themselves.
- Organizational and technical functions are delegated to the group (e.g., planning of staffing, who does what, cost calculation, technical improvements of products and equipment, quality control, equipment maintenance, communication system).
- All major decisions must be approved by a joint committee representing both union and management.[46]

Will It Work?

During 1989, the first year of production, as production targets were low, productivity (defined as person-hour per car assembled) was "surprisingly good," according to Volvo. As production volume and workforce doubled in 1990, things slowed down. Some of the problems faced at Uddevalla in its first year of increased production are summarized by Christian Berggren.[47] Though the change from the 700 to the 900 model was accomplished more smoothly than in other Swedish plants and quality was high at times, quality and productivity fluctuated and remained unstable. With unemployment as low as 1 percent in the late 1980s, employee recruitment was difficult, particularly among men over the age of thirty, since entry-level wages based on an anticipated training period of considerable duration were lower than the wages in the nearby more traditional Trollhättan assembly plant. This made it difficult to recruit employees qualified for this type of demanding work and had a negative effect on the work flow in the work groups in charge of training newly arriving members.

The decentralized organization also led to considerable variation among teams; in some, workers are more likely to cling to established methods and work patterns, and in others highly qualified workers take iniative and continuously strive to develop new methods and improvements. In 1990 differences among teams were considerable: some had no problem achieving the productivity and quality standards, while others lagged far behind. In response, the company tried to create an economic incentive for the weaker teams through a bonus system at the work group level. The union's response was reluctance, pointing out the danger that certain group members might be pushed out of the group.

It is still too early to evaluate this unusual work reorganization experiment in terms of standard productivity, cost, and quality measures. As Volvo's leadership stated in 1989, Uddevalla represents a strategic measure to solve assembly problems in Sweden and is thus a long-term strategy. Volvo's first objective is for Uddevalla to achieve the economic and quality performance of its Torslanda plant, and in the long run to reach the level of its "best" facility in Ghent, Belgium.[48]

The U.S. news media does not take kindly to such longer-term perspectives, and some critical articles have questioned the viability of the concept, arguing that it is unlikely ever to achieve its production goals.[49] Proponents of lean production have already pronounced it a "dead horse,"[50] looking, one might almost suspect, for confirmation of earlier predictions, made before Uddevalla even started production, that it would fail. Though it is mentioned in passing that the "workers seem happier" at Uddevalla and that quality targets have been achieved, these aspects carry little weight in the discussion about world-class productivity levels.

COMPARISONS AND IMPLICATIONS

The differences in the production design concepts and forms of work organization illustrated by these examples are the result of a variety of factors, among them labor market conditions, the economic positions of the companies involved, the market niche served, the system of labor-management relations in a given nation, as well as management philosophies and values.

It has been argued that the stringent Japanese management system requires a certain social context for it to function. It is not surprising that Japanese transplants in the United States and Europe (mostly Great Britain) were typically located in areas with high unemployment, allowing for a very selective recruitment of a workforce with few alternative choices. Where possible, they also tried to avoid unionization of transplants or negotiated labor contracts with weak union influence over job classifications, work assignments, overtime requests, and so forth. In countries such as Germany, the application of Japanese management principles has run into considerable difficulties. The permanent violation of worker codetermination rights has led to a number of court disputes. Management requests that employees work great amounts of overtime or not us all their legally granted vacation days were a frequent source of conflict.[51]

Contrasting the Japanese "multiskilling" concept with European "work humanization" efforts, Kumazawa Makoto, a Japanese scholar, denies any comparability between the two approaches: "The so-called multi-skilled versatility required of an employee is very frequently no other than an adaptive capability to perform a number of simplified operations as swiftly as possible. ... An image of a skilled worker who can decide autonomously the most appropriate plan, method and place of work would be rather disharmonious with the Japanese-style production management."[52]

On the other hand, experimentation by Swedish and in some cases German auto manufacturers with new forms of work organization aimed at enhancing the quality of work and working life might have been much less likely without the pressures of a tight labor market and strong unions who set forth their own agenda for the increased autonomy of work groups and work redesign aimed at ongoing skill and competence development. Volvo's highly successful plant in Belgium, which operates with a very traditional assembly line, is an example of the company's adaptation to local conditions which require few innovations.

Table 4.1   Similarities and Differences in Three Production Design Concepts

	MAZDA	SATURN	VOLVO UDDEVALLA
Mission/Values	Everyone will work together to achieve Mazda's corporate goals through management policies; "everlasting effort for everlasting competition"	To market vehicles ... that are world leaders in quality, cost and customer satisfaction through the integration of people, technology, and business systems	Complete Cars – Complete Products: High productivity, quality, flexibility; equal emphasis on learning and competence development
Decision-making procedures	Achieving decision-making by consensus: ... success [is] based on a common understanding and recognition of the mutual goals of management and employees	The consensus process is the primary method for making decisions; any party may block a potential decision, but the party blocking the decisions must search for alternatives	Legally required trade union consultation regarding supervision and allocation of work; introduction of new technologies
Level of union/employee influence in determining production concept and work organization	Low-none: Management designed production process, detailed job descriptions for every single task; management determined work assignments	High: Union full partner in all strategic decisions regarding production concept, marketing, work organization. Right to veto any decision and make alternative suggestions at all organizational levels	High: Full union partnership in designing production concept; work groups determine the best way to assemble each car

(continued next page)

(Table 4.1 cont.)	MAZDA	SATURN	VOLVO UDDEVALLA
Organizational hierarchy (levels)	Plant manager Area managers Unit leaders (supervise 20-30 workers) Work team with UAW team leader (4 levels)	Strategic advisory committee Manufacturing advisory committee Business unit Work unit module Work unit (5 levels with UAW advisor at each level)	Plant manager Product area managers (80-100 people) Work groups (3 levels)
Work organization	Teams of 6-10 workers; some multiskilling (skilled trades only) and some job rotation for production workers (management determined)	Work units of 6-15 members; responsible for meeting schedule, budget, quality, job assignments, work planning, maintenance, housekeeping, material planning and inventory control, absenteeism, health and safety; UAW coordinator	Work groups of 8-10 workers responsible for complete assembly of car; planning of materials needed, repairs, personnel scheduling, tools and equipment maintenance; rotating group speaker
Production system	Assembly line, short work cycles (less than 2 min.); management determines pace and work assignments	Assembly line with adjustable skillets allowing for some stationary work; multiskilling, work cycles up to 10 minutes	Stationary car assembly, each worker able to assemble 25% or more of the car; 120 minute work cycles, pace determined by work group
Technology	Flexible manufacturing system MIS; robotics CAD/CAM; SPC synchronous manufacturing total quality management	Flexible manufacturing system MIS; robotics CAD/CAM; SPC synchronous manufacturing total quality management	Electronic carriers deliver painted bodies and component groups to each assembly station; computerized inventory control system

(continued next page)

(Table 4.1 cont.)	MAZDA	SATURN	VOLVO UDDEVALLA
Worker selection and training	Criteria: young, mostly without previous factory experience; cooperative attitude; 3-week orientation, focus: interpersonal relations, problem-solving; kanban and kaizen concept; application of kaizen; on the job technical training (six weeks cross-training for skilled trades; 10-80 hours for initially hired production workers; minimal for new employees/temporary workers	Criteria: UAW members with transfer rights from other GM plants; interested in new work concepts and extensive training Extensive pre-job training for all workers; ongoing team development training; work unit selects new group members	Criteria: Basic education (high school); to reflect Swedish labor market structure (40% women; not more than 25% younger than 25; and at least 25% over 45). 16 month process of competence development; 20 days of theory modules spread over time interspersed with on the job learning; competence development plan for each worker; bonus system for increased individual and group qualifications

Finally, Volvo's Uddevalla project and GM's expensive Saturn experiment were conceived at a time when both companies had a sound financial cushion. Table 4.1 highlights some of the key differences and similarities among the production concepts at Mazda, Volvo Uddevalla, and Saturn. It compares the underlying mission and values and shows how these varying philosophies were translated into different decision-making processes, structures of influence, characteristics of work organization, technology applications, and employee selection and training.

While espousing a similar philosophy of worker involvement, input, and multiskilling at the outset, the outcomes at Mazda suggest that such goals are likely to fall by the wayside as production pressures grow. The implicit assumption that employees will participate in a joint effort aimed at achieving management's goals ignores the existence of conflicting interests. There are no negotiated, clearly defined structures for union or employee influence.

At Mazda, the production process was determined and planned by engineers; worker and union input was limited to suggestions for how to improve productivity and efficiency rather than the quality of work itself. By contrast, the original Uddevalla concept as well as the Saturn concept changed considerably during a lengthy planning process extending over several years. The radically different final production concept at Volvo is said to be the result of company initiated reform ambitions strongly supported by Volvo chairman Pehr Gyllenhammar, the experimental space provided to some creative production engineers, and trade union demands for alternative forms of work organization. Gyllenhammar is quoted as saying, "I want people to go home and say, 'I really built this car.' That is my dream."

Roger Smith, on the other hand, wanted Saturn to use the latest technology available; little thought was given to the way in which work would be organized. Though his vision was reshaped considerably, to his credit, he did not force the Saturn group back on his course.

In terms of the degree to which these production concepts provide opportunities for competence development and collective decision-making latitude at the work group and individual level, the three plants can be viewed on a continuum. While production at all three plants is based on work groups, the range of responsibilities and the scope of activities performed by the individual and the group vary greatly. At one end is Mazda, where the work units as they are currently operating seem to provide very little opportunity for individual and group competence development or multiskilling at all levels. Uddevalla, at the other end of the continuum, offers the greatest task variety, with long work cycles and broad responsibilities assigned to the work teams.[53] At Saturn, which embodies many lean production principles in structuring supplier relationships, just-in-time, and so on, individual work tasks resemble more closely those of the traditional assembly line, yet many indirect planning, scheduling, maintenance, and quality control functions are delegated to the work unit.

The participatory planning process at Uddevalla and Saturn gave unions and employees real influence in the design phase. It fostered a discourse as to what constitutes meaningful human activity and how work might be organized to meet human needs for learning and development as well as economic goals of productivity, flexibility, and quality. Needless to say, this process requires patience and is fraught with many difficulties, as it demands the rethinking of traditional roles for all parties involved and the honest search for new ways of working together. For managers it may mean relinquishing traditional arenas of control and unilateral decision-making. For unions it poses the question of how to counteract possible threats to solidarity and the potential for group competition, as work groups gain in autonomy and influence in the decision-making process.

It is thus not the purpose of this comparison simply to point to one of these concepts as the best one. Each developed in a particular context, and all have their advantages and their limitations. Particularly in the case of Uddevalla and Saturn, the jury is still out; it is too early to tell if the currently implemented forms of work organization will and can be maintained. Some skeptics argue that the Uddevalla concept might be workable in the production of expensive luxury cars built to customer specifications, but that it cannot become a model for the production of large numbers of smaller, less expensive cars for which there is a greater demand.[54] From this perspective, Saturn may be an experiment more easily transferable to the car manufacturing process in general.

In the end, the choice of alternative work design concepts is really a choice of purpose shaped by values. If our vision of the workplace of the future is based solely on the criterion of output per person-hour, then indeed the Japanese model may be the preferred choice, though the human costs resulting from stress and a fast work pace appear to be mounting, as recent reports from Japan suggest.[55] Is *karoshi* (the Japanese term for death from overwork) the price to be paid for *muda* (elimination of waste) and *kaizen,* "with its focus on the continuous improvement of product and productivity rather than on the continuing improvement of individual and group skills and competences?"[56]

NOTES

1. Bureau of National Affairs, *Employer Bargaining Objectives – Survey* (Washington, D.C., 1990).
2. Michael Goldfield, *The Decline of Organized Labor in the United States* (Chicago: University of Chicago Press, 1987).
3. Jerome S. Rosow, ed., *Teamwork: Joint Labor-Management Programs in America* (New York: Pergamon Press, 1986); William N. Cooke, *Labor-*

Management Cooperation: New Partnership or Going in Circles? (Kalamazoo, Mich.: Upjohn, 1990).

4. James P. Womack, Daniel T. Jones, and Daniel Roos, *The Machine that Changed the World* (New York: Rawson Associates Macmillan, 1990).

5. Ibid., p. 278.

6. Ibid., p. 13.

7. For a critique of Womack, Jones, and Roos, *Machine that Changed the World*, see David E. Cole and Michael S. Flynn, *Sloan Management Review* (Spring 1991): 104-106.

8. Sean McAlinden, "Commentary: A U.S. Perspective on the Globalization of the Automotive Industry," International Automotive Industry Forum, Phoenix, Ariz., December 1990, p. 3.

9. Jeffrey Liker and Lee Sanborn, "The Team Approach at the Ford Romeo Assembly Plant," Conference Presentation Summaries: Healthy Work Environments – Healthy People: Participatory Approaches to Improving Workplace Health, Labor Studies Center, University of Michigan, Labor Studies Center, Ann Arbor, June 1991, pp. 33-38.

10. Ibid., pp. 101-102.

11. Christian Berggren, *Von Ford zu Volvo: Automobilherstellung in Schweden* (Berlin: Springer, 1991); Christian Berggren, Torsten Björkman, and Ernst Hollander, *"Are They Unbeatable?"* Royal Institute of Technology, Stockholm; published in English by Labor Studies Center, University of Michigan, Ann Arbor, 1991.

12. Satoshi Kamata, *Japan in the Passing Lane: An Insider's Account of Life in a Japanese Auto Factory* (New York: Pantheon Books, 1982), pp. 22-23, 102, 107.

13. Joseph J. Fucini and Suzy Fucini, *Working for the Japanese: Inside Mazda's American Auto Plant* (New York: Free Press, 1990), p. 218.

14. The description of the Mazda transplant in Flat Rock is based on discussions by the authors with the local union leadership and a number of skilled trades as well as production workers. We also rely on the encompassing description of developments at Mazda between 1987 and 1990 provided by Fucini and Fucini, *Working for the Japanese*; and the report of a visit to various Japanese transplants in the United States by a group of Swedish researchers in 1990; see Berggren, Björkman, and Hollander, *"Are They Unbeatable?"*

15. The employee selection and orientation procedures used at the Mazda Flat Rock plant are described in detail by Mike Parker, who himself went through the application process; see Mike Parker and Jane Slaughter, *Choosing Sides: Unions and the Team Concept* (Boston: South End Press, 1988), pp. 178-184.

16. Ford owns 35 percent of Mazda stock, and the Mazda Flat Rock plant produces the Ford Probe, which it sells to Ford.

17. Fucini and Fucini, *Working for the Japanese*, p. 17.

18. Summarized from ibid., pp. 73-78.

19. Ibid., pp. 132-138.

20. Ibid., p. 174.

21. For a summary of the results of this survey, which achieved an 85 percent response rate, see Steve Babson, "Lean or Mean: The M.I.T. Model and Lean Production at Mazda," draft manuscript, Wayne State University Labor Studies Center, Detroit, 1992, p. 16.

22. Berggren, Björkman, and Hollander, "*Are They Unbeatable?*"

23. Ibid.

24. Albert Lee, *Call Me Roger* (Chicago: Contemporary Books, 1988).

25. Amal Nag, "Tricky Technology: Automakers Discover 'Factory of the Future' Is Headache Just Now," *Wall Street Journal* (May 13, 1986).

26. Albert Lee, *Call Me Roger*.

27. For a critical review of team concept implementations at GM, see Parker and Slaughter, *Choosing Sides*.

28. Neil Chethik, "The Intercultural Honeymoon Ends," *San Jose Mercury News* (February 8, 1987).

29. Neil Chethik, "Japanese Auto Ideal Is Hard Taskmaster," *San Jose Mercury News* (February 9, 1987).

30. Lee, *Call Me Roger*, p. 241.

31. Quoted in ibid., pp. 243-244.

32. Ibid.

33. Colin Clipson, "Participatory Work Design at Saturn," Conference Presentation Summaries: Healthy Work Environments – Healthy People, pp. 31-32.

34. Berggren, Björkman, and Hollander, "*Are They Unbeatable?*" pp. 46-47.

35. For a description of semi-autonomous work groups see Chapter 7.

36. David C. Smith, "Saturn Begins to Shed First-Year Growing Pains," *Ward's Auto World* 27 (September 1991): 7.

37. Doron P. Levin, "Saturn Stands Out Brightly amid the Car-Sales Gloom," *New York Times* (December 17, 1991).

38. Ibid., p. 1.

39. Lindsay Brooke, "Slow But Steady: Saturn Overcomes Paint Pitfalls as the Production Amp-Up Continues," *Automotive Industries* 171 (August 1991): 41.

40. Berggren, *Von Ford zu Volvo*, p. 317.

41. Manfred Muster and Udo Richter, eds., *Mit Vollgas in the Stau: Automobilproduktion, Unternehmensstrategien und die Perspektiven eines ökologischen Verkehrssystems* (Hamburg: VSA Verlag, 1990).

42. Quoted in *Ny Teknik* 1984, see Berggren, *Von Ford zu Volvo*, p. 143.

43. Kajsa Ellegard, Tomas Engström, and Lennart Nilsson, *Reforming Industrial Work: Principles and Realities in the Planning of Volvo's Car Assembly Plant in Uddevalla* (Stockholm: Swedish Work Environment Fund, 1990).

44. Figure and text adapted from ibid., p. 22.

45. Ibid., pp. 27-29.

46. Dieter Budde and Manfred Muster, "Die Alternativen kommen ins Hauptwerk zurück," in Muster and Richter, *Mit Vollgas in den Stau*, pp. 99-100.

47. Berggren, *Von Ford zu Volvo*, pp. 189-191.

48. Volvo's assembly plant in Ghent has been its most productive since the mid-eighties. Here Volvo retained the traditional assembly line. In a labor market with an unemployment rate hovering around 10 percent, Volvo had no trouble recruiting workers and achieving a stable workforce with low absenteeism and turnover rates. In Belgium workers can be fired if they are sick too often or don't produce quality work. A factionalized union movement weakens the influence of collective interest representation in the workplace. The fact that in this very different context Volvo made no efforts to depart from traditional production methods points to the importance of the sociopolitical and labor market context in influencing the emergence of Volvo's innovative organizational culture in Sweden. For a more in-depth discussion of these differences, see ibid., p. 321.

49. Steven Prokesch, "Edges Fray on Volvo's Brave New Humanistic World," *New York Times* (July 7, 1991).

50. James Womack, quoted in ibid., p. 5.

51. Christoph Deutschman, quoted in Christian Berggren, *The Limitations of Transplantation: A Summary of Papers from the International Symposium: Production Strategies and Industrial Relations in the Process of Internationalization* (Sendai, Japan, October 14-16, 1991), p. 4.

52. Quoted in ibid., p. 3.

53. In the Uddevalla plant in 1990, workers' ability to completely assemble a Volvo 740 in twenty hours with a maximum of four minor defects was celebrated as the equivalent of achieving journeyperson status. In addition, workers receive qualification bonuses depending on how much of the total car a worker is able to assemble. See Berggren, *Von Ford zu Volvo*, p. 188.

54. In late 1992, Volvo announced the closing of its assembly plants in Kalmar and Uddevalla due to a serious decline in car sales and increasing production overcapacity. Volvo's new chairman, Sören Gyll, emphasized that Uddevalla had reached its productivity and quality goals and proved to be highly flexible in adapting to production changes, and that the decision to close the facility was based on the need to consolidate production of its upscale models in one plant *(Neue Zürcher Zeitung*, November 25, 1992). Assembly will be moved to Torslanda which is the only stamping plant that builds bodies for these models. Volvo also noted that it still considers the organizational model developed at Uddevalla to be of great value and that it is to be integrated at Torslanda as far as possible. Given that production at Torslanda is based on a traditional assembly line concept, however, the extent to which the Uddevalla approach can be transferred is likely to be very limited.

55. See various recent news articles; for example, Tim Jackson, "Japan Counts the Human Cost of Its Economic Miracle," *Independent* (February 9, 1991); Sebastian Moffett, "Japan's Kamikaze Businessmen Are Working Themselves to Death," *Reuter Library Report* (March 12, 1991).

56.   Peter Unterweger, Winter Leadership Conference Panel on the Team Concept, Labor Studies Center, University of Michigan (Ann Arbor, January 1991).

PART II

THE CHANGE PROCESS

5. A Model and Principles for Social System Change

In Part I we described the process of developing competence through work activity, how work design concepts reflect characteristics of the social and economic context, and the challenges faced by today's organizations, confronted with new market demands, new technologies, and changing workforce characteristics. The three examples of different production systems in one manufacturing sector illustrate the range of available choices and their implications for work design. In this part, we will discuss the process of organizational change and the practical implications for how to undertake such a change effort. We start by returning to Lewin's model of change, briefly discussed in Chapter 1, and then propose a set of principles to guide organizational redesign and change.

Before returning to our change model, let us examine the starting point from which processes of participation and competence development are set in motion.

THE STARTING POINT

The term *starting point* does not imply that competence development starts somewhere at "point zero." At any point at which such a process is to be initiated in an existing organization it affects and changes an already existing *dynamic social system* characterized by patterns of overlapping and conflicting interests, variations in people's perceptions about the organization, hierarchies of authority, and an organizational ideology that carries beliefs and assumptions about what is and what ought to be. We can assume that at any point in time, particularly in today's rapidly changing environment, there may be one or several organization members, in whatever function, who perceive a need to change some aspect of the system and how it operates. They have certain ideas about the future of the organization and a preliminary diagnosis of problems, leading them to believe that something needs to be changed in order to prepare the organization for future demands.

But we can also assume that other individuals and groups in the organization – frequently the majority – might not agree with this assessment, are not really concerned with the need for change, or may at best have a sense of uneasiness about the status quo. Depending on people's experience and function in the organization, their perception of what and how things should change is likely to vary considerably. And it is only when the change process is initiated that these different problem definitions, perceptions, and conflicting interests emerge. Social system change is thus a process of developing goals, negotiating different interests, and fostering willingness to change, both individually and collectively. Since it is not a linear and simultaneous process and since what actually happened in a change process frequently becomes transparent only in hindsight, it is useful to return to Kurt Lewin's model of change to help us understand what occurs in the change process.[1] While, as is true for all models, it reduces the complexity of reality and is thus a simplification of what happens in real life, it nevertheless is a useful analytical tool, particularly if we adapt the terminology Lewin used almost 50 years ago for the present context.

THE PROCESS OF CHANGE

What Is a Social System?

People in organizations, departments, work groups, and teams work together in different fashions. The social sciences therefore call them social systems. The term *social system* refers to all forms of people working, learning, playing, or cooperating with each other, such as families, universities, or political parties.

Figure 5.1   Equilibrium of Social Systems

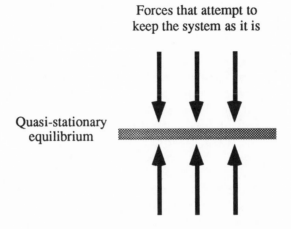

Forces that attempt to
keep the system as it is

Quasi-stationary
equilibrium

Forces that aim at change

The functioning of social systems is characterized by a set of underlying rules or regulations. "Normally," if no change is anticipated, systems appear to be relatively stable. Members are familiar with the variety of norms and rules guiding the system, and they tend to adapt them to their own needs. Lewin, a social scientist, defined this situation as "quasi-stationary" equilibrium (see Figure 5.1). This definition suggests that a social system only *appears* to be stable. There is always movement, but the totality of all movement equals zero; the system remains in what appears to be a state of balance. Another way of expressing this is to say that the balance is achieved by forces that are aimed at change and forces that attempt to stabilize and maintain the system as it is. Many barriers to change in organizations result from the interplay of these forces.

Every major change in a social system, such as the introduction of a new production process or an employee participation project, threatens this "stable state." These changes can arouse fear, since a stable equilibrium is the result of a lot of "invisible negotiation" processes as different individuals and groups try to get their interests and needs met. This equilibrium serves important psychological functions even if it is not completely satisfactory to everyone. As long as the system is undisturbed,

• we know exactly what we can and can't do

- we know what is and can be expected of us
- we know what we can and may expect of others
- we know how the system works and feel comfortable
- in short, it makes the workplace predictable and allows us to feel safe

All this and more are at risk if the quasi-stationary equilibrium of a social system is disturbed. A new situation is created that members have to confront and possibly adapt to. To the degree to which disturbing the system's "stable" state decreases the predictability and understanding of what is happening, what is expected, and so forth, it threatens the basic human desire for mastery and control over one's life. If the change process demands increased participation and influence from organization members who have not previously been able to exert such influence, it upsets existing hierarchies of authority and the way in which power is distributed in the system. Depending on the perception of different actors in the organization as to who loses and who gains as a result of such a change effort, resistance will come from different groups. Even if this is recognized and if all organizational members affected by the change are involved, the previous equilibrium will still be disturbed and changed. Successful change thus requires paying very close attention to the forces at work in a specific social system. Change in every social system requires three basic steps (see Figure 5.2).[2]

Step 1: Open the Existing Situation

As outlined in Chapter 1, change, in Lewin's terms, begins with the mental "unfreezing" of the patterns of norms, values, and beliefs that hold a system together. Changes have to be conceivable if they are to be doable. This applies not only to the initiators of change but eventually to everybody affected by change. For many organizations operating in today's changing environment and faced with pressures for adaptation, the process of unfreezing has been imposed externally. Yet, while the sense that things have to change may be widespread, it is often unclear what needs to be done, why, and how. Opening of the existing situation occurs through reduction of the change-inhibiting forces and strengthening of the forces supporting change. For example, as fears and prejudices are reduced and old habits are changed, trust can develop.

Figure 5.2   "Three-Step" Process of Social System Change

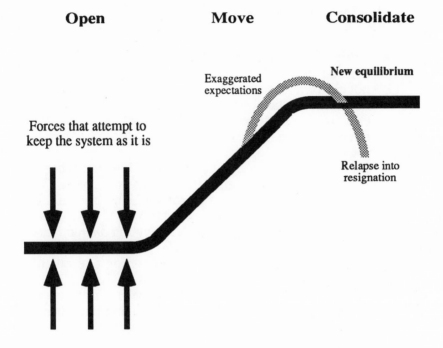

Open   **Move**   **Consolidate**

While all change creates increased uncertainty, resistance to change is frequently not a "personality problem" or an expression of rigidity. Resistance more often signals that the changes fail to take the experiences, needs, and goals of the people affected into account. Resistance is thus most likely to develop if decisions are made without involving the people affected. Resistance reflects the clash of different interests and "developmental states." As discussed in Chapter 1, the process of growth, differentiation, and integration (GDI) does not occur simultaneously in all individuals making up a social system. Only if the individual learning loops become connected through communication, influence, and active involvement in change activities will the system as a whole start to move. Three rules, developed 2,000 years ago by the Greek philosopher Plato, are important:

　　1. Focus on the *goals of the other person*. Put your own interests, needs, and expectations aside and try to put yourself in the other person's situation. Only when you know the mo-

tivation and interests of the other can you try to bring your
goals in line with the other person's needs.
2. Find out the *emotional basis for the resistance*. There are
   three basic types of resistance, which can occur separately
   or simultaneously:
   - Antipathy: people dont't like each other. If that is ad-
     dressed up front this barrier can be overcome, though
     not easily.
   - Rational resistance: The resistance is based on a differ-
     ent logic being used by each person. It is easiest to
     overcome if one tries to understand the other person's
     logic.
   - Emotional resistance and conflicts of interest: These as-
     pects are important and difficult to overcome. They
     have to be addressed and negotiated, and give and take
     may be necessary.
3. Find out *what the other person is trying to communicate to
   you*. Each conversation is aimed at gaining certain information, establishing contact, and expressing oneself (need
   for self-expression). The conversation ought to allow the
   other person to express himself or herself. Try to become
   clear about the relationship between you and the other person, communicate openly, and avoid hidden prodding (I
   would like you to ...).[3]

In the "open" phase, expectations of the people affected are
important. Thwarted expectations often create frustration, resignation, or resistance to change. It is important, therefore, not to
create unrealistic expectations that might not be met. Many participation projects have failed for exactly this reason. They
promised more than they could deliver. The frequent response is,
"We've tried a lot of things already, but nothing succeeds anyway."

The initial open phase is aimed at individual and collective
reflection on the existing situation and the identification of areas
of desired change. The key is open communication among all the
individuals and groups involved. This process of dialogue, in
which individuals can present, clarify, and reflect on their position and come to understand the needs and perceptions of others,
is a prerequisite for individual as well as system change.

Step 2: Move or Change the Existing Situation

The decisive factor that signals the transition from the "open" to the "move" phase is if the people affected start to become really interested in the change. Participation in the open phase stimulates willingness and interest in behavioral change. Willingness to change may not refer to the total change process or all of its outcomes, but that is not important at this point. What matters is the desire to really change something and to get started. It is important not to get impatient in this phase, assuming that enough has been discussed, and the change can now be pulled off. People respond with fear of losing control. It is crucial for people to participate in the different steps, to agree on a time line, and to remain open to changes and adaptations at any point in time. It is insufficient if somebody, somewhere in the organization, is working on the agreed upon changes. Communication and involvement have to be ongoing and transparent.

Thus, while the process cannot be precipitated, it is important that things are starting to happen. The readiness for change created in the open phase now becomes a need for change. Visible changes have to respond to the often small problems that participants see as barriers to change. It makes sense to think carefully about how to achieve the broader goal of change and to focus on small steps first. Just as any work organization change has to be tailored to the specific goals of a particular organization and its members, there is no "one best way" to change social systems. Every situation requires a unique approach that has to be "invented," experimented with, and modified as needed.

Planning in the move phase ought to encompass discrete steps or partial goals which can be evaluated on an ongoing basis. The success of a change process cannot be visible at the end only, but must become transparent as it moves along. The development of partial goals allows the participants to assess when the process gets off track and to avoid possible unintended side effects. This only happens, however, if the participants' experiences and assessment of what is happening are taken seriously and influence the course of the change process. Originally formulated goals may become the subject of corrective action if they turn out to be double-edged, unrealistic, or otherwise undesirable. Initially, partial goals are often formulated to avoid the repetition of previous negative experiences. New goals may emerge as the change process unfolds.

Step 3: Consolidate or Integrate

Once a visible change has occurred – for example, work activities have been redesigned to support competence development – the process of social system change is *by no means completed*. The next stage, consolidation or integration, is an essential and independent phase, which if neglected may lead the system to relapse into old patterns or may prevent the advantages of new systems from taking hold.

This phase is not necessarily short. Its purpose is to establish a new "quasi-stationary" equilibrium of the system. This is why Lewin used the term *freeze* for this phase. We prefer the terms *consolidate* and *integrate,* as they have a less mechanistic or static connotation. This phase, first of all, requires *time*. But it also requires the focused support of the change initiators and those with the authority to make the new system work. Depending on the context and the particular change project, the new system may be reflected in contractual agreements; it may become the focus of symbolic acts (e.g., celebrations, certification, etc.); or consolidation may require further support measures such as additional training.

Once again, the employees affected should be involved in determining what is needed to support and consolidate the new system. Glitches and problems often point to the areas where modifications and further development are needed. It is important to publicly identify the consolidation phase as such and to encourage the participants to take an active part in it. If this phase is not actively planned, and the process just somehow stops, participants' expectations may be frustrated, and they may fall back into resignation (see Figure 5.2).

It is important to remember that social system change is not a steady, ongoing process, but rather occurs in spurts consisting of periods of movement and standstill. In this respect social system development is somewhat analogous to the kind of physical development that occurs through weight training. First the muscle is stimulated through responding to the increased demand of the weights. Real growth and development occur, however, during the invisible recovery periods between training sessions. Similarly, learning and change phases in social systems have to alternate with phases of stabilization in order for change to take hold and for individuals to regain a sense of predictability and mastery. This is often difficult to accept, particularly for managers. If they are future and change oriented, their minds may be busy with new projects and ideas even though the changes are only beginning to become consolidated.

The consolidation phase involves an additional problem. A variety of proven methods exist to initiate the open phase. And the move phase poses no particular methodological problems either, at least not if the process has been planned and implemented in a participatory format. The consolidation or integration phase, on the other hand, has to rely on locally "invented" specific means, appropriate to the change goals and the participants involved. Years of research have demonstrated that specific solutions have to be self-designed by the people who will enact them. Canned or prepackaged solutions seldom succeed. This requires an in-depth understanding of what might be required to consolidate the new situation. Once again, the participants are likely to know best what needs to be done.

It is important to underscore that the Lewinian three-step model of social system change, like all models, is primarily of *heuristic* value. In reality these three phases cannot be clearly distinguished from each other or neatly planned. Rather, they represent stages in a fluid process, since individuals and groups in an organization are likely to be at a different developmental stage at any point in time. What the model suggests is, first, that social systems, in contrast to physical systems, cannot be changed directly, but have to be prepared for change and movement, and second, that a social change process has to be followed by consolidation and integration, providing a new state of balance and a new sense of "normality" and predictability.

Theoretical models such as the one proposed are helpful in understanding the dynamics of social processes and point to important practical implications. At the same time, they offer no simple tricks that, properly applied, guarantee success. The purpose of our approach is not to suggest optimal ways for changing a system or manipulating it to move in a specific direction, but rather to describe a developmental process that integrates individual learning and competence development with broader system change. This endeavor requires that we learn to *think developmentally,* which often is difficult for people who have been raised in the scientific traditions of Western civilization. There are probably many reasons that contribute to this difficulty, the most important, in our view, being the attribution fallacy and the linear cause-effect fallacy, discussed briefly below.

The Attribution Fallacy

In some ways we are all still heirs to Aristotle's logical system, in which it is impossible, for example, to accept both the statement "My neighbor is a good person" and its opposite, "My neighbor is a bad person," as simultaneously true. Even though we know full well that most people's behavior includes some aspects we judge to be good and others we judge to be bad (often in response to different life challenges), our normal tendency is to classify the person in either/or terms: either good or bad. Period. He's either a good worker or a bad worker; she's either a good supervisor or a bad supervisor.

This tendency to classify people's behavior in either/or terms is often accompanied by a tendency to attribute the *causes* or *motivation* of the behavior to aspects of the person's "personality," while ignoring important circumstances of the person's life situation that may be triggering the behavior. Together these tendencies are commonly called the "attribution fallacy." Solid research evidence shows that factors related to the situation usually play at least as important a role in determining behavior as do factors internal to people's "personalities."[4] But these same studies have also shown that Americans consistently ignore even obvious situational factors in explaining other people's behavior, though they often emphasize the importance of the situation in explaining their own behavior. In our culture we learn to prefer explanations that attribute cause or "blame" for behavior to persons, especially when the behavior is negatively evaluated. Thus, even though we know "objectively" that many people become addicted to alcohol or drugs, for example, as a result of socializing in a peer group that enables and rewards consuming the chemical ("show me who your friends are and I'll tell you who you are"), we still tend to *explain* addiction as the result of some defect in the person's character: "He lacks self-discipline." "It runs in that family." This can be true even when our recommended solutions (e.g., remove the person from the "bad" environment) demonstrate that we recognize full well the power of situational factors in triggering behavior. Unfortunately, our explanations can become self-fulfilling prophecies that both limit our own ability to think creatively about solutions and also become internalized by the other person, interfering with our efforts to be a positive force in their lives and inhibiting their efforts to change.

This research also shows that Americans attribute a much higher degree of consistency to other people's behavior than is actually the case when measured objectively. That is, once having classified a person – usually in either/or terms – we are prone to "see" him or her through the lens of our classification, irrespective of changing situations or the passage of time. In other words, we do not easily think of other people, especially once they reach adulthood, as capable of *variable* behavior, sometimes positive, sometimes negative (as judged by us, of course) in response to what to us appear to be either the same circumstances, different circumstances or circumstances changing over time. Instead, it is more as if, having token a mental snapshot of the person at one time and place, that image becomes the one we see when we look at the person. In short, we do not think developmentally. While this habit of thought may work fine in everyday life, as it simplifies the complexities of the world and makes it more predictable, it is counterproductive in efforts to enable developmental change to occur. Lewin's emphasis on "unfreezing" is in large part aimed at these "frozen" or static images of people's potential, which are the corollary of frozen, static roles.

In order to think developmentally we have to try to see people's behavior as a function of their efforts to achieve the outcomes they want in the situations in which they find themselves. That means we have to believe that people can and do learn, change, and grow in response to new goals and opportunities. We can't pigeonhole them as "unmotivated," "incompetent," or any of the other labels that are so casually applied without first looking closely at the factors of their situations.

The Fallacy of Linear Cause-Effect Reasoning

The other legacy of our Western socialization that interferes with developmental thinking is the kind of linear "cause-effect" thinking that we have inherited from efforts to apply scientific models developed for the physical sciences to the study of human behavior. These models, often called mechanistic, work very well for the study of many phenomena in the physical world, where it is often possible, through carefully controlled experimental designs, to isolate one variable, x, that "causes" the appearance or disappearance of another variable, y. Thus, in quality control, for example, we can often, through the use of statistical quality control methods, isolate the source of a defect in the product (y) as caused by the malfunctioning of a certain valve in the machine (x), improper setup by the operator (z), or both: x + z = y. By changing x or z or both, depending on the exact circumstance, we can cause y to disappear.

Much human behavior does not follow linear cause-effect laws or principles. Unlike physical objects, which do not have goals and cannot be said to engage in purposeful behavior (lightning does not "intentionally" strike an object), human beings possess both the desire and the capability to make choices – to exercise preferences in their life situations. In striving to realize their preferences, people engage in purposeful transactions with their environments. This may mean changing some aspect of the physical environment, building a house or chopping a tree, for example, or it may mean interacting with other people who also have preferences. Whenever two or more people interact, each seeking to exercise his or her own preferences in a situation where resources are limited, the possibility for conflicting interests arises. This raises the issue of power or the ability to exercise one's choices in one's environment(s). In most cultures power is not distributed equally among everyone but is allocated on the basis of properties specific to individual or groups. People who have more power than other people, based on, say, physical strength or higher competence or positions of authority have more opportunities to exercise their preferences than those with less power. People tend to join together with others who have similar interests in order to increase their power to exercise their preferences. Thus, people who perceive themselves to have overlapping interests often collaborate to achieve commonly held goals, while people who perceive themselves to have conflicting interests with others engage in various types of conflict, including violence, to achieve their goals. In fact, a number of observers have suggested that the most common form of cooperation exists to enhance the persons' abilities to compete against some commonly perceived rival.[5]

Human behavior is thus a complex matter of purposeful individuals engaging in cooperative and conflicting transactions with each other and with the natural world. Linear cause-effect explanations can never really capture the true complexity of people's motivations, choice of action, and so forth. Although we're all fond of these kinds of explanations – "She's absent from work a lot (y) because she hates her job (x)", or "He behaves that way (y) because his parents didn't love him (x)" – the "truth" is always much more complicated, as many a well-meaning manager who failed to improve attendance by improving job conditions has discovered. Thinking developmentally means unlearning all those clichés based on linear cause-effect, and learning instead to think of human behavior in "multivariable" and "interaction" terms. Multivariable, in this sense, means that some parts of behavior are contributed by characteristics of the person (his or her aspirations and perceived choices, previous experiences, knowledge and competences, acquired beliefs and values, and so forth) and some part by characteristics of the environments in which the person behaves (job demands, reward systems, attitudes and values of important other people, available resources, rules and regulations, and so forth). Behavior itself results from (is caused by) the interaction of many different factors as a person tries to determine what choices are available and how to exercise preference in his or her environment.

Such multivariate and interactional thinking is not easy to do since, according to some experts, the average person usually can only deal comfortably with two "causes" at a time without some kind of special tool or technique. Yet, if we are to think developmentally about improving human competence in complex organizations, we must seek means to overcome both the simplistic understanding of human behavior derived from our early socialization and the limitations of our personal information-processing capacities to address the multivariate and interactional nature of the causes of human behavior at work. The "K.I.S.S. Principle" (keep it simple, stupid) that many of us are so fond of no doubt has a place in the developmentalist's tool kit, but only in regard to specific interventions, not with initial conceptualizations.

This is particularly true for the application of the following four basic principles that should guide processes of work design for competence development. The principles, in a sense, represent the application-oriented essence of the concepts discussed in this chapter.

FOUR BASIC PRINCIPLES

Processes of competence development vary in each individual case as they need to be tailored to the particular situation of the organization and its members. However, relying on the following four basic principles when engaging in a process of social system change aimed at employee competence development is central to success. We have given each of these principles a label that can easily be remembered.[6]

The Judo Principle

Processes of work design for competence development are unlikely to be initiated just because somebody thinks they are a good idea. Economic pressures, quality problems, the planning and introduction of a new production process, and so forth, may trigger the search for alternative solutions and can be used to pursue new approaches to doing things that foster competence development. As with judo, you don't have to be strong yourself; you can, once you master it, use the strength of your opponent and channel it in the direction of your goals.

> *The judo principle means: Use the forces already in motion to benefit you.*

Relying on the judo principle has the advantage that a "real need" of the organization is the driving force behind the change effort. We can rely on it even if the going gets rough and barriers appear. The dynamic tension created by technological innovation as well as market and workforce changes, as described in Chapter 3, offers many reasons and triggers for organizational change. These can be utilized and expanded toward competence development supporting work design. Whenever an organization responds to any of the three conditions mentioned, either through rationalization, innovation, competence development, or a combination of such strategies, it is relatively easy to influence these change processes in the direction of competence development. Chapter 8 presents an example in which the economic necessity to reduce throughput time in an electronic component assembly from forty-five to ten days was the driving force in overcoming obstacles and problems encountered by the change project. Chapter 11 provides a practical step-by-step approach to analyzing ongoing technological and organizational innovations in order to identify opportunities for employee involvement and competence development.

Participation: The Principle of Self-Design

The second building block for competence development is participation. It addresses the question of who should design and move the change process. This touches on an area where our approach differs the most from Taylorist or other "expertocratic" design principles. We believe that when it comes to changing the work situation, there is really only one true group of experts: the people doing the work.

Participation means: The people affected need to be involved.

As we have argued in Chapter 1, competence is developed through active involvement in new activities. Participation is thus at the core of competence development. There is no single best solution to any particular problem across different organizations. As the goals, processes, and characteristics of each organization and its members vary, the principle of self-design implies that the best solution is the one invented by the people who have to live with the consequences of that solution. As external consultants, supervisors, technical planners, trainers, or union representatives, we can provide expertise in the coordination and facilitation of competence development processes. But our main task is to facilitate the type of participation that allows employees to actually contribute their expert knowledge and to formulate their goals. The case study in Chapter 8 shows what "unskilled" or "semiskilled" workers can accomplish if they become engaged in a participatory process.

Heuristic Procedures

It is important to understand that no one single "right" solution exists for any problem. No solution is good enough simply to be transferred from one situation to another. If nothing else, the people are different; they have to be involved and make the solution their own. Successful solutions – and that also applies to this book – should be invented, not copied! The term *heuristics* is rooted in the Greek work "Heureka," which means "I've found it – that's it." A heuristic is the guide to finding one's own solutions.

Heuristic procedures mean: There is no one best way.

This may appear trivial, but in the reality of organizational change it is this basic principle for competence development that is most often violated. The frequently offered justification is that it is useless to reinvent the wheel. This is an inappropriate comparison, as the conditions for turning a wheel are much more stable than those that determine the appropriateness of a certain type of work organization in a unique organizational context. What is needed is a co-evolution of solutions developing simultaneously with a changing environmental context.

Double Helix

Many companies consider the goals of competence development to be unrealistic. "Our employees are not yet mature enough or ready or capable of such developments," the argument goes, or "the existing organizational constraints do not permit it." Both of these arguments are right as well as wrong. It is true that there is often resistance to change and participation among employees at first, and indeed there are many structural problems (that's why change is needed in the first place). But there is no reason to conclude that nothing can be done until the people are mature enough or the structural barriers have disappeared. Our research and practice indicate that processes of individual and social development are linked. As we have shown in more detail in Chapter 1, the interdependence of individual and social learning and change processes has to be seen as a helix or spiral in which the "inside" spiral of psychological change processes is embedded in the "external" spiral of social system change processes.

Double helix means: Individual development has to be linked with social system development.

Individual and social system change processes must be linked. That is, either one of these processes can be ahead of the other only to a certain degree. If individuals are changing, but the system remains the same, sooner or later they become frustrated and may withdraw into resignation. Alternatively, if the system changes too rapidly, and individuals are left behind, feeling threatened by an unpredictable situation, resistance will be the result. The case studies in Part III illustrate that employees' willingness to take on responsibility and autonomy has to follow its own pace: initial willingness to move ahead can develop further only if the structural conditions support taking on more responsibility and autonomy. At that point, new demands for even more responsibility and autonomy can develop. Where the process starts is almost irrelevant. What matters is that individual and social change processes drive each other and thus continue to move forward together. The double helix concept also helps to assess why, in a given situation, the change process suddenly stagnates and stops. In many such cases, all the energy is focused on only one of the two processes, individual development or system change.

The emphasis in this chapter was on the change process itself and the core principles to be adhered to in the initiation and implementation of change projects aimed at fostering competence development. The next chapter provides a set of practical steps for how to proceed with such an endeavor.

NOTES

1. Lewin, *Field Theory*.
2. This illustration represents a modification of Lewin's model; see Andreas Alioth, *Entwicklung und Einführung alternativer Arbeitsformen* (Bern, Switzerland: Huber, 1980), p. 142.
3. See Rupert Lay, *Dialektik für Manager* (Frankfurt, Germany: Ullstein, 1989).
4. See Lee Ross and Richard Nisbett, *The Person and the Situation: Perspectives of Social Psychology* (Philadelphia: Temple University Press, 1991), for a good overview of the attribution fallacy.
5. Richard D. Alexander, *The Biology of Moral Systems* (Hawthorne, NY: Aldine de Gruyter, 1987).
6. Felix Frei, "Qualifizierende Arbeitsgestaltung," in Peter Meyer-Dohm, Michael Lacher, and Jürgen Rubelt, eds., *Produktionsarbeiter in angelernten Tätigkeiten: Eine Herausforderung für die Bildungsarbeit* (Frankfurt, Germany: Campus, 1989), pp. 147-168.

6. How to Implement a Competence Development Process

Following the judo principle discussed in Chapter 5, a good starting point for initiating an employee competence development process is to focus on a particular problem or set of problems widely perceived as in need of addressing. The specific focus may center on a quality improvement effort, the design and implementation of a new production process, the acquisition of new equipment, or the perceived need to upgrade employee skills. The initial proposition to use such a planned organizational change or modification as the starting point for enhancing employee competence may come from management, the union, an employee, or an external consultant.

Since, in American firms at least, management has final authority over most organizational policies and practices, the understanding of and commitment to engage in such a process by top managers is a necessary first step. By top management, we refer to decision-makers with the authority to implement planned changes in organizational structure and functioning. These individuals will ultimately have to change their own behavior in order for the change process to succeed.

The commitment of top management is necessary but not sufficient. As the double helix model makes clear, the change process will eventually have to include plans to incorporate all levels of management as well as technical and professional support staff and, of course the nonmanagerial employees. In unionized settings, the understanding and commitment of the union leadership are equally essential, since the change process is likely to affect aspects of formally and informally negotiated work arrangements and working conditions. The union, as the legally constituted representative of employees' interests, will play a central role in either supporting or undermining the change process. If left out of the design phase, union leaders are unlikely to develop the understanding required for them to change their behavior and modify their traditional role. (For a more in-depth discussion of the union's role in participatory competence development projects, see Chapter 13).

Before suggesting a step-by-step approach to initiating and implementing a competence development project, let's review the central propositions that guide the process and thus influence the way in which to proceed:

1. *Competence develops through engagement in new activities*. The process of competence development begins with direct participation in new activities. These new activities expand the range and scope of task demands and response possibilities. The critical exploration of existing work arrangements, in relation to both organizational and individual goals, reveals contradictions and problems between how things are and how they could be. This kind of "gap analysis" lays the foundation for inventing alternative possibilities. Envisioning and implementing changes in current work activities and arrangements allow for continuous adaptation and reassessment, help identify additional training and skill requirements, and foster the development of new goals and employee interest in taking on new challenges. A structure and process have to be created to make this happen.

2. *Start with contradictions*. Most employees are aware of many problems and contradictions that interfere with optimal job performance in line with their own goals and those of the organization. But many of them have never been asked about their perception and ideas or, if they volunteered them anyway, quickly found out that nobody cared. First and foremost, employees have to realize and to be able to believe that work activities can be changed. Contradictions between the reality of their work situation and their subjective goals, even if recognized, do not automatically result in change-oriented action as long as the situation is

defined as "resistant to change." The willingness to change and think about alternatives grows with a heightened awareness of contradictions in existing work arrangements if the situation is perceived as open to change and if the changes proposed seem desirable and feasible.[1]

3. *Construct a dialogue concerning desired futures.* A process must be invented that allows people to coordinate their individual perceptions of contradictions and problems in order to construct a shared vision. This can occur through the dialectic of collectively reflecting on problems, taking action to implement improvements, and then reflecting again on the effectiveness of the changes. The need to create a mechanism for an ongoing dialogue is central to the processes of both individual competence development and social system change.

4. *Build a "good dialectic" through open information and communication.*[2] Information and communication are key ingredients in constructing a dialogue in which employees can invent alternatives and develop new goals. Most organizations make little effort to communicate their goals, the challenges they face, and their strategies for addressing them all the way down to the shop floor or the "front line" of their operation. The manufacturing worker who has never been informed about where the part that he or she produces goes is not a rare exception. The more employees know about the "bigger picture" and how their work fits into it, the more aligned their creativity becomes with future work demands. Yet communication has to be a two-way process. Communication not only has to flow top-down, involving more than newsletters and piles of memos, it also has to flow bottom-up. Through direct, verbal, two-way communication a dialectical process of mutual learning and dialogue can be initiated. The most valuable information often comes from employees' experience. Such information is generated if employees are given the opportunity to experience and link aspects of work activities that they did not perceive before or saw as unrelated. In order for the dialectic to foster competence development, people must feel free to ask questions about "the way we've always done it."

The following procedure for planning and implementing *Qualifizierung* by means of employee participation is not a simple step-by-step process, as that creates the danger that only secondary goals or objectives are pursued and the primary goal might get lost. Any specific technological or organizational innovation is only a means to the end of encouraging employee participation in the process. Every secondary goal or step in the process has to be analyzed in terms of the degree to which it serves the overall goal and the interests of developing broader employee competence.

The process proposed below represents one way of approaching and initiating an employee participation process geared toward competence development. Depending on the situation and the specific project in which the process is embedded (e.g., technological change; change in organizational structures and policies; change affecting just one department or change aimed at the whole organization), the steps may vary somewhat, and different specific tools may be used.

STEP #1 – ESTABLISHING A STEERING COMMITTEE

The first step is to assemble a project steering committee. The question of who should be involved in a particular organization can usually be answered by asking, "Who are the stakeholders here? In other words, which individuals and groups might be affected by this change?" Many well-intentioned projects have failed or run into snags because some person or group affected was deliberately or accidentally left out. A steering committee often consists of planning staff already involved in work activity planning, the employees affected by the innovation, their supervisors, and representatives from union and middle and higher level management. Not all affected employees need to be involved in this group, but they have to be represented. Such representatives should be respected and trusted by their peers, and preferably selected by their co-workers. Different organizational units may have to be represented if they are affected by the innovation. Participation should be voluntary. The team might be complemented by internal or external consultants on an as-needed basis. Management representatives involved must have decision-making authority. The team has to be authorized either to prepare or make necessary decisions itself. The team's activities have to be actively supported by the organizational authorities.

Following is a list of the positive aspects of working in steering committees:

Teamwork

- fosters creativity and willingness to learn, which in turn leads to increased flexibility and openness for innovation;
- provides employees with insights and knowledge about the organization of work activities beyond the limits of their own work situation. They learn to see and understand problems from the perspective of others. A mutual learning process occurs;
- makes supervisors aware of the skills and abilities of their employees;
- supports a joint needs assessment;
- helps alleviate fears and doubts;
- fosters communication skills;
- helps to resolve conflicts;
- promotes willingness to cooperate;
- improves the quality of problem analysis and decisions made, as the knowledge and perspectives of multiple actors are shared;
- encourages mutual assistance and support;
- fosters the readiness to ask for help from outside if needed;
- promotes planning and working together;
- fosters external contacts;
- contributes to the reduction of hierarchical barriers.

At every stage in the process, there are potential pitfalls to be avoided. The following list, based largely on our own experience, is not inclusive. Other issues, some related to organizational beliefs, values, and ways of doing things, that may create problems if unexpectedly violated.

Pitfalls to be avoided:
- Top management "doesn't have time" to get involved.
- Middle and lower level managers or the union are left out.
- Some other group affected is not involved.
- Employees (and this includes supervisors) are not replaced on their job while participating in the project group. This may mean more work for others or an increased workload for participants. Resentment and envy by colleagues may be the result and may lead these participants to drop out.

STEP #2 – DESIGNING A CHANGE PROCESS: CREATING PROCESS GUIDELINES AND PREPARING FOR ACTION

Establishing a set of process guidelines agreed to by group members, greatly improves the effectiveness of task-oriented work groups. Frequently group participants have different educational and work backgrounds, different amounts of experience in working in groups, and partially conflicting interests. Establishing and then following a set of ground rules greatly enhances the development of trust and fosters mutual learning and equal participation from members with different levels of authority. Group members should be asked to think about how the group should function; by generating their own ground rules, they feel comfortable taking an active part in meetings. Guidelines can be amended over time as problems emerge that interfere with the group's effective functioning.

Process guidelines adopted by such project groups may include the following:
- Everyone's perspective is important.
- Listen for the content of what group members are trying to say.
- One person speaks at a time.
- Keep information discussed confidential.
- No retaliation for things said in meetings outside meetings (paybacks).
- Decisions are made by consensus.

Consensus decision-making helps to democratize the process and equalize power among participants. It means that for a decision to be adopted by the group, every participant has to be willing to support it or to suggest alternatives that others will accept. The bottom line: decisions are not made by majority rule but are only implemented if carried by the group as a whole. Though initially time-consuming to establish, consensus decision-making has consistently been shown to result in better decisions and better implementation.

STEP #3 – CLEARING THE GOALS

As mentioned earlier, participatory processes aimed at competence development are frequently initiated in conjunction with a technological or organizational innovation already in the planning or implementation stage. Using the analysis process described in Chapter 11 helps the steering committee identify opportunities for where and how to introduce participatory involvement, and who else might have to become involved. It is also a very valuable tool for identifying problem areas in an organization's "typical" approach to innovating and for becoming aware of the reasons why past employee involvement efforts may have failed. One project team that two of the authors worked with had a goal of reducing organizational sources of stress through projects aimed at increasing employees' influence and involvement in decision-making. The team identified the following set of do's and don'ts based on the history of experiences with past programs in their workplace.

Programs need to
- be considered relevant and important by employees
- have commitment and support from management and the union
- provide an optimal level of participation for the target group
- be planned and carried out in a way that assures that the stated goals will be met
- provide information and feedback to participants on their actions and on the program's development
- have built-in "maintenance" procedures (e.g., ongoing evaluation)
- address problems, not just symptoms
- be coordinated with existing programs, since they affect each other
- pay attention to possible unexpected outcomes that may create sources of stress and disincentives for participation
- be coordinated by people who are people-oriented and not make too much of their role
- be offered in a pleasant environment
- focus on their stated objectives rather than serving some people's hidden agenda

At this point, the goals to be achieved through the innovation need to be clarified. Goals are likely to include economic as well as social aspects; for example:

Economic goals: It is useful to determine the specific economic goals to be achieved, for example, the amount of desired productivity increase; reduction in workforce fluctuations (e.g., absenteeism); utilization of equipment; quality standards; overtime, personnel, or transition costs. The social goals should be determined simultaneously so that the excitement about possible economic improvements does not backfire in the form of unintended side effects such as increased job stress or job elimination. Again, the involvement of various stakeholders in the project team improves the likelihood that differences can be negotiated, avoiding "negative surprises" later on.

Social goals: These involve an agreed upon understanding of the discretion employees will have in terms of activities, decision-making and work redesign (combining planning, execution, and control functions); identification of the extent and type of competence development potential; identification of possibilities for mutual cooperation and support; determination of the limits of job demands and stress; determination of wages and compensation systems, work as well as break times; and identification of the possibilities for promoting job security and future development potential.

Don't overdetermine the goals and objectives at this point; rather, set the broad parameters within which the innovation is to take place. New goals may emerge and originally envisioned outcomes may have to be modified as employees become actively involved in the change process.

THE OPEN PHASE: ACTIVATING EMPLOYEES

How do employees get involved in the process? How can they be activated to become engaged in the rethinking and redesign of work activities? This process can be initiated by encouraging people to compare their current work experience with what might be different, more rewarding, more effective. In many organizations, however, employees may respond with initial mistrust. They may have experienced many years on the job with little interest expressed for their concerns. The may have been "burned" by previous so-called employee involvement programs that did little to improve their work situation. Or they may fear that any changes may negatively affect social relationships at work, change things they like about their job, or disrupt (not officially sanctioned) ways they've found to make life at work easier for them.

Such problems can be addressed by giving the employees to be involved in the innovation the opportunity to discuss their expectations, desires, and fears, and the problems in their current work situations. This might be done by interviewing employees, asking them to describe and comment on the following areas:

- their workplace and work activities; how long they have been on this job; how they got trained
- their history with the company: how long they have been employed, how well they know the company, the different areas they have worked in
- their occupational and work history
- their feeling about their job, the kinds of stress they experience, health and safety problems, the work atmosphere, and their relationships with their co-workers and supervisors
- problems that occur in the work process: problems with equipment, tools, materials, work organization, management, and so forth; unexpected events; how work disruptions are currently addressed
- expectations about their future in the department, in the company
- suggestions for improvements, how their occupational development might be positively influenced
- overall expectations about the future of their worklife and how these expectations might be supported
- interests and activities outside of work

These interviews can be accompanied by a more structured analysis of the existing work situation (for an example see Table 6.1).

Such interviews and analyses are best conducted by members of the organization itself. Sometimes, however, an external moderator may help get the process started. If there is mistrust or concern about confidentiality, employees interviewed may be reluctant to discuss their concerns or share personal information with "insiders" about future plans, work climate, or relationships with supervisors, or to talk about "things already well known" to another member of the organization. In addition to yielding rich information about the current situation in a workplace, these conversations may start employees thinking about aspects of their work that they have previously seen as givens rather than as variables that could be changed. This may encourage taking a fresh look at the work situation, resulting in new ideas for improvements.

Table 6.1   Analysis of the Existing Work Situation

ACTIVITY:		
Criteria	**Description**	**Acceptability**
Job content / Competence requirements		
External working conditions		
Cooperation requirements		
Stress / Demands		
Organizational priorities		
Wages / Salaries		
Personal development possibilities		
Daily hassles		

Along with employee interviews, a sociotechnical systems analysis should be conducted.[3] Its main focus should in the following areas:
- Analysis of the Structure and Flow of Work Processes
    - determination of operational units
    - analysis of work flow connections (flow, technology)
    - analysis of the organizational structure (horizontal/-vertical)
- Variance Analysis
    - identification of system fluctuations/variances and deviations
    - analysis of sources of system variances
    - analysis of the effects of system variances (social and technological)
- Analysis of Subjective Cause Attribution
    - analysis of organizational planning (including information strategies)

- analysis of subjective cause attribution for system variances and deviations
- analysis of strategies for coping with system variances
  (official, prescribed strategies – actual strategies used)

Table 6.2 shows an abbreviated version of a variance analysis.[4]

Table 6.2   A Schema for Variance Analysis

Type of variance	Where does it occur?	Where is it caused?	Who controls / regulates it?	Why does it occur?

These analyses usually expose a more or less extensive list of
deficiencies in the work process. Major problems must be addressed immediately. If not, employees' willingness to participate and change things may quickly turn into resignation and resistance. Taking care of immediate problems is an important step
in supporting employee activation. If the little things that cause
anger and frustration every day are not fixed, people will not be
very interested in participating in larger innovations. A successful involvement in solving everyday problems encourages participation and interest in tackling the bigger problems. Employees
have to be able to see that change is not to their detriment but
rather improves existing work situations and opens up new possibilities.

THE MOVE PHASE: DEFINING WORK ACTIVITIES AND DESIGNING WORK ORGANIZATION

The actual work of the employee teams begins now, after basic improvements in the work situation have occurred or after determination that these changes will be made. The process involves the search for a form of cooperation that allows employees to continuously influence the improvement of their work situation as well as to participate in the innovation. At this point project teams might be formed, or existing structures of work team cooperation may be utilized. It is important that employees find the form that best suits them, and that records are kept of all the meetings. Project teams can consist of employees only, or they can include supervisors, union representatives, or external consultants. In general, a mix of supervisors and employees is preferable. But meeting without supervisors, at least occasionally, may help the group to articulate its interests more fully and to address fears or conflicts. In unionized settings, the active participation of union representatives is essential in order to coordinate the process with the terms of labor contracts and in general to protect the unions' legal duty to represent all members' interests.

This step involves a more in-depth joint analysis of problems in the existing work situation, the determination of the relationship between work activities (work flow), and the redesign of individual activities and tasks. This is the main task of the project team. A number of proven tools are available to initiate this phase. They are described in more detail in the tool box in Chapter 12. Tools #2 (Subjective Task Analysis) and #3 ("The Ideal Job") are particularly helpful in evaluating individual work activities according to a set of competence development criteria. At the same time, these tools help generate alternative work designs that better meet employees' needs and contribute to organizational goals.

The key to the optimal utilization of human and technological potential lies in the organization of work, the interplay between people and technology. That means using technological potential as well as human potential. In designing work organization and work activities the criteria described in Chapter 7 should be used as guidelines.

The design of work organization involves:
- Identifying primary and secondary tasks

- Distinguishing between tasks according to competence requirements, the level of job demands and pressures, etc.
- Developing work teams with high competence requirements
- Distributing less demanding and less taxing tasks among all group members
- Assigning members to the different activity groups, making sure that members with different competence levels work together
- Determining additional competence development needs
- Determining changes in supervisory functions

Education and Training

The redesign of work activities also involves the joint definition of competence requirements for these activities. The identification of such competence requirements is based on comparing previously required skills and types of knowledge with emerging demands in relationship to the planned change. Competence "gaps" are addressed by planning and initiating the necessary education and training measures. Planners of production systems as well as employees affected are to be involved in training.

Workplace Design and Work Environment

Finally, the individual workplaces are designed following criteria of sound ergonomics. It is useful to appoint an "ergonomics coordinator" for each organizational unit whose task it is to examine changes in working conditions resulting from future technological and organization change.

Implementation

Implementation of the planned work organization is to be based on time, cost, and personnel requirement calculations. A test phase might be necessary. Periodic progress assessment comparing "what is" with "what should be" will help keep the project from getting sidetracked. The process should be accompanied by ongoing documentation assessing if the steps and means used are in line with the overall goal of supporting employee participation and continuing competence development. Such ongoing process evaluation prevents the project from getting sidetracked in the pursuit of other objectives, as important as they might appear. Periodic evaluation of the overall goals makes the process transparent, as each step or method is reviewed in light of the overall purpose. Transparency of the process steps also reduces reluctance and mistrust. Ongoing evaluation helps to identify problems and deviations early on and allows for corrections and the resolution of problems. Needless to say, employees are to be part of this evaluation process.

In addition, outcomes of subgoals developed in the course of the process, particularly those related to the improvement of working conditions, should be evaluated. The overall goal as well as subgoals should be listed. This helps to evaluate wether the outcomes at each step and the subgoals listed are still in line with the overall purpose of the project.

THE INTEGRATION PHASE: CONSOLIDATING EMPLOYEE PARTICIPATION

After the desired changes have been successfully implemented, they have to be consolidated, and the process has to be firmly integrated in the organizational structure. Subsequent innovations should be utilized to develop new project teams. Participation structures and processes should be integrated and defined in written agreements (e.g., labor contracts). The goal is to make employee participation not just a one-time project, but a part of organizational culture and employees' everyday work activities. Figure 6.1 presents an overview of the process of planning and implementing *Qualifizierung*.

Involving employees in innovation processes presents two basic difficulties. The first problem is to demonstrate to employees that they stand to benefit from cooperating in the process. The prospect of participation in planning and decision-making may arouse fears and possibly resistance among employees new to this process, based on their previous experience that workplace changes are frequently accompanied by deskilling and the elimination of jobs. They know that too often they bear the negative consequences of "work improvement" projects. In addition, many employees have found that management has failed to act on their input and suggestions for improvements in the past. These types of experiences do not provide positive reinforcement for continuing to participate.

Figure 6.1   How to Implement a Competence Development
                  Process

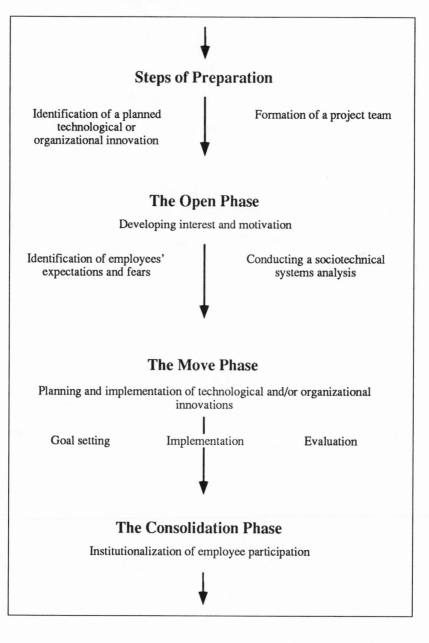

Other barriers emerge from the concern that employee participation may eliminate the privileges of some groups in the organization. Many supervisors fear the loss of control and decision-making power. They are worried that employee participation means less decision-making latitude and influence for them. Employee participation, however, is intended to open up new domains of responsibility and decision-making for supervisors as they are freed, for example, from certain tasks that the work group can take on.

Other obstacles are related to the discomfort of having to give up cherished old habits. "We've always done it this way, why change?" is a frequently heard argument. Much of the resistance is rooted in the history of previous attempts to involve employees. Perceptions and expectations are strongly influenced by experiences of success or failure.

The structure of the organization presents an additional set of barriers. An ingrained piece rate system can present an insurmountable obstacle to employees' desire to rotate activities and work on different tasks. Other difficulties may result from an elaborate seniority system or great variation in existing skill and competence levels.

This list of barriers is not all-encompassing, as many of them are specific to the individuals and structure peculiar to an organization. But obstacles are not insurmountable. To overcome them, it is important to explore why they exist. Once that is known, ways can be found to address them.

In this and the preceding chapter we have focused on the change process and how it might be initiated and implemented. The next chapter describes the goals for which these processes aim: the joint optimization of the social system and the technical system. It thus presents a method for organizational design with self-regulation and competence development at its core.

NOTES

1. Christof Baitsch and Andreas Alioth, "Entwicklung von Organisationen – vom Umgang mit Widersprüchen," in Felix Frei and Ivars Udris, eds., *Das Bild der Arbeit* (Bern, Switzerland: Huber, 1990), pp. 244-257.

2. Chris Argyris and Donald Schon propose the term *good dialectic* in *Organizational Learning: A Theory of Action Perspective* (Reading, Mass.: Addison-Wesley, 1978), p. 42.

3. See Emery and Emery, *Participative Design: Work and Community Life* (Canberra, Australia: Centre for Continuing Education, 1974).

4. Ibid.

7.   Optimizing the Social and the Technical System

All work organizations have the characteristics of sociotechnical systems, whether we conceptualize them in that manner or not. The sociotechnical system principles discussed in this chapter should not be viewed as a *prescription* for an organizational form, but rather as a *method* of creating the conditions for people to exercise new choice opportunities in the various relationships characterizing work systems.[1]

Like every other system, work organizations consist of parts or elements but also of the relationship between them. The three main types of relationships are:
* relationships between machines (technical equipment)
* relationships between people
* relationships between machines (technical equipment) and people

The technical system and the social system are independent of each other inasmuch as they follow different laws: the technical system is subject to the laws of the natural sciences, while the social system is purposeful and follows the laws of the human sciences. Yet the systems are correlative, as the functional task of the work system requires the interaction of both. Thus, the system as a whole cannot be optimized by improving either of these systems independently. Only by *jointly optimizing* both systems can the best match be achieved.

The flaw in most types of work system designs is that they are planned from a functional perspective only, focusing largely on the design of the technical system. On the blueprint it all looks good. The equipment is expected to do x. People should do y. The outcome should be z. And if something does not work as expected, the repairman, supervisor, or engineer is called in to "fix" it. Planning becomes focused on problem-free functioning, though hardly any organizational production flow is without disturbances:

• Equipment breaks down or does not function properly
• People have a "bad day," get sick, or go on vacations
• The right materials or parts are not available
• The quality of raw materials and parts fluctuates
• An urgent customer order disrupts the flow
• The preceding department did not do its job

The minimization of work flow disruptions can only be achieved if planning anticipates the occurrence of all kinds of problems and ways of addressing them. As all possible disruptions are never foreseeable, and since technical problems have to be solved by people, technical and social systems have to be jointly optimized. Sociotechnical system analysis thus often starts with the identification of production problems and fluctuations, the so-called variance analysis (see Chapter 6).

JOINT OPTIMIZATION

Joint optimization means more than merely adapting the technical system to the social system or vice versa; it involves the *design of the sociotechnical system as a whole.* This does not mean that joint optimization has to focus on the organization as a whole or even encompass a department. System design or re-design can start in smaller units that perform a relatively independent task. Such units, however, always encompass more than a single job on an assembly line, for example, because each such job is dependent on preceding and subsequent tasks. This leads to the search for "natural work groups" or groups of jobs that, together, make up a self-contained part of the total production process or primary task.

At the core of each sociotechnical system unit is its *primary task.* Each unit's task is derived from the primary task of the organization as a whole and the primary tasks of other higher level system units. The primary task is the transformation process of a given (sub)system. In an automotive engine plant, for example, the primary task of a sociotechnical unit might be to produce pistons. This task is derived from the plant's task of producing engines, which in turn contributes to the organization's primary purpose, producing cars.

Primary tasks can be determined by a quantitative and qualitative definition of the input-output relationship. The primary task can be distinguished from secondary tasks like system support (e.g., repair, maintenance, training) and regulation functions (e.g., input planning, control, coordination of tasks). The primary task is a heuristic concept used in the sociotechnical system approach that helps identify organizational units which engage in a clearly identifiable, relatively self-contained set of activities.

The principles discussed below are not be be understood as a cookbook recipe for the joint optimization of sociotechnical systems. Rather, they suggest ways of reconstructing the characteristics of existing systems by creating the conditions for organizational members to exercise more influence and expand their range of choices toward making the system as a whole more functionally effective.[2]

1. The Design of Relatively Independent Organizational Units

Independence refers to the identification of the smallest organizational units (work groups or teams, for example), which are assigned a primary task that can be executed relatively independently. The design of such units sometimes requires a technical solution first. For example, the production process may have to be reorganized into relatively self-contained, indirectly linked processes that are connected to each other in a modular design with built-in production flow buffers for each unit.

> Example: Production of a group of parts in a manufacturing cell. The definition of the cell depends on which primary task (e.g., machining of parts A-Z) and which secondary tasks (e.g., material disposition, programming, equipment repair, maintenance, etc.) should be combined in order to minimize disruptions and potentially conflicting interdependencies with other organizational units. Technically, this involves the design of an equipment configuration that can meet these requirements.

2. Unity of Product and Work Organization

The production of a product or the performance of a service ought to be clearly attributable to a specific organizational unit.

In other words, the technical and organizational flow has to be designed in a way that allows for the identification of each (sub)product with its production unit in terms of quantity as well as quality of output. Input elements or problems resulting from other units have to be identifiable as such. If we compare work systems to circuits, the work systems within an organization should be as "closed" as possible. This facilitates direct feedback and a quick response to problems. The unity of product and organization is a motivational prerequisite for the work group's orientation toward a common task.

> Negative example: For the production of a number of different parts, the technical system is "optimized" for the serial production of parts that are checked for quality later in a different department. The social system is "optimized" by establishing a piece rate for individual part production jobs: the more parts produced, the higher the pay. Result: Quantity is achieved at the expense of quality. Scrap is high.

Thus, the primary task – in the example above, the production of quantity and quality – must not be divided. Secondary tasks such as quality control should be integrated into the sociotechnical system unit.

3.   Activation Through Task Orientation

If work is designed from a purely technical perspective, people often end up with a job that in itself has no meaning. Work motivation through external means such as financial incentives or pressure has great limitations. Instead, the concept of activation is based on the notion that meaningful work design stimulates a person's interest and the use of knowledge and problem-solving skills.

Activation through task orientation will be enhanced if:
* work activities have meaning and encompass a set of related tasks
* the relationship of each activity to the unit's primary task is evident
* work activities can be regulated and controlled by the work group members themselves
* work activities allow for both self-reliance and cooperation
* work activities provide opportunities for new learning; they are neither too difficult nor too simple

- work activities represent a manageable level of challenge and are neither too monotonous nor too demanding or overwhelming

4.   Self-Regulation

Self-regulation means having the resources, competences, and desire to solve problems where they occur. Work unit members thus gain a sense of control, as uncertainties about fluctuations and problems arising from the organizational context can be largely eliminated. Production problems can be addressed quickly and with greater flexibility.

For example, members of a sociotechnical system unit ought to be in a position to execute and make decisions about all aspects related to the accomplishment of the unit's primary task. This includes minor repair and maintenance work (if necessary, a technical expert can be called upon). The supervisor, in general, does not make decisions internal to the sociotechnical unit but focuses on boundary management in order to minimize disruptions to the unit's functioning. This often involves coordination with other units whose work may influence or depend on this unit's work. The supervisor's responsibility, for example, is to make sure all necessary materials and documents are available, technical experts are at hand when needed, and so forth.

5.   The Prerequisite: Appropriate Interdependence of Individual Tasks

All previously mentioned principles are difficult to implement if the tasks of the work group members in a sociotechnical unit are inadequately linked.

Task interdependence is inadequate if:
- the ability to complete an individual task depends on how well the previous task has been accomplished (e.g., assembly line)
- all tasks are dependent on a larger technical system and thus completely determined by it
- all tasks are essentially identical and only connected through output standards and piece rate incentives
- the various tasks are completely disconnected; each employee could just as well work independently

By contrast, meaningful task interdependence requires that:

- the primary task is separated into a variety of meaningful subactivities
- the relationship between all subactivities is obvious
- cooperation is perceived as advantageous
- the mutual interdependence does not limit the autonomy of the individual too much
- coordination within the group is left to the group itself
- superordinate norms and policies protect the individual from the "tyranny of the majority"

6.   Boundary Maintenance

If the technical and organizational design creates self-regulating, relatively independent organizational units, the supervisor takes on a support rather than a control function, aimed at fostering self-regulation and independence of the unit within the organizational environment. This involves managing the relationships and linkages between the unit and other parts of the organization, thus providing a buffer function. Direct supervisory interference and control of the activities of the unit's group members becomes unnecessary. (For a discussion of the changed role of supervisors in sociotechnical systems, see Chapter 14).

Table 7.1 contrasts the key elements and characteristics of sociotechnical systems with those of the Taylorist-bureaucratic approach.[3]

Table 7.1   Paradigms of Work Design

	Taylorist-Bureaucratic Approach	Sociotechnical System Approach
1. Unit of design	"one person – one task"	integrated work system (usually a work group)
2. Information flow	top-down; separate from work activities	self-regulating, informal within and between work group
(continued next page)		

(Table 7.1 cont.)	*(Taylorist-Bureaucratic Approach)*	*(Sociotechnical System Approach)*
3. Locus of control (regarding production decisions, variances)	upward, following chain of command, external regulation	at the production, work group level, self-regulating
4. Design principle	a) total specification of all tasks	a) minimum critical specification (decision latitude)
	b) redundancy of parts (e.g., stock chaser)	b) redundancy of functions (multiskilling)
5. Technology	technical imperative (person as extension of the machine)	joint optimization (person as complementary to the machine)
6. Task characteristics	fragmentation, repetitiveness, isolation, little training, externally determined	holistic, task variety, cooperation, continuous learning, autonomy
7. Supervisory role	ongoing control, direct interference in work activities	output "control" and feedback, consultation aimed at self-regulation
8. Motivation	instrumental, extrinsic, individual, and pay oriented	occupational identity, intrinsic, social support and task oriented
9. Occupational development	hierarchical promotions, titles	competence development, also horizontally, multiskilling and occupational flexibility, mobility

AUTONOMOUS WORK GROUPS/SELF-MANAGED TEAMS

The determination of a meaningful primary task usually involves a number of interdependent work activities. The design of sociotechnical systems thus leads to mostly team-oriented forms of work organization. These teams are called autonomous or self-managed work groups. Of course, no single group in any organization can be completely autonomous or independent from other organizational units; it can only be semi-autonomous. Autonomous groups are learning systems focused on a meaningful primary task usually involving a number of interrelated jobs or sets of work tasks. As groups are able to control more and more of the variances encountered, their problem-solving capabilities increase, which can be used to enhance performance and to accommodate group members' personal needs.[4]

Self-management can take different forms depending on the degree of autonomy. The autonomy of a work group is determined by the degree of decision latitude along the three different dimensions proposed by Susman:[5]

1. *Decisions of Self-Regulation.* These decisions concern the regulation of the system, involving:
   - coordination of work activities in terms of cooperation and deadlines
   - allocation of labor, materials, and equipment as well as decisions about equipment maintenance, timing, breaks, etc.
   - boundary maintenance, the management of input and output conditions
2. *Decisions of Task Independence.* These decisions refer to issues of work task design and planning:
   - decisions about when a specific part or product is to be produced (planning of production schedules)
   - decisions about the sequence in which different parts/products are to be produced (prerequisite: work flow is not predetermined by technology)
   - decisions about the sequence in which different tasks are performed in order to meet the final output goals (prerequisite: work flow is not predetermined and allows for alternative routes)
3. *Decisions of Self-Governance.* These decisions refer to the material and psychosocial needs of the group members. The extent of group members' influence over these deci-

sions depends on legislative or contractual rights of employees and their representatives (unions) and the value system held by the organization's management:
- decisions made by the group about the selection of supervisors or new group members, and decisions about mechanisms for dealing with disciplinary issues
- decisions referring to the type and volume of production output

Regardless of the particular form of the work group, the following aspects are important for the successful functioning of self-managed teams.[6]

A Common Primary Task

In order for people to work cooperatively, the primary task must be defined so the group members see it as a team project. This includes all activities involved, such as machine operating, setup, production planning, and clerical tasks. If tasks are assigned so that each team member has a specific area of responsibility for which only he or she is held accountable, the overarching common interest is missing. Mutual support – a condition for flexibility in the work team – requires task interdependence, a sense of collegiality, and an occasional "thank you." If the group as a whole is responsible for the overall task, mutual support becomes based on common interest.

Coherence

The notion of a team project implies that the work activities required for the completion of the overall task are perceived by the group as internally coherent. The product or task outcome ought to be clearly identifiable both qualitatively and quantitatively. In other words, a work group can hardly be held accountable for its product if task elements or errors from other groups in the organization might influence the outcome but cannot be traced to their original source in the final product. Among other things, the internal coherence of a work process is determined by the equipment layout and the design of the technical system.

Comprehensibility

The work area ought to be comprehensible for all group members in terms of its spatial arrangement as well as its complexity.

The work team has to have access to all the means of information and communication necessary to accomplish the overall task. Comprehensibility is enhanced if the spatial organization of each workplace allows for spontaneous communication and if the group has its own clearly identifiable "territory."

Task Distribution

If a work group sees its overall task as a collective activity with mutual responsibilities, the group, within the constraints of agreed upon quality and health and safety standards, takes on the responsibility for internal task allocation and with it the self-regulation of individual activities. Internal coordination and control by a supervisor are replaced by outcome-oriented process supervision on the part of the group as a whole.

Competence

The decision latitude for internal task distribution depends on the skill and competence level of the work group members. The range of competences has to be seen in the context of group size and the complexity of the overall task. In larger groups with more complex tasks, overlapping competences might be sufficient; in other words, not every person has to be able to do everything Competence increases as time goes on, as individuals acquire new skills and problem-solving capabilities. Multiskilling and task rotation can vary according to individual preferences and their current level of competence, allowing group members to find suitable niches. Competence is essential to successful teamwork because if a person fails to perform competently, team members are likely to resent the person and behave negatively.

Disposition Latitude

In order to rely on internal flexibility to deal with personnel fluctuations due to absences or changing output requirements, adequate personnel resources and sufficient time for planning are needed in addition to a certain degree of multiskilling of group members. Then the group will be able to balance the variances on its own. This also allows the group to plan its work activities over a longer time period.

Group Norms

Based on the principle of self-regulation, the work group has to be able to set its own norms and rules for internal cooperation and the resolution of problems and conflicts. These norms and rules are likely to reflect the characteristics of the group's composition. The group, therefore, should have input in the selection of its members. Group norms and values, however, have to be consistent with overarching values, principles, and guidelines of the total organization or, in the case of unionized firms, with both the employer's and the union's beliefs and values. This will prevent the emergence of narrow group self-interest and will help preserve equities among the entire workforce. Thus a balance must be maintained between decentralization of rules and unit functional autonomy and consistency of certain principles and practices across units. Otherwise, autonomous units will tend to develop animosity and competitive relations with other units.

Coordination and Boundary Management

A coordinator might be elected by the group to handle external communication. To avoid the development of hierarchies or unintended supervisory roles and conflicts of interest, the role of the coordinator should be rotated. Regardless of the particular system adopted (e.g., if the group decides to work without a coordinator), communication rules with external units have to be specified to clarify responsibilities and communication flow.

Wages

The pay system can play an important role in work groups. Job-based wage differentials can lead to status differences and status related distribution of work tasks within the group, which may inhibit the development of multiple competences. Any performance bonuses in addition to basic pay scales should be calculated for the group as a whole, as groups work on a common task. However, individual differentiation according to levels of competence achieved, that is, how many tasks a group member has mastered, should provide an incentive to acquire additional knowledge and skills. Each group member should be able to increase his or her competence and with it the pay for knowledge share. In unionized settings, wage systems are contractual issues and have to be negotiated accordingly. (For a discussion of the pros and cons of different compensation systems, see Chapter 15.)

Cost Accountability

Administratively, each work group should represent a cost center. If the work group is to take on responsibility for individual cost factors, it has to be able to manage its own budget. This may involve cost accounting for materials, tools, and equipment used, including planning of staffing requirements and scheduling. A personal computer available to the group could thus be used for budget assessment and cost control.

PRINCIPLES OF JOB DESIGN

The above discussion of sociotechnical design criteria focused on functional work organization characteristics in support of joint optimization. It described the structural arrangements that foster competence development processes and optimal organizational performance. For the design of individual work activities, however, additional criteria have to be considered that address the needs of the individual for physical and psychological well-being and development.

Each individual is different. We all know that, and yet we tend to design jobs as if such differences didn't exist. Different strokes for different folks – what is good for one person may not be appropriate for another. In order to take people's varying abilities, skills, and needs into account two basic principles have to be considered in the design of work activities: variable job design and developmental job design.[7]

Variable Job Design

Some people like to work alone, others prefers to work in a group. Not everyone likes to take on the same amount of responsibility. The principle of variable job design takes such differing preferences into account. Jobs should offer the possibility of choosing among various forms of work organization, for example:
- individual-based or group-based activities
- jobs involving more or less responsibility
- jobs requiring the utilization of different technologies

- jobs with more or less demanding work activities

But not only are there differences between people; individuals themselves change over time. A young person might be more willing and able to do a job involving heavy physical labor. A person might be interested in changing jobs and learning new tasks at some point in time, but might like to stay in a more stable position at another time in his or her life.

Developmental Job Design

The principle of developmental job design takes into account the potential for individual change over time. That means that options to change and move into different jobs ought to be available in the course of a person's work life. The job I like today may not be the job I'd like to do tomorrow.

The frequently voiced statement about finding the right person for the job is based on a static perspective that different people fit in different predetermined slots. As job demands and/or individuals needs, preferences, and competences change, work assignments should be reexamined periodically together with the employee affected. Rather than seeing individual needs and motivations as barriers to job design, they should be viewed as opportunities to respond to changing demands as flexibly as possible. Both of these principles are based on the premise of voluntariness.

Assessing the Quality of Jobs

The design of work systems requires additional evaluation criteria against which we can judge specific work activities. These criteria protect the physical and psychosocial health and well-being of employees and provide opportunities for learning, development, and growth.

Absence of Physical and Psychosocial Health Hazards

Harmful physical and psychological health effects are often objectively identifiable. There is a multitude of known occupational illnesses, injuries, and work-related negative health effects, for example, long-term exposure to high noise levels, hazardous chemicals, or ergonomically unsound machinery, equipment, or work procedures. In addition, the link between psychosocial health hazards resulting from work-related stress (for example, high job demands combined with low decision-making latitude, job insecurity, and so forth) and negative health outcomes such as cardiovascular problems, hypertension, ulcers, and depression, is well documented.[8]

People respond differently to certain working conditions or task demands. What is seen as a challenge by one individual may be experienced as stressful by another person. Negative effects on psychological and social well-being occur if a person feels qualitatively or quantitatively overloaded or underutilized. While such limitations are subjectively experienced, they have an objective, external cause, for example, noise, monotony, work overload, time pressures, unclear or contradictory instructions by a supervisor, racism, sexism, or fast work pace. The persistence of such factors over time can result in symptoms of stress-related illnesses and long-term negative health effects.

Many of these job constraints can be avoided if individuals have some discretion and influence over their job. In addition, people have to experience that "things can be changed." The sense that one's work situation cannot be changed and the resulting feeling of resignation itself can be major sources of stress.

Presence of Developmental Opportunities

Good jobs are characterized not only by the absence of health and safety hazards but by the opportunity to exert influence, use and further develop skills and competences, and so forth. Table 7.2 shows the key features of good jobs proposed by Karasek and Theorell.[9]

In general, the potential a job offers for personal development increases with more individual and collective discretion in decision-making and organization of work activities. For all of the above principles, the key is that people, individually or collectively, ought to have the opportunity to influence their working conditions according to their interests and preferences.

The above discussion focused largely on relatively small face-to-face groups and criteria for a development-supporting design of individual work activities. The design features characterizing individual jobs and small group work systems, however, are embedded in a broader context, which has to be structured accordingly in order to support the proposed elements of individual and group work organization.

Table 7.2   Characteristics of Good Jobs

Decision Latitude: Skill Discretion	The job offers possibilities to make the maximum use of one's skill and provides further opportunities to increase skills on the job. New technologies are created to be effective tools in the workers' hands, extending their power of production.
Decision Latitude: Autonomy	There is freedom from rigid worker-as-child factory discipline. Machine interface allows workers to assume control. Workers have influence over selection of work routines and work colleagues and can participate in long-term planning. It may be possible to work at home during flexible hours.
Psychological Demands	The job has routine demands mixed with a liberal element of new learning challenges, in a predictable manner. The magnitude of demands is mediated by interpersonal decision-making between parties of relatively equal status.
Social Relations	Social contacts are encouraged as a basis for new learning and are augmented by new telecommunications technologies that allow contact when isolation was previously a necessity. New contacts multiply the possibilities for self-realization through collaboration.
Social Rights	There are democratic procedures in the workplace. A bill of rights protects workers from arbitrary authority. Workers are represented by a grievance council or union, which reviews common worker problems periodically.
Meaning-fulness: Customer/ Social Feedback	Workers gain direct feedback from customers, because they can complete enough of a product or service that the customer can evaluate their contribution. The power of new production technologies, placed in workers' hands, enables customers and workers to work together, customizing the product to meet customers' needs and providing new challenges to workers.
Family/Work Interface	Work-load sharing between sexes promotes sharing of family responsibilities and allows more energy for family activities.

PRIMARY WORK SYSTEMS

Another unit of sociotechnical systems is the *primary work system*, a functional system with a semi-independent operational identity as a production or service unit in which an individual has several group memberships. This may be a product area consisting of a number of departments, with each producing part of the complete product. Involvement in primary work system arrangements increases the competences that may be acquired (e.g., the addition of quality control, maintenance, and administrative functions in addition to process jobs), thus opening career paths and creating roles rather than mere jobs.[10]

Multiple membership in larger social aggregates also lessens the danger of overidentification with small work teams. In addition to increasing the primary work system's influence in the overall organization, these larger organizational units counteract the tendency toward work group competition and address labor union concerns about the development of competing loyalty in autonomous groups that may undermine the union.

THE ORGANIZATION AS A SOCIOTECHNICAL SYSTEM

Though the process of designing sociotechnical systems can be initiated at the small unit level, studies of the implementation of the sociotechnical system approach in various types of organizations indicate that the most common reason for the failure of autonomous work groups is the lack of support in the surrounding organization. Innovations at the subunit level are unlikely to survive if the organization as a whole is not changing in the same direction.

The traditional technocratic bureaucracy characteristic of work organizations based on scientific management principles finds it increasingly difficult to cope with the interdependencies, complexity, and uncertainty of the changing economic, political, and social environment. The changing context, along with the characteristics of the more widespread application of computer-based technologies (see chapters 3 and 4), poses a new challenge to traditional organizations. The new organizational paradigm founded on the principle of joint optimization, in addition to embodying the sociotechnical work design principles illustrated in Table 7.1, replaces tall organization charts and autocratic leadership styles with flat hierarchies and participative management styles; it emphasizes cooperation over competition; it fosters commitment instead of alienation; it moves from low risk-taking to innovation, and takes into account the broader goals of society and its members rather than focusing on the organization's objectives alone.[11]

THE CAVEAT

The above discussion suggests that a new organizational paradigm implies much more than the application of sociotechnical work design principles. It requires a new organizational philosophy based on different values and assumptions. Employers' attempts to use sociotechnical system principles in a prescriptive sense in order to reap the obvious functional benefits of drawing on workers' intelligent action, without changing the control and reward structure of the existing activity patterns, will "inevitably lead to a form of social engineering in which people are reduced to objects ... the transition from the old to the new paradigm comprises a complex process of decision-making, learning and commitment that can neither be understood nor managed by means of the socio-technical approach."[12]

As discussed in Chapter 4, the Japanese production system, based on the principle of *kaizen* (continuous improvement), is carefully designed "not only to enable intelligent action but to demand it."[13]   Its system of quality circles carefully determines the parameters of choice and substitutes intrinsic (self) control mechanisms – reinforced by the combination of applied social psychological and engineering methods – for the extrinsic control mechanisms of the mass production paradigm.[14]   This system, often based on setting up units of cooperation and competition at different levels, attempts to create the perception that employee and organizational goals are identical, and that no conflicts of interest among different organizational groups exist. In this application of selected participatory design principles, employee input remains very restricted and is channeled toward the achievement of organizational productivity and quality goals only, and not toward broader workplace democracy goals of shared influence and competence development at all levels.

If, as is our premise, the broadening of opportunities for choice in the context of employee participation in the organization of work activities is both a functional and a moral imperative, it must involve recognition and fair representation of the interests of all organizational stakeholders based on democratic structures and processes that support "the establishment of a negotiated order in which multiple and mutually agreed tradeoffs are continuously arrived at."[15]

NOTES

1. For a critical discussion of the misconceptualization of sociotechnical systems, see Schurman, "Reconstructing Work", pp. 268-274.
2. Alioth, *Entwicklung und Einführung alternativer Arbeitsformen.*
3. See Alioth, "Selbststeuerungskonzepte," in A. Kieser, G. Reber, and R. Wunderer, eds., *Handwörterbuch der Führung* (Stuttgart: Pöschel, 1987) for an adaptation of work design paradigms originally proposed by Trist.
4. Trist, "Evolution of Socio-technical Systems,"
5. Gerald I. Susman, *Autonomy at Work: A Socio-technical Analysis of Participative Management* (New York: Praeger, 1976).
6. Andreas Alioth, "Die Gruppe als Kern der Organisation," in Gottlieb Duttweiler Institut, eds., *Arbeit – Beispiele für ihre Humanisierung* (Olten, Switzerland: Walter, 1983), p. 86.
7. These criteria have been adapted from Eberhard Ulich, "Psychologie der Arbeit."
8. See, for example, Karasek and Theorell, *Healthy Work.*
9. Ibid., pp. 316-317.
10. Trist, "Evolution of Socio-technical Systems."
11. Ibid., p. 42.
12. Hans van Beinum, "Observations on the Development of a New Organizational Paradigm," paper presented at the seminar on Industrial Democracy in Western Europe (Cologne, Germany, 1990), p. 7.
13. Schurman, "Reconstructing Work", p. 272.
14. Ibid.
15. Trist, "Evolution of Socio-technical Systems," p. 43.

PART III

CASE STUDIES

8. Alcatel STR: Bottom-Up Approach

Alcatel STR Incorporated (formerly Standard Telephone and Radio Inc.) was an ITT subsidiary until it became part of the Alcatel Telecommunications group in 1987.[1] While its headquarters are in Zurich, its major manufacturing plant is located in one of the city's suburbs (Au), with a second production facility in the mountain region of western Switzerland (Brig). Alcatel STR produces a variety of electronic products, including telephone switchboards. These electronic printed board assemblies (PBAs) are circuit boards involving the assembly of numerous electronic components. Annual production totals about 100,000 PBAs with hundreds of different PBA types. PBA assembly is part of a larger department and involves roughly 100 employees. With the exception of the supervisors and a small number of technical apprentices, who all are Swiss males, PBA assembly is done by women, mostly "unskilled" immigrant workers from Italy, Spain, Turkey, and other countries.

Changing market conditions provided the impetus for developing a new PBA production system. The existing system was incapable of meeting demands for increased flexibility and the 150 different, custom-designed PBA types produced annually. Furthermore, Alcatel STR management saw the development of a new production process as an opportunity to create humane and thus more attractive jobs that could prove that there was a place for manufacturing jobs in the Swiss economy of the future. "We don't want to plan the technology first and then adapt the work organization to predetermined technological structures," said the project manager in charge of planning the new PBA production when he contacted one of the authors in November 1987. He was interested in creating a people-oriented work organization that could be developed jointly with an appropriate technical system.

Though not based on an assembly line or quota system, work in the existing PBA production system was largely organized according to Taylorist principles. Every woman had her assigned workplace and received the parts she was to work on from her supervisor. While a number of women were skilled in doing a variety of work tasks, most of them did the same thing every day: for example, bending the tiny wires of a resistor to be inserted into the circuit board. Overall, the jobs were monotonous and required little training or thinking. Needless to say, the women were unable to adequately understand and interpret electronic blueprints. This was the task of the supervisors. There was little information and communication about what happened in other departments or what happened to a specific part once work on it was completed. In general, the women did not even know what the part they worked on actually was.

In an initial two-day seminar, supervisors and other management involved in the existing PBA production process were introduced to the concept of sociotechnical system design (see Chapter 7). The key outcome of these two days was the insight that neither the project task force nor the external consultant knew what the new production process should look like, and that additional expertise was needed to design a PBA assembly process that would both provide attractive jobs and increase productivity. Alcatel STR had about 100 such experts, namely, the women workers in PBA production and their supervisors. The external consultant's task was to get these experts involved as quickly and successfully as possible. Working together, a form of work organization was to be developed that reduced order throughput time from forty-five days to ten days. This economic objective was to be achieved in a way that made work more interesting and challenging for everybody involved.

Shortly afterwards, the employees were introduced to the project goals and the idea of participation. A group of fifteen to twenty women was to become involved in the design, planning, and implementation of a new system. Forty women were interested in participating, however, which led to the formation of two project groups rather than one. One group worked on "Production System 1," involving a DIP-Inserter (double in-line package) robot capable of assembling integrated circuits; the second group tackled "Production System 2," involving SMD technology (surface mounted devices), a robot capable of assembling tiny electronic components. "Production System 3," located in a different geographical area, was to be redesigned at a later time. Table 8.1 presents an overview of the project development steps.

Table 8.1   Alcatel STR Project Development Steps

0	Site visit	December 1987
	Sociotechnical analysis of the old PBA production system	
1	Task force seminar: "future-oriented" work design	January 1988
	· Project goals · Experiences elsewhere · Development of a common understanding	
2	Employee orientation	February 1988
	Information about the project and the participation process	
3	Selection of project groups for PS-1 and PS-2	February 1988
	15-20 employees each	
4	Criteria for reorganization	February 1988
	Group discussion to develop criteria for a future work design	
5	Variance and task analysis	February 1988
	Analysis of variances and their effects	
6	Work organization	March 1988
	Development of "building blocks" for work design and task combinations	
7	Layout	March 1988
	Development and simulation of physical layout models	
8	Future roles of front-line and general supervisors	March 1988
	Development of a new leadership model in cooperation with the people affected	
9	Proposal presentation to steering committee	April 1988
	Request/Approval of proposals	
10	Employee orientation	April 1988
	Feedback to employees about steering committee decisions	

11	Support measures	May/June 1988

· Identification of employee *Qualifizierung* goals
· Coordination with other departments: PPS, etc.

12	Training phase	Summer 1988

Initial instructional modules and skill certification
("training pass")

13	Taking stock	September 1988

Process evaluation and correction where necessary

14	Gradual process restructuring and utilization of new equipment	Summer 1988 - Spring 1989

PS-2 followed by PS-1

15	Reorganization of PBA function testing	Starting 1989

Development of a multiskilled testing group

16	Reorientation and assessment of leadership roles	Spring - Summer 1989

· Distinction between "red" and "green" tasks for the advisors:
  "red" = trouble shooting; "green" = supervisory assistance
· Leadership function returned to supervisor

17	Extension of reorganization process to PS-3	Spring - Fall 1989

Independent design process in the Brig facility

18	Stabilization	Fall - Winter 1989

Development of support measures for self-regulation and group
autonomy including new leadership functions

19	Coordination with "the environment"	Winter 1989

Coordinate production and leadership concept with other
organizational units (buy-in)

20	"Routine" operation	Winter 1989

Start of "routine" operation phase

The reorganization parameters thus set were the development of three similarly sized production systems with the goal of completing each order within ten days. After ten days, at least 70 percent of the orders were to be passed on to the next higher production level for systems assembly, while 25 percent were to be marked for functional testing (within a maximum of five days). Functional testing was to be integrated in each production system, and employees in charge of testing would be involved in the

design of their tasks at a later time. The overall production concept shown in Figure 8.1 had been developed by a technical project group.

Figure 8.1   Alcatel STR Production Concept for the PBA
                    Department

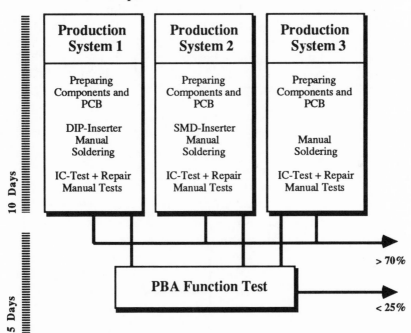

Work design for each production system was now the task of
the employee project groups. Employees' competence and task
orientation were impressive. The consultant saw his main function as helping the group to look at things with "fresh eyes," in
order to explore new possibilities.

The participation process was made more difficult because the
women involved represented many different nationalities.
Though the majority of them had lived in Switzerland for more
than ten years, most of them barely spoke German. The earlier
production system required minimal communication, as nothing
had to be discussed or decided. It thus provided little incentive to
learn the language. To witness how the women overcame these

communication barriers in the participation process was fascinating. The work group meetings were organized using the "Metaplan technique,"[2] which allowed for written documentation of the discussion. Each woman received a photocopy of the Metaplan charts generated at each meeting. Because of the language barrier, the external consultant did the Metaplan recording. He described the meetings as follows: "I started out by asking a question; this was usually followed by a seemingly chaotic, yet very lively discussion conducted in various different languages – with me being the only one not understanding what was going on. Then suddenly there was silence and one of the women sufficiently fluent in German told me what to write on the chart. When I looked around in disbelief to check if this really reflected a consensus, the women nodded firmly and assured me that, indeed, it was their answer to the question."

Figure 8.2   Organization Chart for One of the Alcatel STR
                    Production Systems

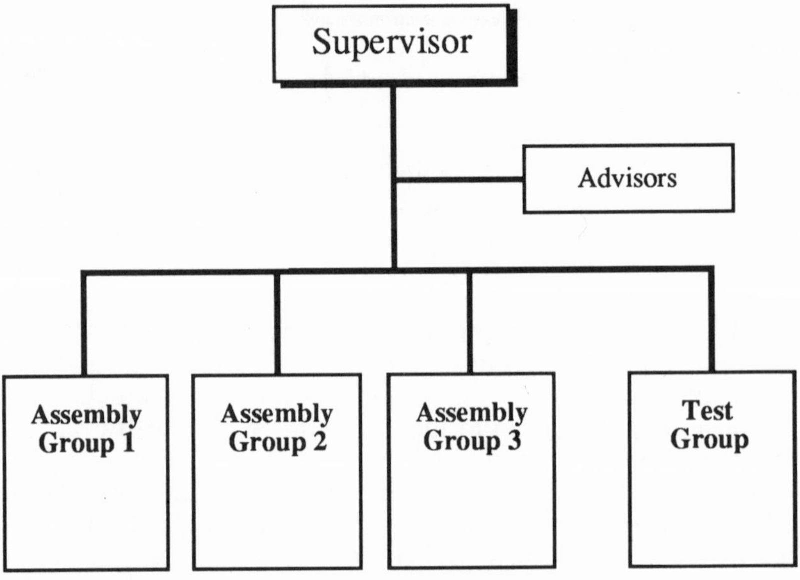

After three months, the groups had developed a model for the future work organization. Figure 8.2 presents the organization chart for one of the production systems. Two things are noteworthy:

- Groups of five or six women were in charge of the complete assembly of a PBA, including the internal task distribution as well as the nonelectronic testing. In other words, only the electronic testing would be done by a separate group. The integration of electronic testing into the assembly groups would have required too much technical equipment. The tasks to be accomplished by the assembly as well as the test groups are shown in Table 8.2.
- The hierarchical structure was changed, with all groups reporting directly to the general supervisor. Previous front-line supervisors became advisors with an instructional and trouble shooting role rather than a direct management and control function.

One thousand hours were spent in careful planning and preparation before the first changes were implemented. This was worthwhile as it helped get people oriented and pulling in the same direction once the solutions were implemented. It also helped unfreeze old patterns and habits, a precondition for movement and change in an existing social system (see Chapter 5).

In the early implementation phase of the new PBA production system, the women sometimes ran out of work if the job setup person lagged behind in preparing work orders. When this happened, the women tended to go back to the old production system to help out their co-workers there even when they were under no particular production pressure. The reason was not just solidarity; rather the women found it difficult to hang around waiting, not doing anything. Instead of struggling with the problems presented by the newly developing production system, they preferred to avoid them and to go back to the old way of doing things. The production manager observed that the advisors went along with this simply because these tasks were easier for the women. In order to avoid this relapse into old patterns, the production manager suggested that the women bring their knitting projects to work in order to occupy themselves during waiting times. The women did as told but felt guilty at first when other employees, walking through their department, saw them knitting. If there was not much to do, sometimes the product manager simply sent them home at lunch (while paying them for the afternoon, of course). All this was to emphasize support for the new system and to encourage the women to confront the difficulties involved in the implementation of a new, very different production system.

Table 8.2   Alcatel STR Assembly and Test Group Tasks

ASSEMBLY GROUP TASKS
• Internal Task Distribution • Review of Work Order Forms • Preparation of PCBs • Preparation of PBAs • PS-1: DIP-Inserter: Manual Assembly, Soldering • PS-2: SMD: Manual Assembly, Soldering • PBA Assembly • Inserting PBAs into Soldering Frame/Removal • Final Assembly • Touch-up • Testing • Delivery to Test Group
TEST GROUP TASKS
• Internal Task Distribution • Review of Work Order Forms • Incircuit Testing • Repair • Manual Testing • Final Assembly • Delivery to PBA, Stock, or System Testing

The groups' planning and preparation meetings were moderated by the external consultant and took place in a specially assigned training room. The Metaplan technique was used to document the process. Big pin boards were covered with large sheets of paper on which four-by-eight-inch cards of different colors were pinned. Ideas and problems in connection with the topic of discussion were listed and then regrouped on the board according to theme or category. Everybody could see everything that was listed and could intervene if they felt that their statement was misgrouped or misinterpreted. Disagreements among group members thus could be identified but did not have to be resolved at the time. At the end of each meeting, the cards were photographed in their last position, and photocopies were distributed to the group members a few days later. These meeting "protocols" were also publicly displayed in the department. Sessions usually lasted two to four hours during working hours. Sometimes a full day was allocated, as in the case of planning the production layout, for example. Various possible layout models were developed, using Fisher construction sets. Using a Polaroid camera, a picture was taken of each model. The picture was then put up on the pin board, and arguments for and against this design were listed next to it. If the groups met for a full day, they sometimes went "offsite" to a restaurant in a nearby town. This created some envy among some of the other women, who suspected the groups of eating and drinking well instead of working. Indeed, they did both.

The group proposals were submitted to the project steering committee and were accepted with only minor changes.

The step-by-step implementation of the new PBA production began in April 1988. The project groups decided that the proposal would be implemented during the first five months without revising and second guessing the plan. At the same time, however, a public log was to be kept where employees recorded all problems and unsatisfactory aspects as well as ideas for how to address the problems. A date was set for five months later to assess the development and make changes and corrections where necessary. This agreement was based on the assumption that some time was necessary to give the new process a chance to work and to try to iron out the bugs. At the same time, employees knew that things that did not really work could be changed eventually.

The evaluation meeting in September 1988 showed that the work redesign demanded a lot of change from everybody. When difficulties arose, advisors as well as employees tended to revert to traditional role behavior. Not only were advisors likely to interfere too much with the groups, but the women frequently called for the advisors if problems occurred, rather than experimenting with solutions within the group.

The implementation of this new work organization concept not only demanded changes in the role definitions of all employees involved, but required major *technological innovations*, possible and affordable only because of advances in computer-based technology. For example, each group had its own computer terminal, which provided access to the information necessary to complete the tasks. A new job setup system was created, and the product planning system was changed considerably based on input by the work group. Flexible assembly stations were now supplied on-line with assembly blueprints. In addition, SMD technology, likely to find increasing application, was introduced.

Though one production system was singled out for initial implementation, there was surprisingly little internal conflict and envy. The project team tried very hard not to present the PBA project as something special. Instead, it emphasized that this group was merely the first one to try a new form of work organization and that other departments would follow. In terms of the relationship between "old" versus "new" PBA production, it was clear that the simultaneous existence of old and new PBA production areas would last only one year. The issue, therefore, was who would implement the actual change first. This problem was discussed and decided within the work group, so nobody felt that it reflected management's preference.

Some problems arose within and between the groups, however. There was envy sometimes when one group felt that the other was praised more by an advisor or supervisor. Supervisors were encouraged to deal with this issue. With performance figures accessible to all group members, discussion about sudden downturns in performance took place, but it also created a mildly competitive atmosphere. This had to be addressed so as to avoid an undesired "speed-up" system. Conflicts within the groups most often resulted from leadership ambitions of individual women. While the advisors offered help in mediating the problem, they encouraged the groups to learn to address these conflicts internally. An internal trainer (from the company's training and education department) conducted team development training sessions that were extremely successful. Advisors frequently commented on the social competence with which the women tackled and solved their problems. This was a more difficult issue later, when other – mostly male – departments started the same process.

In addition to the cost of technological equipment, the new form of work organization required major investments in employee qualification. A former supervisor was put in charge of training. Together with other advisors who now had instructional functions, including some of the most experienced women from the different assembly groups, lesson plans were developed to convey the necessary knowledge and skills. Each employee now received a training pass, which was a binder including an overview of twenty-seven instructional units, each encompassing several days of education and training. The overview listed the title of the unit, the learning objectives, the prerequisites for the course, and its duration. Upon completion of an instructional unit, the employee received a certificate from the instructor. Employees could sign up for individual units based on their own initiative or upon recommendation by the supervisor. Individuals could thus increase their competence level and flexibility over time. As an employee becomes more qualified, she becomes eligible for more varied work tasks and higher pay. Experience indicated that self-regulation worked well in this respect, but that some effort was needed to keep the process going. This involved a semiannual qualification assessment in which the supervisor meets with each employee to discuss the qualification level attained and to jointly set goals for the next half year. Included in this process might be the repetition of previously learned materials if an employee feels insufficiently competent in an area.

Some time after the work groups had started to function well, the consultants observed that some women had become visibly more self-confident. This was reflected in their body posture; they were literally walking more upright than before. Asked about this change, the women agreed with the consultants' interpretation but added that their increased self-confidence had created some difficulties, too. For example, there were more fights at home, as they had become unwilling to let their husbands tell them what to do. And sometimes they talked about their work at home, something not all husbands liked. "Because now," they said, "our work has become important, too."

As the women's competences increased, the advisors' problems with their new function intensified. They had a hard time abandoning the old supervisory role, and, one year into the project, still behaved like traditional supervisors. The women were increasingly unwilling to be patronized as they themselves had now acquired the necessary competence to accomplish their tasks. To address this growing conflict, advisors and supervisors met with the external consultants to discuss the problems and reassess the concept of leadership in self-managed teams. The following issues emerged:

- The advisors spent little time on instruction; instead they helped out wherever problems occurred. This kind of trouble shooting took up all their time.
- Regardless of whether one, two, or three advisors were present in a production unit on any single day, all problems were solved by the end of the day. This suggested that the women relied on these advisors as additional resources if they were available, but that the group members were able to solve problems themselves if fewer advisors were there.
- The advisors not only were very eager to help the women out, they needed the opportunity to help in order to feel useful. Afraid of becoming redundant, they tried to cling to their old functions.
- As a result they were overloaded and had no time to take on the new tasks of providing instruction to group members and searching for long-term solutions to everyday problems, which trouble shooting "fixed" only temporarily.
- At the same time, advisors expressed interest in these new activities, particularly because they perceived them as opportunities for further qualification.

In order to solve the difficult problem of trying to overcome ingrained habits, the following plan was agreed upon:

- Leadership of the production unit was the basic responsibility of the unit supervisor. However, it was up to the supervisor to delegate parts of his leadership function to the advisors. This involved tasks such as clarification/documentation of technical matters; problem-solving in cooperation with other departments; instruction of new and existing employees; maintenance of technical equipment; introduction of new tools and equipment; further development of technical and organizational solutions; and planning their own continuing education. These tasks were labeled as "green" tasks.
- Where necessary, advisors would still be available for trouble shooting. However, they were to get involved in these activities only in response to explicit work group requests, and would try to reduce these types of activities. These trouble shooting activities were defined as "red" tasks.
- To avoid red tasks taking up all the time at the expense of the green tasks, advisors were to distinguish between times

when they wore the red hat, so to speak, versus times when they wore the green hat.

- The time allocation for green and red tasks would be decided at a weekly planning meeting with the unit supervisor.
- To clarify which advisor was available for red tasks at what time, and thus could be asked for help by the work group, for example, the green times for all advisors were listed on a bulletin board. During green times, advisors were not to be disturbed. Meetings for green activities could be arranged with advisors at all times, however.

Central to this concept was that each advisor was to take on green as well as red tasks so as to avoid the development of green staff only who would be increasingly removed from the production process. Half a year later, this model was operating well and continues to work to the satisfaction of the employees involved. The advisors had to learn how to work differently, and it was a new experience to plan and allocate their time according to different tasks. At this point, none of them would like to return to the old system.

At about the same time the reorganization of the third PBA production unit, located in the western part of Switzerland, was to be undertaken.

The women in the Brig production facility, as well as their supervisors, thought that the "Zurich System" was not something *they* wanted to adopt. They were not convinced that the women in Zurich actually liked the new form of work organization. Instead, they thought that the consultant had talked them into it. In order to challenge this perception, all women were invited to visit the Zurich facility. A bus was organized and they arrived for a one-day visit during which the Zurich management – without the external consultant – showed them the new production process. On the way home, the women concluded that there was a lot of "happy dust," that they had been shown only the "pretty picture" and that there had been insufficient opportunity to ask critical questions of their colleagues. Luckily, the department head heard about this. The women in Brig were asked to select a delegation of four women who would come back for a second visit. This time there would be no "program"; in other words, the visitors should decide what they wanted to see and whom they wanted to talk to for as long as they liked. Following these visits the four delegates had completely changed their mind. They returned home and convinced their co-workers to engage in their own participation and work reorganization process.

It was important to realize that the reorganization experiences of production systems 1 and 2 could not simply be transferred. The employees in Brig needed to develop their own system. To illustrate the independence of the Brig project, the consultant guiding the original project was not directly involved but served as an advisor only to an internal "change agent." The third production system has operated as a self-managed team since December 1989, though its workflow and organizational structure are slightly different.

In the meantime, the production units also achieved their economic goals. Operating with the same number of employees, throughput times have been reduced from forty-five to ten days, and quality meets the desired standards. In view of this success, the company decided to gradually reorganize other production areas following the same principle: each area was to develop its own solution. The design was to follow sociotechnical systems principles aimed at increased self-regulation of work groups and a reduction of hierarchical structures. This was to be achieved by a participatory process involving all employees affected. A number of projects are currently under way and are starting to show some success.

WHAT MATTERS

Alcatel STR illustrates the promise of a successfully implemented process of work design for competence development, improving the quality of jobs, and working life and achieving the economic goals set for the project. It also points to a number of key issues raised in the preceding chapters:

- The success of this process is not dependent on previous worker skill and education level. In addition, the project had to overcome communication barriers resulting from the very limited knowledge of German many of these women had. This is of particular importance, as predictions for the future U.S. workforce include a growing number of under-educated immigrant workers.
- Changes in the distribution of competences are not without tension, as they upset the previous hierarchy of power and authority. The difficulties confronted by advisors could only be overcome as they redefined their role in a way that

provided meaningful new tasks and alleviated their fears of becoming obsolete. At the same time, competence development at work may have effects beyond the workplace. The growing self-confidence resulting from their new work experience created conflicts at home as the women started to question the dominant role played by husbands in many of the immigrant cultures.

- Mechanisms have to be established addressing the issue of envy and intra- and intergroup competition. To the degree to which work groups take charge of their activities and develop a stake in achieving their goals, intergroup competition can easily lead to speed-up and peer pressure on the "weaker" members of the group.
- The principle of self-design is critical. Just because the process worked well for the women in Zurich in no way meant that the women in Brig were willing to adopt the same system. They had to be given the opportunity to ask critical questions and to develop their own participation and design process.
- And finally, major productivity increases without simultaneously growing demand are likely to result in a reduction of jobs. Though at Alcatel STR no jobs were lost, this is an issue to be negotiated if unions are to participate and support this type of work redesign process.

NOTES

1. The authors would like to thank Alcatel STR for permission to publish this case study revealing the company's identity. The consulting firm involved was AOC AG, Zurich; the consultant was Felix Frei.

2. T. Schnelle-Cölln, ed., *Metaplan-Visualisierungstechnik. Die optische Sprache in der Moderation*. Metaplan Reihe, Heft 6 (Quickborn, Germany: Metaplan GmbH, 1983).

9.   Swissair: Top-Down Approach

This case study describes the work reorganization and restructuring process at Swissair, the national airline of Switzerland.[1] Though this project affected the organization as a whole, we will focus here on the approach taken to restructure work organization at the front line, seen as central to the company's future success. Swissair has a workforce of about 20,000 employees worldwide, with about 12,000 employees working in Switzerland.

In 1987 Swissair management decided to launch a four-pronged reorganization/restructuring project aimed at securing the future of the enterprise. The work reorganization project described here, and initiated in 1988, was one of four areas of strategic interventions. Product/service improvement was to be the focus for 1989, cooperation with other airlines was initiated in 1990, and in 1991 a cost improvement program was to be implemented. The latter three areas of intervention will not be addressed here.

When the reorganization project was initiated in 1987 the company was doing well financially. The project was given impetus not by existing economic pressures, but by a number of strategic issues seen as threatening the viability of the organization in the future. The appointment of a new chief executive officer in 1988 facilitated the process of fundamentally reexamining Swissair's way of doing business. The following problem areas were identified:

- The organizational environment – markets, technologies, and societal values – was changing at an accelerated pace. In order to take advantage of business opportunities and to ensure organizational survival, two success factors were deemed critical: market or customer orientation, and flexibility and mobility. The existing organizational structures inadequately met these challenges.

- The optimal utilization of qualified employees at all levels, but in particular those at the front line interacting with customers, required increased scope of activities and more decision latitude. The currently centralized structure, characterized by a high degree of functional specialization, made this impossible. As a result, employee motivation and identification with company goals were threatened.

- The growing complexity of work tasks dramatically increased expenditures for administration and coordination activities in the functionally specialized organizational structure. Rising costs and difficulties in organizational decision-making processes called for structural solutions to reduce expenditures for coordination and to foster more effective decision-making processes.

The broad goals of the reorganization project were to develop an overall organizational strategy and to establish structural conditions that would improve flexibility, efficiency, and customer orientation. This was to be achieved by creating easily identifiable organizational units that, limited only by coordination requirements, would be characterized by a high degree of autonomy and potential for self-regulation. This reorganization was to be applied to the overall organizational structure (vertical dimension) as well as to the internal structure of individual departments or organizational units, addressing in particular the organization of work at the front line (horizontal dimension).

Rather than creating a new set of fixed structures, the reorganization was to focus on flexible arrangements that would allow for further adjustments in response to emerging market conditions or other environmental changes. In addition to requiring flexible and adaptable structures, this called for a willingness on the part of management and employees to accept and actively confront change and to perceive ongoing change as an integral part of the business. The process of *Qualifizierung*, or competence development through work reorganization, was seen as useful in fostering innovative, cooperative, and flexible attitudes among employees in a less rigidly structured and more dynamic organizational environment.

Four task forces were established to tackle the project. They were to work independently, playfully competing with each other, in order to avoid a narrow-minded or biased solution. Three of the task forces were to address the overall structure and management hierarchy of the company. Task Force 4 was in charge of developing the front-line or bottom-up perspective for the new organizational structure. Among other things, proposals made by Task Forces 1-3 were to be evaluated by how well they supported and facilitated the implementation of the criteria developed by Task Force 4. This approach was to ensure that top-down planning would include bottom-up perspectives from the beginning. Or as the new CEO suggested, "Day after day, our staff are called upon to deliver high performance. Management must be there to help them – and not the reverse."

Each task force was assisted by external consultants recruited from four different well-known consulting firms. For Task Forces 1-3 the external consultants were available upon request; in other words, they were not to develop a "consultant solution" but assist the task forces as needed. In Task Force 4, by contrast, two external consultants (among the authors of this book) were full members of the task force and thus carried joint responsibility for the outcome of the task force activities.

Together, the members of the four task forces formed the project team in charge of the overall reorganization project. They had been hand-picked by the CEO and represented upper management as well as the personnel and organizational development departments. This selection of influential and high-ranking organizational members fostered motivation among the task force members to explore and develop truly innovative solutions.

The work of the four task forces was to be guided by the following organizational goals and objectives:
• market and customer orientation
• flexibility and mobility
• clearly defined, comprehensible, and responsive organizational units
• adequate discretion and decision latitude at the front line
• cross-utilization of employees
• adequate variety of organizational structures
• development of required organizational linkages
• direct information, decision, and response channels
• clearly identified and easily accessible contact channels for external partners (less red tape for customers and suppliers in dealing with Swissair)
• clearly defined leadership responsibilities

More specifically, the different task forces had the following charges:

Task Forces 1-3: Overall Organizational Structure. Working independently of each other, each of these task forces was to design an overall structural concept ranging from the top management level down to the existing departmental level. Their challenge was to produce viable alternatives, evaluating advantages and disadvantages in the following areas:

- overall department organization
- marketing and sales
- financial management and accounting
- personnel management
- centralized corporate planning and development
- information systems
- air transport policy
- management
- chain of command and hierarchical designations
- report system
- task force/project management

Task Force 4: Basic Workflow Organization. The goal here was to develop a set of general criteria for work organization at the departmental level. The task force was to examine workflow organization in the various departments and develop proposals for broadening staff responsibilities and increasing task variety for individual jobs or work activities. It consisted of two line managers, one personnel manager, an internal organizational development expert, and two external consultants.

The discussion below summarizes the outcomes of the overall reorganization project. In particular, the activities of Task Force 4 are central to this book. First, it is relatively unusual, though very important, that good forms of work organization should be at the center of an organizational restructuring process. Second, it illustrates how the process of *Qualifizierung* and the goal of competence development cannot be pursued independently from changing organizational structures.

Based on Swissair's customer orientation and flexibility goals, the design criteria for the lower levels and front-line work organization were guided by two considerations. First, customer orientation means friendly interaction with customers, unbureaucratic behavior, and providing correct and reliable information. In short, competent customer service requires competent and knowledgeable employees. Such employees require freedom to make decisions and attractive jobs and, in turn, want to be treated as customers by other organizational departments. Customer orientation thus becomes a concept guiding employee interactions as well as those between employees and external customers. Second, the demand for simplified decision-making structures and a reduction in existing hierarchical levels requires more self-regulation and concomitant decision-making at the front line and lower organizational levels.

Based on these goals, the task force developed the following *vision:* The focus of organizational functioning is the place where work activities are executed, that is, at the organizational base. From this perspective, the organizational "superstructure" becomes a support function, facilitating lower level task accomplishment. Employees at the base must (1) be able to work efficiently, (2) like what they are doing, (3) take on responsibility, (4) keep coordination and administration expenditures low, and (5) be utilized flexibly. Accomplishing this requires work teams with clearly defined and comprehensible areas of responsibilities. To the degree possible, these teams are to be organized as if they were independent businesses. That is, they

- are responsible for their product/service
- plan, regulate, and organize their work activities themselves
- have their own budget
- regulate their own working hours
- handle administrative tasks on their own
- are not to be tied by boundaries between hierarchically regulated organizational units
- can introduce innovations in their areas
- create a sense of belonging for the individual team member

As every employee takes on managerial functions, fewer people remain in functions where they exclusively manage, plan, control, and coordinate.

Based on this vision, the task force selected six departments (check-in, cargo handling, aircraft handling, telephone sales, aircraft maintenance, and central purchasing) for an analysis of barriers in the current organization that obstruct the work organization envisioned for the future. The members of the task force developed a set of case studies based on extensive interviews with one or two persons from each of these departments. The interviewees selected – mostly managers from the different areas – were very knowledgeable about their department. The interviews focused on the customer needs to be satisfied by each department and tried to explore the degree to which the existing conditions could optimally meet these requirements. The results of this analysis provided the basis on which the task force developed the following design criteria for work organization, against which the overall structural reorganization proposals were to be evaluated.

DESIGN CRITERIA

for Primary/Front-Line Work Structures

by P. Truniger (OP), L. Tanner (PBK), O. Fontana (RM), H.U. Berger (POE), A. Alioth, and F. Frei (AOC), 2/19/1988

Preliminary remark: The message of this paper may also be applied to the paper itself: its value lies in its further development!

The authors are well aware that some statements made in this paper are open to a number of interpretations. However, in the interest of furthering discussion, they prefer to refrain from closer definition or elaboration, and to make themselves available to discuss the material presented here.

Goals

The requirements for the organizational structure of the company, as well as the criteria for primary work structures stated below, are designed to achieve the following goals:

- to make staff increasingly aware of customer needs, and enable them to respond to these in an entrepreneurial fashion;
- to encourage staff to become more flexible (in competence and in commitment), and to bring greater variety to the content of their work;
- to provide both staff and the work organization in general with greater flexibility in responding to changes in staff's own wishes and demands;
- to increase scope for action at the primary-function level, with more possibility for self-regulation of variances and disturbances. This should ensure faster decision-making, greater staff motivation, and increased informal lateral communication;
- to reduce the number of interfaces, and thus the effort expended on coordination and administrative tasks.

Basic position

On the basis of the goals outlined above, the *work team* should be regarded as the smallest organizational unit. (Smaller units of individual work positions should be permitted in exceptional and well-justified cases.) Work teams should operate like small businesses, with a clear and comprehensible field of responsibility. They should be encouraged to assume full responsibility for a product or service. All of this will, of course, place special demands on the structure of the *organizational unit* of which they form a part.

The following elements of primary work structures have to be designed in accordance with the organizational structure of the company as a whole:

1. the *primary task* (function/main task of the *work team)*, and with it the amount of scope available to the team and its individual members;

2. the *mission* of the larger *organizational unit,* from which the primary task of the work team can be deduced and understood (i.e., everyone knows and understands how the primary task fits into the broader goals and activities of the organizational unit);

3. the degree to which *support and control functions* (e.g., current staff units and specialist services, etc.) are to be integrated. This refers to the inevitable friction between the autonomy/initiative of the work team and its embeddedness in the organization as a whole (in other words, the right balance needs to be found between centralization and decentralization);

4. *support measures* to ensure that the structures devised are actually adhered to (behavioral aspect).

The "work structures" group has studied the above four points, and formulated the following requirements. The basic principles to be followed are:

- autonomy at the primary/front level is possible only if there is sufficient (i.e., considerable) scope of action at higher levels, because the amount of scope that can be delegated will become progressively diminished further down the line;

- the procedures required to produce products and services that best satisfy the requirements of the customer are to determine the structures to be adopted.

1.   Concerning the primary task

1.1   The performance of every work team must be defined in terms of the customer it serves. In other words, we are striving to offer a *service to the customer.* This applies not only to external "real" customers, but equally to internal customers: front-line personnel will only be able to orient them-selves toward the outside customer if they themselves are treated as customers by the internal units supporting them. Thus, customer-oriented activities may be aimed directly at a customer group, or they may be affected indirectly, through product orientation. A prerequisite of both is that the per-formance requirements are stated in a clear and comprehen-sible manner.

1.2   Customer needs which belong inseparably together should be assigned to *one* work team, which will have sole responsibility for them. In other words, the structure of the company must ensure that the needs of both external and internal customers are not jeopardized by an excess of interfaces or problems with delimitations of responsibility.

1.3   This sole responsibility should permit each individual work team to be given its own *corporate assignment,* which will then be carried out individually, with collective responsibil-ity, by the team concerned. These assignments should spec-ify the following targets:

- quality
- quantity
- cost, with team budgeting responsibility
- revenue targets (wherever feasible) and/or other success criteria

These targets are to be seen as threshold values, to be estab-lished in consultation with those concerned. If some or parts of these targets are subsequently changed, others dependent upon them will need to be modified accordingly.

In order to ensure that such assignments may be delegated, the larger organizational unit itself must enjoy an appropriate degree of autonomy regarding such targets, within the broader overall budget constraints.

1.4   These targets will also set the standard for evaluation of per-formance. Wherever work needs to be performed in teams, evaluation should be of the team as a whole (e.g., group "performance reviews" should be conducted). This does not, however, rule out the possibility for differentiating salaries according to an individual's competence/skill, as well as ac-cording to team behavior (see 4.5). Every team member should be able to see whether and how well the team has fulfilled its assignments; the appropriate *management tools* should be used to this end. *Feedback* from both internal and external customers must also be guaranteed.

1.5   The work team must generally be given enough scope to:

- fulfill its task (resources and their provision; see 3);

- stimulate individual initiative in serving the customer (a minimum of regulations);
- encourage a feeling of belonging to the team;
- allow the introduction of different and group-specific procedures within the overall company policy framework.

In general, the organizational structure must permit a number of different substructures, and the achievement of these targets is not to result in more bureaucracy; the spoken word is to be given more prominence.

2. Concerning the "mission"

2.1   The individual assignment of a work team should be *clearly derivable from* and *understandable* in the light of the mission of the larger organizational unit. In other words, in structural terms, the larger organizational unit should not be some kind of a "supermarket"; it should have a specified task within the company as a whole, a task which is clearly outlined and can be communicated as a "mission."

2.2   Within this larger unit, there must be a *functional link* between the various work teams. This link must be both simple and transparent. There should be few and clearly defined interfaces. All relevant interfaces have to be within the same unit.

2.3   In the interest of *bottom-up transparency* and *top-down manageability,* the establishment of the organizational structure should take into account the following considerations:

- location of spatial units (geography, social contact) in addition to functional interdependence based on mission;
- the size of the organizational unit should be limited to about 250 staff members (this limit should only be exceeded if the work cannot be effectively further subdivided, or if other pressing reasons such as shift work exist);
- there should be no more than three management levels per "mission unit."

2.4   This means that there should be no more than *six hierarchical levels* for the organization as a whole.

3. Concerning support and control functions

3.1   To the degree to which they are required, planning and control functions should be decentralized, and performed as close to the lowest level/front line as possible (e.g., material should be prepared for individual groups or sections). *Allo-*

cation of day-to-day work in particular should be done by the work team itself. In addition, support functions essential for the customer should not be delegated to other units.

3.2   *Budgeting responsibility* should be seen in line within the framework of the overall budget (see 1.3).

3.3   *Planning of the means of production* (including specification of computer equipment) for the field of operations must also be executed at the lowest possible operational level. This entails decentralization of the required expertise.

3.4   *Internal services* performed or offered by separate support organizations should be *monitored* by the intended *user*, who is to be viewed as an internal customer (see 1.1).

3.5   Responsibility for *selection, care, assessment, and salaries* of staff lies with line managers. In particular, salaries should take into account the *versatility* of the staff member (pay for knowledge) and his or her *behavior within the team*.

4.   Additional support and development measures

4.1   *Promotion of understanding and empathy:* Bringing the product/service into line with the customer's needs means being able and willing to see the situation from a user/customer perspective. This can be fostered through:

- information (awareness of the customer's/supplier's situation; see also 1);
- personal experience (job rotation, temporary assignments to other units);
- social contact (direct communication channels, spoken word; see also 2).

4.2   *Career orientation:* Increased autonomy at the primary level/front line, fewer hierarchical levels, and the integration of support functions all mean fewer prospects of promotion. For this reason, the development of career models appropriate to the profession and career in question must be encouraged. For status reasons, such models must also be externally defensible and comprehensible.

4.3   *Leadership:*

- Management staff should increasingly be selected, trained, and evaluated with human resource objectives in mind (staff training, workplace improvements, flexibility, and organizational development). One key point here is the training of management staff to lead and develop groups.
- Management must see itself much more as leading a team rather than a group of individuals.

- Management responsibility will and should grow; at the same time, responsibility for directly performing task assignments should be delegated more and more to others (the setting of parameters is a management task; self-regulation is up to the team and the individual). The principle of group responsibility involved here will in many cases entail the breaking of a "taboo" and will require time and support in the initial stages.

4.4   *Management:* Management staff needs to think and act strategically, i.e., in broader time and planning terms (future needs, management succession, organizational development, system modification). The higher up the manager is, the greater this breadth of perspective should be.

4.5   *Salaries:* Staff salary arrangements must above all provide some incentive for developing flexibility and showing initiative. They must also encourage a willingness to cooperate (multiskilling, team spirit, including rewards for special knowledge and performance).

4.6   *Collective bargaining agreement:* If the above structural criteria are to be successfully implemented, they must be reflected in the content of future collective bargaining agreements, and thus given explicit support.

4.7   *Infrastructure:* Infrastructure will need to be adapted, through the availability of computer equipment (management tools at basic-function level), appropriate facilities (geographical proximity), and rationalization (automation of mindless, monotonous work).

4.8   *Bookkeeping and accounts:* The information required for self-monitoring will need to be made locally available (see 1.3 and 1.4).

This list of criteria contained a number of potentially controversial issues with considerable implications for the organization and many of its members. As these may be obvious only to the insider, some of the key issues are highlighted below:

- Defining the work group as the smallest organizational unit: As tasks were being redefined for work teams rather than for individuals, each team would develop its own flexible form of task distribution and regulate and change its activities. This also meant that tasks considered irrelevant to the overall team task could be eliminated quickly and unbureaucratically. New tasks aimed at improving customer service could be integrated flexibly and more easily.

- Placing the concept of customer needs/service at the core of organizational redesign made it possible to question some of the traditional fiefdoms of upper management and to redistribute the management "pie" without managers losing face.
- By clarifying the relationship between work team goals and the larger unit's mission, it was possible to reduce unit size and restructure some of the larger units into more easily accessible and understandable units.
- The flattening of the organizational hierarchy from nine to six levels created the preconditions for expanding the range and scope of activities for the front-line employees. Eliminated were one of two top executive levels, a middle management level, and the traditional first-line supervision level. Elimination of first-line supervision resulted in a structure in which the team, rather than individuals, reported to the next level of management. (Though all of the affected employees retained employment, this structural reorganization led to a status demotion for some of them.)
- By reintegrating support and control functions into existing line functions as much possible, a lot of bureaucracy could be eliminated. At the same time, the line function's ability to respond quickly to changing situations and problems was enhanced. This again was a prerequisite for broadening the range and scope of work activities at the front line.

Looking back, the very humane treatment of the "reorganization losers" (no layoffs or salary cuts) had its disadvantages. Savings badly needed only two years later could have been achieved. But, more important, many employees were left with the impression that management's reorganization was largely cosmetic in nature. This impression was used by some to try to survive the process without making any real changes in their area, while others were demotivated in their efforts to change.

The authors working with Task Force 4 believe that it would have been better to confront the topic of reorganization losers head on and to offer an attractive alternative to those expected to lose in the process. At the same time, this would have sent a clear message to the remaining staff that the gaps thus created were to be bridged through the proposed restructuring of existing forms of work organization.

IMPLEMENTATION

In order to illustrate the importance of these criteria to the leadership and to gain a better understanding of the discrepancy between the current and the desired situation, the existing work organization at the organization base was analyzed. Task Force 4 conducted an extensive survey among existing organizational units involving about 1,200 employees and 35 moderators trained by the task force. These moderators conducted some 120 workshops aimed at developing a comprehensive picture of the current work situation. The emphasis was on how employees felt about their work and the kinds of problems encountered in their jobs. Again, questions were asked from the perspective of who the customer is (internal or external) and how the unit identifies and serves customers' needs.[2]

In general, the results showed that employees lacked recognition and needed information, and that the scope for individual action was very narrow. In addition, work environment problems like noise, drafts, and lack of space were identified. The findings also suggested that teamwork would be popular in most organizational units. Finally, it was very clear that people had high expectations concerning the restructuring project.

On August 1, 1988, the company was reorganized into eleven new departments. Department heads and line managers were responsible for the development and implementation of reorganization projects in their unit. On the first day at work, the new department heads received the detailed survey results, with specific recommendations regarding reorganizing the work structure in their units and retraining their departmental staff. Work redesign was to be planned and developed at the departmental level, tailored to the specific needs of the unit. This reflected the overall reorganization philosophy that new forms of work organization with increased scope and decision latitude cannot be developed centrally, but have to emerge at the front line, allowing for different forms and structures based on the needs and preferences of a particular unit. In trying to implement the new forms of work organization, Swissair could rely on previous experiences with self-managed work teams that had been introduced in various parts of the organization in the past years.

This example of the implementation of the proposed new work organization structure at the departmental level describes the changes in a technical department. After the original supervisor had been assigned another task, a semi-autonomous work

team was established. The twelve team members are now responsible for all repair orders of pneumatic equipment, including
the delivery of the assigned equipment and quality control.
Declaring the repaired equipment operational, indicated by a
specific code at the airline terminal, was basically the most important control function of the supervisor. This function has now
been taken over by the employee who repaired the equipment. In
addition, the group plans work schedules (e.g., schedule changes
due to sick leaves and other absences), elects a rotating group
speaker, and will foster multiskilling among its members.

The work reorganization was developed together with the
team members. The participation process started with a workshop
in which the team members compared their own tasks with those
of the supervisor and the department manager. Based on this
comparison, the new task assignments without a direct supervisor
were discussed and determined.

It is typical for Swissair's work redesign efforts to focus on
those areas where an opportunity for change presents itself. This
adaptation of the judo principle means, however, that many different forms of work organization coexist simultaneously. Under
the same department head in the pneumatic area, for example,
two other groups continue to work in the traditional way with a
supervisor.

Different departments approached the task in different ways.
In some departments, task forces analogous to the overall reorganization project were established in order to initiate a similar
problem identification process and to "invent" department-spe-
cific solutions. Reorganization efforts are currently at different
stages of implementation in the various departments. Though the
list of design criteria developed by Task Force 4 is not well
known throughout the company, the underlying ideas seem to
have taken hold.

The principle of "self-designed" implementation has the dis-
advantage that more conservative departments can hang on to
outdated forms of work organization and traditional management
styles. On the other hand, in those departments where change is
happening, a real learning process is taking place; people buy in
and are actively involved.

Since work organization restructuring at the lower organizational levels is proceeding slowly, the unions are urging management to move faster. Union representatives know what they
are asking for, as all eighty members of the work council were

trained (by the authors) on the process of work design for competence development in early 1989.

An important intervention to strengthen management's efforts to diffuse work reorganization was the start of a training program for lower-level management in 1991, aimed at educating them about the process of work design for competence development. Already established work teams are being supported through training courses about working and problem-solving in teams.

Overall, this approach to restructuring work at the front line promises to be successful, but is much more demanding and time-consuming than initially expected by most participants.

WHAT MATTERS

- Top-down design can provide meaningful guidelines but is likely to lead to limited action/implementation if the managerial structure and incentive system remain largely unchanged, and if managers themselves are not engaged in a participatory process that reassesses their roles and tasks.
- Although successful work design for competence development is premised on the involvement of the affected employees in designing a system that fits their particular needs, support programs are needed to guide the process by helping lower-level management (whose traditional role is often most threatened by such changes) define a new role and to support the work group with the training needed to foster autonomous functioning and team problem-solving.
- Union involvement can be important in supporting the change process. However, this is likely to happen only if the union is informed about and supports the intended reorganization. In the case of Swissair, the union took the initiative and demanded its own education on the work design for competence development concept. As the American literature suggests, where unions are not supportive of participatory projects, the effect of such efforts is negligible.[3]

NOTES

1.   The authors would like to thank Swissair for permission to publish this case study revealing the company's identity. The consulting firm involved was AOC AG, Zurich; the consultants were Andreas Alioth and Felix Frei.

2.   See tool #4 in Chapter 12.

3.   Cooke, *Labor-Management Cooperation.*

10. Tetra Pak: Organizational Assessment as Impetus for Change

The setting of this project was the German subsidiary of a leading international corporation involved in the production of cardboard packaging for liquids such as milk and fruit juices.[1]

Tetra Pak was founded in 1951 by the Swedish entrepreneur Ruben Rausing following extensive research conducted by him in the forties. Rausing set out to meet the self-imposed challenge of ensuring that, in spite of increasing urbanization, every child should be able to find fresh, high-quality milk on his or her breakfast table. The solution, as he defined it, was packaging that would maintain milk quality over a longer period of time, that was easy to transport, and whose benefits would outweigh its total costs. The results were the well-known cardboard containers and conservation technologies such as UHT (ultra-high temperature). The company remains a family-owned business.

Tetra Pak's business policy is to retain ownership of all packaging equipment produced in the company's own, mostly Swedish factories. Equipment is leased to customers all over the world. The customer buys the cardboard from Tetra Pak. The German subsidiary, the site of the project described here, produces packaging material which includes cardboard coating and customer-specific labeling. All wood pulp used for Tetra Pak packaging is produced in Sweden, where the company's natural resource conservation policy guarantees reforestation at a faster pace than lumber is used.

In terms of environmental concerns, cardboard packaging receives a good rating. It can be burned without residue and has a high incineration value. The heat generation value is half that of oil; the more cardboard added to household waste, the less oil is required for incineration. The glass bottle – often cited as a major alternative from an environmental protection and energy conservation perspective – would be rated more highly only if recycling greatly surpassed current efforts.

Tetra Pak Germany produces about 10 percent of the total business packaging volume. The subsidiary encompasses two production plants (Limburg and Berlin), a research and development facility in Darmstadt, as well as additional research facilities in other locations. The headquarters are in Hochheim, a suburb of Frankfurt. Tetra Pak Germany employs approximately 1,000 people.

At the time of project initiation, the company was organized into eight functional areas: finance/personnel, sales, marketing, technical department, planning, customer services, production, and R&D. The project, conducted between 1986 and 1990, involved all areas except production. With the exception of R&D, all areas were part of central administration. A total of 480 employees participated in the project.

The organizational hierarchy was comprised of five levels: chief executive officer, corporate area managers, department managers, supervisors, and employees. Executive management consisted of the chief executive officer and the area managers.

PROJECT HISTORY

In 1986 one of the authors was asked to give a talk to executive management and the department heads on the topic "Improvement of the Quality of Work." The key point emphasized was that quality of work is not a question of discipline or employee motivation, but, first and foremost, a result of organizational structures and leadership style. Quality of work, it was argued, could not be separated from *quality of work life.*

The CEO liked these ideas and was eager to move into an organizational change project. His management staff pointed out, however, that such an undertaking was meaningful only if the key problems were first identified and clearly documented. Following discussions with the external consultant, it was decided to limit intervention to an organizational assessment.

The CEO was the founding father of the German subsidiary. He had greatly influenced the growth and development of the company from its modest beginning in the sixties. For twenty-five years the business philosophy of his management team successfully focused on quantitative expansion, with sometimes enormous growth rates. Increasing market saturation in the eighties led management to start emphasizing qualitative development, the goal the project described here was intended to help achieve.

A model for the planned organizational assessment was to be developed by the executive management group in cooperation with the external consultant. Executive management and the external consultant gathered for a one-day offsite meeting in 1987, later referred to as the "sweater meeting." (so named, because the managers invited were told to attend in casual attire rather than formal business suits, something very unusual for this organization's culture).

A Diagnostic Model for Organizational Assessment

The model developed at the offsite meeting was to be guided by the following general questions: (1) Will the company still be in a position to meet the quality standards demanded by the market in five years? and (2) What changes might be required to achieve this goal?

The assessment was to be based on a five-phase *diagnostic model*, following the method developed by Kolb, Rubin, and McIntyre.[2] It involved a participatory research process in which the implicit assumptions or theories the managers held about key variables affecting business success were explored. The emerging model was then to be "tested" in a subsequent organizational assessment.

Phase 1

First, the managers identified the following key areas they felt needed to be addressed in order to arrive at a meaningful organizational diagnosis:

• Identify the strengths and weaknesses of the organization.

- Discover the structures and patterns of organizational decision-making processes and identify possible areas of improvement.
- Get a sense of how people feel about the organization and explore the presence of important shared values.
- Identify areas of change of interest to employees and possible sources of resistance to change.
- Gain insight about positive and negative aspects of the overall organization and different functional areas.
- Strengthen organizational leadership.

Phase 2

Now the participants determined the variables they thought had to be addressed in order to answer their questions.

Hierarchical structure	Performance of staff units
Informal awards	Work atmosphere/ organizational climate
Span of control	Organizational goals
Production process: technology and organization	Availability of resources
Informal social structures	Information flow and channels
External relationships: market and government	Leadership style and atmosphere
Benefits and bonuses	Quality and output control
Management selection	Customer demands
Training	Employee quality consciousness
Organizational culture: values and norms	Self-reliance and employee participation
Finances: costs, profits	Decision planning and execution

Fluctuation

Employee job satisfaction

Employee performance

Innovation

Employee competence development

Definitions of tasks and responsibilities

Willingness to take on responsibility

Leadership

Phase 3

The variables selected were grouped into the following major categories, considered to be interrelated:
1. Organizational structure
2. Leadership style
3. Personnel policies
4. Performance/output
5. Environment
6. Decision-making processes
7. Employees

Phase 4

In this phase the managers tried to identify the degree to which change in one category would affect the other categories. For example, by changing one category substantially, another category might be very much affected, only slightly affected, or probably not affected.

Phase 5

An organizational assessment model was now developed by placing each category in a box. Based on the previous assessment of the relationship between these categories, the boxes were then connected to each other with arrows indicating the direction and strength of relationships (see Figure 10.1).

This model created a "lens" through which the company could be looked at more closely. The organizational assessment explored the seven key variables and their relationship to each other. The main questions were how decisions were made in the company, what determined them, and what their positive or negative effects were.

Figure 10.1   The Tetra Pak Diagnostic Model for Organizational Assessment

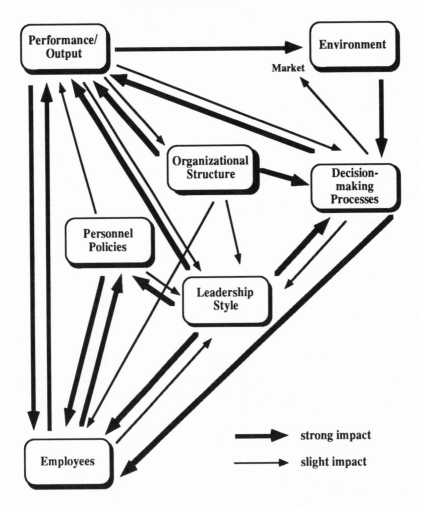

Following the sweater meeting, it was agreed that two of the
authors/consultants would conduct the actual organizational assessment through employee interviews. The goal was not to col-
lect vague complaints, but rather to identify specific information
helpful in developing measures for improved decision-making
and implementation. The data collected were to be specific
enough to provide insights that could guide changes within functional areas as well as departments. In order to make the decision-making process more transparent and to assess and improve

leadership qualities, employees at all hierarchical levels were to be interviewed.

Data collection addressed the following topics, derived by the external consultants from the model presented in Figure 10.1:

1. General Information about the Organization
   - Organizational goals and contributions of specific departments
   - Overall strengths and weaknesses: company/department
   - Perception of organizational philosophy and corporate identity/culture

2. Organizational Structure (considered a key area of inquiry)
   - Formal and informal hierarchies
   - Organization chart from the perspective of supplier-customer relationships
   - Task distribution between departments
   - Characteristics of organizational structure below department manager level
   - Effects of organizational structure on cooperation and communication (especially top-down patterns)
   - Dependencies between internal administration and international headquarters

3. Leadership Style (considered a key area of inquiry)
   - Management information patterns/policies
   - Perceptions of leadership styles and behavior (form and content)
   - Clarity of directions and orders
   - Prerequisites for successful leadership (including delegation, representation)
   - Effects of leadership styles on organizational goals
   - Overlapping and divergent perspectives between management and other employees
   - Effects on individual jobs
   - Responses to bottom-up initiatives

4. Personnel Management/Policies
   - Expectations
   - Areas where personnel management affects one's work/department
   - Possibilities for development and *Qualifizierung*
   - Expectations regarding employee benefits

5. Performance/Output
   - Subjective performance evaluation criteria
   - Top-down understanding and tolerance

- Preconditions for good performance
- Quality of product/output
- Customer orientation and responsiveness to customer needs
- Possibilities for quality improvements
- Attitudes toward organizational innovation

6. Environment
   - Market demands: present and future
   - Effects on the company and department
   - Public perception of the organization
   - Environmental demands/regulations
   - Consequences for individual jobs

7. Decision-Making Processes (considered a key area of inquiry)
   - Decision-making scope and latitude
   - Preparation and development of decisions
   - Clarity and transparency of decisions
   - Regulation of decision-making authority
   - Decision implementation and evaluation (control)
   - Overlap of accountability and responsibility
   - Employee involvement in decision-making processes

8. Employees (considered a key area of inquiry)
   - Management perspectives of employees
   - Expectations and cooperation among employees
   - Expectations regarding future work organization and management
   - Sources of motivation (perception of the organization)

9. Interdependencies and Mutual Effects
   - Most important interdependencies and mutual effects between the topics addressed; relationships with other factors
   - Interdependencies/effects between departments (where respondents are able to assess them)

CONDUCTING THE ORGANIZATIONAL ASSESSMENT

Data collection for the organizational assessment was to start at the bottom, beginning with production employees, followed by supervisors, department heads, and so forth. Management expected this process to yield detailed, subjective information, allowing the leadership to find out what employees really thought about the organization. This presupposed leadership willingness at all levels to see their area as open for development. The process was organized so that results obtained at one hierarchical level were to be shared with the next higher level first. Executive management thus deliberately accepted the risk of *being the last ones to find out,* and faced the possibility of organizational movement and unrest whose cause they would be the last to know.

Interview data that could be traced back to an individual were fed back to that person before being shared with the next higher hierarchical level. Thus, the individual interviewed had the right to edit his or her information before authorizing the consultants to share it. A distinction was made between information that people were willing to share publicly (with their name not removed); information that would appear in the form of anonymous statistical data, thus presenting no confidentiality issues; and information that was confidential, divulged only to improve the external interviewer's understanding. The interviewees themselves decided into which of these categories their statements should fall. Furthermore, participation in this process was voluntary and could be refused without the need for justification. The work council of the local labor union agreed to this process.

The workers' council played a marginal role in the whole process. Although the council was informed on a continuing basis and asked for agreement where necessary, the council did not see a role for itself in the project, nor did it recognize the importance and implications of the project from the union's perspective.

Employee Level

First, focus group interviews were conducted with nine selected groups, each involving eight to ten lower-level employees. The participants selected reflected a representative slice of employees at this level.

Group interviews were conducted using the Metaplan technique aimed at documentation and visualization of group discussions.[3] The technique offers an uncomplicated method for documenting the themes of a discussion and for categorizing and evaluating them in terms of importance. Lightweight pin boards are covered with large sheets of brown wrapping paper. Issues emerging in the discussion are written on small colored four-by-eight-inch cards that can be pinned to the boards. Cards can thus be regrouped easily while at the same time providing a visual image of the status of the discussion that can be recorded with a camera if necessary.

After the consultant stated the purpose of the interview, participants briefly introduced themselves and explained where they worked. The interview then addressed the following topic areas:

1. Strengths and weaknesses, in terms of
   - the organization as a whole
   - functional area, department, or work group
2. Information flow
   - Analysis of communication and cooperation
   - Managerial information policies/patterns
   - One's own information policy/pattern
3. Perception and evaluation of management's leadership style
4. Perception and evaluation of directions provided by management
5. Expectations of personnel management/policies
6. Prerequisites for being able to do "a good job"
7. Customer orientation (environment)
   - responsiveness
   - problems with customer service
8. Conflicts among customer, organizational, and employee interests
9. Decision-making processes
10. Problems in the area of work organization regarding:
    - range and scope of activities
    - task variety
    - positive future prospects
    - respect for one's work
    - support in one's work activities
    - potential to take initiative
    - opportunities for competence development
    - promotion prospects
    - options for taking on responsibility
11. Individual work motivation
12. Other problems
13. Expectations about future work organization
    - working hours
    - organizational structure
    - effects on the role of the individual
14. Environmental compatibility of product

Which areas to emphasize and the level of detail were left up to the group. The following list of discussion topics was derived with a focus on employee-relevant issues: On some topics listed previously (e.g., 6. Environment), a number of subquestions were formulated. Other topics (e.g., 8. Employees) were not addressed in employee discussions, but were included in interviews with supervisors and managers at different levels.

Participants' answers were recorded, and the interview protocol was returned to the participants for comments, corrections, and changes. This protocol was confidential and reviewed by group members only. The protocols from all the groups were then combined into a summary report to be used as the basis for the next set of interviews with department supervisors.

Supervisory Level

At the supervisory level, interviews were conducted with five groups of eight to ten supervisors each. These interviews followed a format similar to the one used with production employees. In addition to discussing the fourteen topics outlined above, supervisors were given the summary report from their employees. They were asked to comment on the perspectives of their employees and to discuss how they might respond to the concerns raised. In particular, the leadership role of the supervisors was addressed in terms of the following criteria:
- Self-assessment of leadership style
- Training and education
- Communication with employees
- Motivational strategies
- Knowledge about employees' concerns and situation

Again, this information was returned to the participants for comments in the form of individual group reports. An overall report was then prepared summarizing these findings.

Department Head and Area Manager Level

Next, individual interviews two or three hours in length were conducted with the department and area managers and with the chief executive. The written summary reports from the employee and supervisor group interviews were sent to them ahead of time. The questions to be addressed by management were based on the following key issues raised in the summary reports:

- Information/communication problems (employees are given insufficient information to do the job)
- Authoritarian and contradictory leadership style that negatively affects employee performance
- Lack of clear direction and instructions
- Unequal treatment of employees along with insufficient respect and support
- Too much formality, bureaucracy, and paperwork
- Unclear personnel policies, personnel planning, and evaluation
- Lines of authority are unclear and circumvented
- Organizational culture: externally generous image; internally petty treatment of employees
- Favoritism and perks: pressure for self-aggrandizement
- Obscurity of decision-making process (unclear why and how decisions are made, who is responsible; tendency to avoid mistakes, leading to lack of decision-making where needed; lack of employee involvement in decisions that directly affect them)
- Lack of awareness of environmental issues regarding product disposal
- Insufficient customer orientation (neglect of overall goals)
- Neglect of employees (lack of respect, recognition, feedback, constructive criticism, and qualification possibilities, few prospects for promotion; limited range and scope of activities; little respect for employee concerns and interests)
- Lack of attention to disruptions in organizational climate

Managers were asked which of these problems were relevant in their functional areas or department. Did they think these problems existed in their area? If yes, in what form? How did managers respond to try and solve them? Managers were also asked to react to employee and supervisor suggestions for how to change the work organization. In particular, they were asked if they would implement these proposals in their area, or if they would support them within the broader organization. Employee and supervisor proposals encompassed the following suggestions:

- Job sharing and/or part-time employment
- Expanding the current flex-time system
- More work groups; development of semi-autonomous work teams by combining more and less demanding work activities
- Consolidation of work groups and departments in order to "flatten" the hierarchical structure

Finally, managers were asked to make suggestions and illustrate them graphically in response to the following questions:

- What should the organizational structure look like to be able to respond quickly and flexibly to changing market and environmental demands?
- What should the organizational structure look like in order to make decisions and the decision-making process more transparent without adding additional bureaucratic features?
- What leadership qualities will be central in the future?

In addition, managers were asked to assess their own leadership style.

All interviews were tape recorded, but (for confidentiality reasons) only one group report for the department managers was prepared. The overall summary report was organized according to topic areas and distinguished between respondent groups. The consultants then presented these results to the top management.

This bottom-up assessment approach required considerable trust and willingness to face critique on the part of management. Indeed, some information from the first interview round (involving area management secretarial staff) was "leaked" to the bosses. This created a very difficult situation, as top management had interpreted the agreement of how feedback would be provided differently than the external consultants. Much discussion was necessary to calm things down and to clarify that the price to be paid for management's resolve to tackle some hot issues might include some managers feeling put on the spot. The project's continuation indicated that it was possible, however, to reestablish mutual trust.

PROJECT CONTINUATION

In response to the organizational assessment, top management and the consultants decided to start the project "Z-89" in early 1989. The meaning of "Z" was not to be defined; rather, each employee could interpret it as he or she liked. "Z," for example, could mean *Zukunft* (future), *Zusammenarbeit* (cooperation), *Zufriedenheit* (satisfaction), *Ziel* (goal), and so on. A task force was established in each functional area to address the problems and issues identified. Each task force determined its own objectives and its own approach to solving the problems. In particular, the task forces focused on:

- developing proposals for problem solution based on the results of the organizational assessment for that particular functional area
- completing the organizational assessment and specifying issues
- providing information about task force activities to all employees on a regular basis

Each area task force consisted of the area manager (task force leader), one or two department managers, two or three supervisors (with leadership functions), and a number of employees equal to the total number of managers on the task force. In addition, each task force was assisted by two facilitators: one member of the company's personnel office and one of the consultants. While management representatives were chosen by the chief executive, the employees selected their own representatives to serve on their task force. Employee selection followed a presentation of the project at a corporate area meeting with all employees.

A distinction was made between task force leadership and task force management: Task force *leadership* was the function of the *area manager* (task force leader). He was responsible for keeping the task force focused on goals and task accomplishments, for the planning and organization of task force activities, and for the execution of measures proposed by the task force. Task force *management* was the function of the *external facilitator*. He was responsible for working with the task force to develop problem definitions and to generate solutions and implementation suggestions.

The task forces met regularly every two to four weeks. They determined the meeting dates as well as the length of each meeting. To start with, all task group members received the results of the organizational assessment. In addition, all participants received some guidelines for how the task force was to operate.

Each task force then decided which topics it wanted to tackle first. The topics selected were prioritized, and the group decided how much time should be spent on each issue. Discussions and results of the task force meetings were recorded on a flip chart and summarized in minutes which were distributed to all members. In late 1989/early 1990 the external facilitator withdrew from the task forces, which by then had developed their own style of working together and continued their projects, sometimes working in subcommittees.

In mid-1989 top management also hired another external consultant to conduct leadership seminars for the company's managers (department managers upwards). Complementing the work of the task forces, these seminars addressed issues of leadership and problem-solving processes. At the same time, an internal project group developed a set of leadership principles in cooperation with the original consultants. These leadership guidelines established participatory management principles as the foundation of the company's management philosophy.

Improvement in the quality of work, the original goal of the organizational assessment, was addressed starting in mid-1990 by establishing quality circles. The project detour, however, points to the importance of employee involvement and the improvement of the quality of working life as a precondition for achieving other organizational goals. Employee commitment to new organizational goals is unlikely unless their own concerns and interests are seen as central to organizational change.

Counter to the expectations of top management, the organizational assessment had uncovered a lot of problems. While not a painless process, employee critique was interpreted as a challenge for reorientation and a resource for organizational development. The task forces were central in fostering a new appreciation between management and employees as both sides shared their perspectives and goals.

One of the most important outcomes of the organizational assessment and the Z-89 project was the communication process initiated: management and the organization now appeared changeable and more flexible in the eyes of the employees. Managers, for their part, become aware of employees' ability to develop and change, too. Both sides learned to appreciate the potential for innovation and change in each other.

Management was extremely impressed by one female employee's ability to articulate her views. Before, this woman had been viewed as nondescript, and her supervisors expected nothing special from her. Based on this change in perspective, her abilities were supported and she was encouraged to get involved in much more demanding tasks.

Alternatively, one of the area managers had been particularly criticized for his authoritarian leadership style. He had resisted the project for a long time. Following the work in the task force, he systematically started to work on his weaknesses. He also joined the project group charged with developing leadership principles, were he emphasized the need for guidelines that were clear and binding for both managers and employees.

WHAT MATTERS

While many employee involvement initiatives for workplace improvements have stumbled or failed due to lack of attention, backing, and follow-up by top management, this project shows that top management's commitment and interest in change are insufficient unless support and involvement from middle and lower level management can be developed. The lessons are:

- Middle and if possible lower level management need to be involved and have ownership in the design and implementation of such projects.
- Taking an honest look at one's organization and encouraging bottom-up feedback on leadership style and organizational decision-making and work organization policies may be a painful process for which the participants, especially those who might be at the center of critique, must be prepared in advance. Insufficient clarification of the interview feedback process, combined with a confidentiality leak, put the project in jeopardy at one point.
- Employees' interest in improving the quality of work increases if their own concerns about the quality of working life are granted central importance in an organizational assessment and change effort. Competence development that contributes to the broader organizational purpose will become attractive if it takes employees' personal motivations and goals as a starting point.
- Major efforts at organizational restructuring like this one are likely to impact the union's role and activities. Rather than staying on the sidelines, unions are well advised to take an active role and lend visible support to changes that benefit the membership or raise critical questions where the implications of change may be detrimental to the union and the members it represents.
- Conducting an organizational needs assessment can support an extensive "open" phase, thus creating the willingness to engage in the "move" phase to follow. At the same time, this type of needs assessment itself contributes to competence development as the persons involved start to thoroughly examine their work situation.

NOTES

1. The authors would like to thank Tetra Pak for permission to publish this case study revealing the company's identity. The consulting firm involved was AOC AG, Zurich, and AOC GmbH, Berlin; the consultants were Felix Frei and Werner Duell.

2. D.A. Kolb, I.M. Rubin, and J.M. McIntyre, *Organizational Psychology* (Englewood Cliffs, N.J.: Prentice-Hall, 1984).

3. Schnelle-Cölln, *Metaplan.*

PART IV

TOOLS FOR PLANNING AND IMPLEMENTING CHANGE

11. Organizational Innovation: The Starting Point for Participation

TECHNOLOGICAL AND ORGANIZATIONAL INNOVATIONS: APPLYING THE JUDO PRINCIPLE

In today's changing environment, technological and organizational innovations of one form or another occur almost daily. A new piece of equipment is installed, a new production process is established, work teams or other forms of worker cooperation are initiated, training programs are implemented, and so forth. Every innovation has a purpose, such as reducing costs, increasing productivity or quality, improving worker motivation and morale, decreasing absenteeism, or addressing safety problems.

Innovations are preceded by a more or less extensive planning and decision-making process involving one or several individuals, depending on the size of the company and the type of innovation. All participants in an innovation pursue certain goals and objectives. These can be the goals envisioned by the organization, but innovation participants – depending on how they perceive the innovation to affect them – will also pursue their own objectives, which may or may not be in conflict with the stated objectives.

Innovations have to be implemented somehow. The innovation process starts with an idea and ends with the actual implementation and utilization of a piece of new machinery, for example. Information has to be collected and communicated, employees may have to be trained, departments may have to be reorganized. Every innovation has an impact on those directly and indirectly affected by it. Jobs can change or be lost, or new jobs may be created. New technologies may help eliminate certain problems but may create many others.

Such planned or ongoing organizational innovations can be utilized by applying the judo principle described in Chapter 5, that is, using the forces already at work for the purpose of enhancing competence development through participation. To achieve this, the "typical" approach to planning and implementing technological and organizational innovations in a given organization needs to be explored. The analysis of the innovation process itself provides an opportunity for employee participation and yields information about where and how possibilities for competence development can be strengthened. It also identifies the weaknesses in organizational innovation processes where worker participation may lead to better outcomes.

Analysis of Technological and Organizational Innovations

The better the technological or organizational innovation is understood – the more is known about its goals, the actual innovation process, and all those participating in it – the easier it becomes to identify opportunities for influence. For each innovation a better alternative may exist. There is no one right way to plan and implement an innovation process.

The following overview describes what questions to ask, and how asking the right questions about technological and organizational innovations, the innovation process itself, and the innovation participants can identify alternatives and opportunities to influence the process as well as the outcomes.

What?

What type of innovation is it, and what is its extent?

- What technological or organizational innovation is planned?
- What organizational goals is the innovation to achieve?

- Are the goals genuine and honest? (For example, is improving the quality of work life really the goal? How is productivity calculated? What factors have been included or excluded?)
- What effects will the planned innovation have for the goals of the individuals affected? What will the work situation look like in terms of health and safety, utilization of skills and knowledge, personal development and learning potential?
- What are the alternatives to the planned technological or organizational innovation (based on the criteria of sociotechnical systems design; see Chapter 7)?

Who?

Who will implement the innovation, and who will be affected by it?

- Who are the innovators and who are the people affected? Which of the people affected are not involved, and why not?
- What are the real goals of the innovators? Are their goals identical with those officially described?
- What is the reaction of those affected? Do they accept or resist it? Why?
- Which of the innovators support the goals of a sociotechnical systems approach and job design aimed at competence development? Who can be convinced of the need for getting the people affected involved?

How?

How is the innovation to be implemented?

- Why were certain implementation procedures selected? What were the goals pursued with this approach (e.g., to circumvent resistance)? At what point and to what extent were the people affected informed about the planned innovation?
- What happened as a result of the implementation approach selected (e.g., agreement or resistance, involvement or caution)?
- What steps are necessary to support participatory work design?

THE TEN STEPS TO ANALYZING INNOVATION GOALS, EFFECTS, AND ALTERNATIVES

Steps 1 through 4 help to answer the question *what?* Steps 5 through 7 answer the question *who?* Steps 8 through 10 answer the question *how?*

Step 1: Search for Informants

When you first hear about a planned innovation, look for and talk to competent informants or organizational members who can tell you what is planned, who is in charge, and how the innovation is to be implemented. Using the questions outlined above, try to find out what kind of innovation this is and how it is to be integrated into the organization. This may involve gathering information from a number of internal departments.

Technological and organizational innovations can involve:
* structural and spatial innovations (construction, buildings, etc.)
* elimination of jobs; new hires; personnel transfers
* acquisition of new equipment or tools, introduction of VDTs, improvement of material handling and storage systems, introduction of robots, etc.
* utilization of new products and materials
* introduction of new production processes, e.g., NC and CNC, CAD, CAM, flexible manufacturing systems, CIM
* introduction of training centers, quality circles, organization development
* improvements in material flow as well as information and communication structures, introduction or reduction of hierarchical levels; introduction of individual or team work
* changes in working hours, work schedules, break times, vacations
* competence development and training measures
* change in work content; job enlargements or restrictions
* performance control; quality and output control systems
* new pay or wage systems
* etc.

The key questions to ask are:
* What is the innovation and how is it to be utilized?
* What effect will it have? What is its intent? What can it accomplish?
* Whose interests will be affected positively or negatively?

Step 2: List Innovation Goals

As information about the innovation is obtained, more specific questions about its goals can be asked. These goals should be summarized in a second step. Possible goals might include:
- rationalization through faster production systems
- work intensification
- quality improvements
- increased worker motivation to reduce fluctuation and absenteeism
- utilization of worker expertise to improve solutions to technical or other problems
- improvement of working conditions to maintain or increase job satisfaction (possibly to solve absenteeism or "motivation" problems)
- improved workforce utilization
- reduction of waiting time
- reduction of throughput time
- increase in flexibility and mobility

Ask why the technological or organizational innovation is introduced. If multiple goals exist, what are the expectations regarding performance, quality, efficiency, working conditions, personnel management, employee competence, and so forth? Have alternatives been considered? What made this innovation better than other alternatives considered? Look at the current situation. What does it look like?

Step 3: List Effects of the Innovation

List the likely outcomes of each goal for the organization and particularly for the employees affected by the innovation. Look for additional information about possible effects. Don't rely on information from only the people in charge of the project. Find out what the people affected think. For many technological and organizational innovations, information is also available in academic journals, the organizational development literature, and union and industry publications.

Ask what effects the innovation will have for different organizational stakeholders (e.g., management, union, employees, customers) in terms of the criteria shown in the matrix example in Figure 11.1.

Figure 11.1   Matrix of Innovation Effects

	Situation Gets Better (for whom)	**Situation Un-changed (for whom)**	**Situation Gets Worse (for whom)**
Productivity			
Quality			
Working Hours			
Job Loss/ Reduction			
Competence Development			
Physical and Psychological Pressures/Stress			
Work Environ-ment			

Step 4: Develop a Matrix of Alternatives

Develop a matrix of alternatives to the planned innovation and its goals. Are there alternatives to the proposed innovation that lead to better working conditions and more opportunities for competence development for the people affected? By comparing alternatives the bottom-line advantages and disadvantages of different options can be explored. Considering alternatives is also important because it often shows that planning for innovation has been done very superficially, with little consideration of the variety of possible impacts. This analysis is likely to expose the underlying purpose of a proposed innovation. Robots are sometimes introduced with the argument that they eliminate the health and safety hazards of certain jobs. These goals might be reached in other ways, however, without the job reductions that often accompany the introduction of robots. Talk to the people in charge of planning the innovation, and talk to other people in the organization who are knowledgeable about the subject but are not involved in the planning. Consult experts from labor unions, universities, and other institutions. Ask about the possible effects of alternatives to the planned innovation. Ask about other possibilities that might achieve the same goals.

List the information for each alternative in the matrix. Compare the alternatives. This provides a basis not only for a critical examination of the proposed innovation but for developing constructive suggestions about how a particular problem might be solved.

Step 5: Identify the People Involved and the People Affected by the Innovation

In every innovation process, various individuals or groups take on different functions. Identify which persons or groups play different roles. For example, find out who first came up with the idea, who approved it, who is or is expected to be involved in implementing it, and so on. Develop a list of the people involved in these different functions. Compare the list with the organizational chart. This may uncover the real power centers in the organization.

Ask all the individuals and groups involved about their goals and motivations in relationship to the planned innovation. Find out who benefits the most and in what ways; for example, who gains prestige or influence, who may get promoted, and so forth. Note goals and motivations on your list of people involved. Highlight possible contradictions between officially described and unofficial goals or hidden agendas.

Step 6: Reactions of the People Affected

At this point, find out the reaction of the people affected by the innovation. Ask if somebody has been left out and if that had any effect on planning and implementing the innovation. Were the different individuals and groups involved and affected consulted regarding expectations and concerns they may have? Have functions changed, for example, increase or loss in influence?

Ask about sources of and reasons for opposition and fears about the impact of the innovation.

Step 7: Search for Support

Identify those individuals or groups in charge of planning and implementing the innovation who support your goal of getting employees involved in the process. Who is interested in employee participation?

Step 8: Develop a Time Line and a Chart of the Different Innovation Steps

Four phases can be distinguished in every innovation process.
1. A problem is identified whose solution is seen as requiring some kind of innovation.
2. The innovation is planned and developed. This phase involves the collection of information, an assessment of the situation, and the conceptualization of goals.
3. The innovation is introduced. This phase involves the development of a time line and an action plan, the allocation of financial and other resources, the selection of the people to be involved, and the implementation of the innovation.
4. The innovation becomes integrated in the organization. This phase consists of the evaluation and, if necessary, adjustment of the innovation until it fits smoothly into the existing production process.

At this point identify the steps taken from the planning to the introduction phase of the innovation and list the events in chronological order. An example of such a list is presented in Table 11.1.

Pay attention to when the employees affected are being informed about the innovation.

Table 11.1   Steps of the Innovation Process

Date	Phase	Action taken
2/1993	Innovation planning	Collect information
4/1993		Hire external consultant
5/1993		Prepare budget for three utilization alternatives
6/1993		Elicit and compare bids
2/1994	Innovation decision	Decide how the innovation will be utilized
5/1994	Innovation preparation	Inform supervisors and workers
8/1994	Innovation implementation	Purchase and operation
1/1995		Evaluation

Step 9: List Innovation Process Goals and Effects

Find out why the innovation planners proceeded the way they did. Various goals and standard procedures of doing things may have influenced these decisions. For example, is information withheld because of concern about resistance? Is unrest in the organization to be avoided (though this rarely succeeds, leading instead to uncontrolled rumors), or is critical and constructive feedback from employees to be encouraged? Are there alternative perspectives about how to proceed? Develop a list of all the different steps and measures and the goals associated with them.

Ask about the effects on the organization and its members that a certain way of introducing and implementing the innovation will have. In particular, explore the effects on the social structure of the organization, communication patterns, existing social networks, and so on. In general, resistance often occurs if social relationships are affected by the innovation. Note these effects on your list of procedures.

Step 10: List Alternative Process Steps and Implementation Procedures

In this final step, explore how alternative ways of proceeding might allow for more extensive information and involvement of employees. At what point in the process should information meetings be held? Is it useful to do innovation planning with work teams, at department meetings, and so on? Develop a list of alternative innovation planning and implementation procedures.

Following these ten steps will provide a comprehensive picture of how technological and organizational innovations are planned and implemented in the organization. Though every innovation requires somewhat different procedures, this analysis yields a general understanding of the patterns of the organization's planning and decision-making processes. It also helps identify individuals and groups that will support your goals, and points to the areas and opportunities for developing employee participation in the process.

Obviously, these ten steps have to be adapted to the particular developmental phase of the innovation to be addressed.

The complete analysis of the ten steps results in seven useful tools:

1. A list of goals to be achieved through the innovation
2. A list of the social effects of the planned innovation
3. A matrix of possible alternatives to the planned innovation, its goals and effects
4. A list of all individuals and groups involved in the innovation
5. A time line and process chart
6. A list of all measures taken (goals and effects) to implement the innovation
7. A list of alternative procedures and measures to implement the innovation

12.   Tool Box

The tools described in this chapter are empirically tested methods to involve employees in the process of work redesign and *Qualifizierung,* and to improve organizational performance. Tool #1 helps different organizational stakeholders identify and clarify the ways in which processes of work design for competence development are likely to affect areas of common and conflicting interests. Tools #2 and #3 are aimed at a critical evaluation of existing job characteristics and the identification of opportunities and alternative solutions for redesigning work activities to enhance ongoing competence development and learning. Tool #4 links an assessment of work-related problems and organizational barriers with efforts to improve the organization's customer service orientation. Tool #5, "Card Week," is a structured method for involving employees in identifying problems or daily hassles at work and for generating solutions.

A word of caution: The usefulness of Tools #2 to #5 largely depends on what happens as a result of initiating these types of employee involvement processes. Involvement and participation create expectations. If organizational decision-makers are not committed to taking action and providing feedback to the participants about their suggestions, using these tools may create rather than solve problems. We have argued throughout this book that the people affected are the people to be involved; this means bottom-up as well as top-down. In other words, if middle and upper managers are expected to take action as a result of employee involvement processes, they need to understand what happened and find a way to be involved.

TOOL #1: ASSESSMENT OF OVERLAPPING AND CONFLICTING INTERESTS

Effective organizational functioning requires that organizational stakeholder interests be optimally balanced. The main stakeholders in the modern enterprise may encompass customers, employees/union, management, shareholders, suppliers and other business partners, and the public at large. In some areas the interests of these stakeholders overlap; in other areas they may conflict. For example, union/employee concerns about fair, increasing wages may be in conflict with management efforts to cut costs. Or a company's neglect of environmental protection regulations may save money in the short run, but may negatively affect workers' health or the broader public if spills or soil or water pollution accidents occur.

On the other hand, there are many areas of overlapping interests. Employee skill and competence enhancement, for example, may require the reallocation of resources and thus represent a cost in the short run, but may benefit customers, employees, management, and shareholders in the long run if it results in employee job satisfaction, improved quality, and reduction of waste and thus contributes to organizational competitiveness. Work design for competence development is aimed at utilizing overlapping interests without obscuring areas of conflicting interests.

> GOAL: Identification of areas of conflicting and overlapping interests between union/employee goals and organizational goals.
>
> TARGET: Union/employee representatives and management representatives planning a competence development process.

The matrix presented below provides an analytical tool that can be used to:
* identify the areas in which work design for competence development can promote congruence of organizational and employee interests
* identify the areas that remain conflicting and thus subject to bargaining and negotiation
* help clarify in what ways a competence development process can contribute to the various goals of different organizational stakeholders

Although this matrix subsumes the interests of various stakeholders (e.g., management, customers, shareholders) under the heading "organizational goals" and juxtaposes them with "union/employee" goals, it is important to remember that there may be areas of conflicting interests among these groups. For example, some management cost-cutting strategies may benefit shareholders in the short run but may not be in their long-term interest. Alternatively, unions as organizations may have objectives and needs that do not always benefit their members.

It may be useful for management and union/employee representatives to do their own independent assessment of overlapping and conflicting interests first and then use their different analyses as the basis for discussion and negotiation on how a competence development process can optimize mutual interests.

The matrix in Figure 12.1 shows which of the goals of both parties in the employment relationship might benefit from such a process and which areas of interest remain conflicting. This matrix reflects our assessment of conflicting and overlapping interests. Blank matrices that can be used for your own assessment of common and conflicting interests are found in Appendix A.1. The symbols used in the matrix below are to be interpreted as follows:

✚	Work design for competence development can be utilized to support the goals of both parties.
✌	These goals are in conflict and must be subject to negotiation to protect union/employee interests.
↔	In these areas the potential for conflict exists. Special attention is in order.
(blank)	No immediate relationship is apparent.

Figure 12.1   Matrix of Overlapping and Conflicting Interests

... related to:

Employee goals (interests) \ Organizational goals (interests)	market/competition			Workforce availability (adequate numbers and level of competence)	labor market		
	Adaptation to changing market demands	Competitiveness (price, quality, quantity)	Cost minimization; profitability		Support of consumer purchasing power	Avoidance of external regulations (tariffs, restrictions)	Stabilization of social environment/social progress
Job security	↔	↔	✌	✚	✚	✌	✚
Fair, increasing wages	↔	✌	✌	✚	✚	✌	✚
Preservation of health and continued ability to work			↔	✚	✚	↔	✚
Competence preservation and further development	✚	✚	↔	✚	✚	↔	✚
Participation in organizational decision-making	✚	✚		✚		↔	↔
Decreased separation of planning/execution functions	✚	✚	✚	✚			
Cooperation and meaningful social relationships at work		✚		✚			✚
Socially accepted/valued activity		✚		✚	✚		✚
Profitability not at the expense of society	↔	↔	✌		✚	✌	✚
Meaningful activity	✚	✚	✚	✚			
Task variety and discretion/ decision latitude	✚	✚	✚	✚			
Avoidance of unnecessary work stress	↔	↔	↔	✚		↔	
Positive prospects for promotion/mobility	✚	✚	✚	✚	✚		✚
Identification with the organization	✚	✚	✚	✚			✚

(continued next page)

Figure 12.1   Interest Matrix (continued)

... related to the organization itself

Employee goals (interests) \ Organizational goals (interests)	Optimal resource utilization	Current and future performance demands	Minimization of conflicts	Organization specific competence development	Avoidance of training requirements (demands)	Communication of organizational values/norms	Protection of organizational power hierarchies	Organizational attractiveness (retaining core staff)	Prevention of labor solidarity
Job security	✌		+	↔	✌	+	✌	+	✌
Fair, increasing wages	↔	+	+	↔	✌	+	✌	+	↔
Preservation of health and continued ability to work	+	✌	+	↔	↔	+	↔	+	↔
Competence preservation and further development	+	+	+	↔	✌	+	↔	+	↔
Participation in organizational decision-making	+		+	✌	✌	+	✌	+	✌
Decreased separation of planning/execution functions	+	+	+	↔	↔		✌	+	✌
Cooperation and meaningful social relationships at work	+		+				↔	+	↔
Socially accepted/valued activity			+	↔	✌	+	↔	+	↔
Profitability not at the expense of society	✌	↔		✌	✌	↔	✌		↔
Meaningful activity	+	+	+	↔	↔	+		+	
Task variety and discretion/ decision latitude	+	+	+	↔	↔	+	↔	+	
Avoidance of unnecessary work stress	↔	↔	+				↔	+	
Positive prospects for promotion/mobility	+	+	+	✌	✌	+	↔	+	
Identification with the organization	+	↔	+	↔	↔	+	↔	+	✌

241

TOOL #2: SUBJECTIVE TASK ANALYSIS (STA)

GOAL: The subjective task analysis encourages and enables employees to identify problems in their work situation and to develop alternative solutions.[1]

TARGET: All members in a work group or department of a relatively independent unit with fragmented task organization. (Group size: 5-15)

FORMAT: Group meetings: approximately 4 x 2 hours (or one day)

MATERIALS NEEDED:
- Subjective Task Analysis Questionnaire (see Appendix A.2)
- Flip charts
- Markers
- Masking tape or a big pin board

FACILITATORS:
- Internal education and training facilitators
- Union representatives
- Possibly external consultants

PROCEDURE: Phase 1: Evaluation of each work task in the department
Phase 2: Development of alternatives
Phase 3: Assessment of existing and lacking competences
Phase 4: Planning and implementation of required skill training

Phase 1

a. Group members are asked to list all tasks that have to be performed in the department on a flip chart.

b. The facilitators explain the six evaluation criteria described in Table 12.1. It is not necessary for all group members to interpret these criteria in exactly the same way. Different perspectives and interpretations can enrich the discussion. There is no simple right or wrong interpretation!

c. The group is asked to evaluate all of the tasks listed according to each of the six criteria. This is done by assigning a value of 0 to 10 to each box where 0 = worst and 10 = best.

For example, a task that provides an optimal amount of variety would get a 10. Task evaluation should not focus simply on actual behavior (e.g., "Are co-workers indeed supporting each other in this task?"), but rather should ask, "Is the nature of the task such that people can support each other's activities?"

d. Facilitators should not interfere with the group's discussion and evaluation of the different tasks (possibly leaving the room). However, the group as a whole has to agree on its evaluation of the task; in other words, the person doing the task should not be the only one involved in evaluating it.

e. The points given to each task on each criterion are tallied and entered in the total column.

f. The facilitator joins the group again.

Table 12.1   Subjective Task Analysis

	Task 1	Task 2	Task 3	...	Task n
Elbow Room/ Decision latitude					
Variety					
Learning Opportunities					
Mutual Support/ Respect					
Meaningful Contribution					
Future Prospects					
TOTAL					

CRITERIA FOR WELL DESIGNED WORK TASKS/JOBS

A.   Elbow Room (Decision Latitude)

I feel like I am my own boss. I can make real decisions. Supervisors don't continuously breathe down my neck, but define goals and tasks in a way that makes clear what is important.

B.   Variety

Not having to do the same thing all the time. Activities can be varied from time to time to avoid boredom and fatigue.

C.   Learning Opportunities

Occasionally, the activity presents new problems that cannot be resolved routinely. New learning occurs only, however, if these problems are not just seen as a nuisance but can be viewed as a challenge. I have to be able to set the goals myself, though. And only if I am able to assess whether and how I have achieved my goals can I improve my knowledge and future behavior.

D.   Mutual Support and Respect

The tasks are such that co-workers can help each other. The success of my task also depends on whether my co-workers do a good job. Every task is important enough for the whole so that one can respect others' contributions.

E.   Meaningful Contribution to the Organization and the Customer

The contribution of my job to the goals of the organization is recognizable; the value to the customer is apparent. I could and would tell my kids about what I am doing.

F.   Positive Future Prospects

The job is no dead end. It provides opportunities for personal development as part of and beyond this job. The job offers incentives to learn more as well as material security.

Phase 2

The group is asked to propose suggestions for improvements. The overall goal is to increase the score for the low score tasks without reducing the scores of the more highly rated tasks. The suggestions are listed on a flip chart. Suggestions may vary in terms of:
- extensivity of change proposed
- chances for realization
- cost

Individual suggestions might be worked on more specifically later. This can be the group's task or the function of, for example, a technical expert team.

Phase 3

a. At this point, the degree to which each member of the group can do each of the listed tasks with his or her current knowledge and skill is assessed.
b. The goal of a second step is to identify who would have to have or acquire what competences in order to implement the suggestions for task improvements. This process identifies competence requirements.
c. The comparison between existing skills and knowledge and desirable skills and knowledge points to competence gaps.

The identification of missing competences is not to be viewed as "blaming" anybody. It is a list of competences desired by the group as a whole. Not everything might be doable. If that is the case, the suggestions from phase 2 have to reconsidered.

Phase 4

Now the conditions have to be identified that allow for the development of the additionally required competences. Training involving internal or external resources may be necessary. Where possible, however, competences ought to be developed within the group through mutual learning and on the job instruction. Such agreements should be made in writing and might be integrated in contract language.

Note that the above process describes only the analytical parts of the STA. For the implementation of the suggestions as well as the development of possible training programs, consult Part II, "The Change Process."

In some cases, phases 3 and 4 might not be necessary if the problems identified are exclusively technical or organizational in nature. Also note that the subjective task analysis method is particularly useful in work situations characterized by high task fragmentation.

TOOL #3: "THE IDEAL JOB"

GOAL: This group process for jointly conceptualizing what "ideal jobs" would look like helps identify opportunities to improve work organization.

TARGET: All members in a work group or department of a relatively independent unit with fragmented task organization. (Group size: 10-25)

FORMAT: Group meetings: approximately 4, lasting 1-3 hours

MATERIALS NEEDED:
• Subjective Job Assessment Questionnaire (see Appendix A.3)
• Flip charts
• Markers
• 4 X 8 cards
• Cardboard
• Possibly materials for developing models

FACILITATORS:
• Internal education and training facilitators
• Union representatives
• Possibly external consultants

PROCEDURE: Phase 1: Complete Subjective Job Assessment (SJA)
Phase 2: Feedback of results.
Develop a general picture of "what the group would like their jobs to be like"
Phase 3: Discover existing "positive elements."
Develop "ideal job situations"
Phase 4: Develop training programs

Phase 1

The Subjective Job Assessment Questionnaire is completed in order to evaluate the current work situation. Each member of the group completes the questionnaire for his or her job. The questionnaire covers a variety of work aspects, for example:
- Autonomy
- Variety
- Transparence/Understandability
- Responsibilities
- Possibilities for cooperation
- Work overload and "underload"

These concepts and the purpose of filling in the questionnaire have to be explained first.

The questionnaires are analyzed by the facilitators. The type of analysis conducted is based on the number of questionnaires and whether there are groups or subgroups involved in similar work activities (see Appendix A.3).

Phase 2

The facilitators report the results of the questionnaire analysis to the group. The results represent the common frame of reference for the future planning process. The group discusses, first at a general level, in what direction the current work situation ought to be changed.

Three flip charts are prepared with the following headings:
- *"Keep as is ..."*
  for example: "We want to keep working together as a group"
- *"More of ..."*
  for example: "We want more variety in our jobs"
- *"Less of ..."*
  for example: "We don't need supervisors to watch us as closely as they do"

Phase 3

Each group member notes on four-by-eight-inch cards all the work activities involved in his or her job. It helps if the supervisor of the group participates in this and the following phases. All cards are displayed on a big piece of cardboard. The job activities listed provide the building elements from which each group member now "assembles" his or her "ideal job." The question of training and qualification needed for each activity is not considered at this point.

Obviously, this process does not eliminate all undesirable activities. It has to be followed by a negotiation process between all participants. These negotiations should be guided by the following questions:

- Can job elements be exchanged meeting mutual interests?
- Can the request for certain job elements by several group members be addressed through rotation?
- Are there meaningful job elements which are currently not included but would complement the activities of the groups as a whole?
- Are there job elements that don't have to be included in the activities of the group at all?
- Are there "unpleasant" job elements which cannot be avoided but could be shared by all members of the group?
- Are additional resources or equipment needed in order to create "ideal jobs"?

If the group has come to a solution, it may be useful to simulate the solution as a model. Layout plans can be used for this purpose. Different possibilities can be simulated. Consequences of different variations ought to be discussed in terms of:

- implications for communication and cooperation
- implications for material and work flow
- implications for the esthetics of the work situation

The playful character of this process often initiates "trying out" variations which, if only verbally discussed, may be prematurely discarded as unfeasible.

Phase 4

At this point the group has to come to an agreement on a preliminary or final solution for how to organize its work activities.

The proposed solution may have to be reviewed by technical experts and management. The focus of this process ought to address possible negative effects of the proposed solution on other organizational units. The solution also has to be analyzed for potential violations of legal or contractual agreements. A written agreement about rights and responsibilities involved in the proposal may be necessary.

At this point, additional training and skills/knowledge needed by individual group members for the solution to work have to be identified.

Training programs are to be developed.

TOOL #4: DIAGNOSING WORK-RELATED BARRIERS TO IMPROVING CUSTOMER SERVICE ORIENTATION

GOAL:	This process is aimed at improving organizational/departmental customer orientation and service by addressing work-related problems and organizational barriers to optimal performance.
TARGET:	Groups of 10-15 employees representing similar work areas or organizational functions (e.g., homogeneous with regard to qualifications)
FORMAT:	Group meeting: approximately 3 hours
MATERIALS NEEDED:	• Pin board or wall space • Flip chart/markers/masking tape • Overhead projector • Blank transparencies/markers Transparencies of Display 1 or 2 • Copies of Work Assessment Questionnaire (see Appendix A.4)
FACILITATORS:	Internal education and training facilitator (but not immediate supervisor)
PROCEDURE:	Phase 1: Identification of internal and external customers; identification and evaluation of problems with customer service and interdependencies among employees and organizational units (see Tables 12.2 or 12.3) Phase 2: Assessment of the quality of work design and work organization; identification of positives and

negatives (see Work Assessment
Questionnaire in Appendix A.4.)
Phase 3: Identification of other bar-
riers to optimal performance
Phase 4: Development of recom-
mendations
Phase 5: Evaluation and feedback

Phase 1

a. The facilitator introduces the group to the purpose of the
meeting, which is to focus on the customer (and the idea of
customer service) and on their work itself and, in combining these two perspectives, to identify barriers to optimal
performance and to develop recommendations for action
steps.
b. The facilitator explains the question, answer, and comments
sections on Table 12.2 or 12.3 which are presented on flip
chart sheets or on a big board. (Note: If this process is
done with participants from areas/departments with direct
customer contact, use the questions in Table 12.2; if participants have no direct customer contact, use the questions in
Table 12.3.) The facilitator instructs the group that the "answers" should be factual, but that the "comments" section
should include subjective responses (e.g., how do I react to
this?), experiences, likes, dislikes, ways of exerting influence.
c. Participants split into teams of two or three and discuss
their answers and comments to the questions.
d. The group reassembles, and the facilitator asks participants
to share what they discussed and lists the answers and
comments for each question in the blank boxes on the flip
chart or board. Ample time should be taken to discuss the
various questions in order to really understand the participants' perspectives.

Phase 2

a. The facilitator explains the goal of phase 2, which is for
each participant to evaluate a number of different aspects of
his/her work situation and tasks. This provides the basis for
identifying barriers to optimal performance and areas where
change is needed.

Table 12.2   Analysis of External Service Orientation

(for areas/departments with *direct* customer contact)

QUESTION	ANSWER	COMMENTS Evaluation/ Experience + −
Who are our customers?		
How is customer contact established?		
What do the customers want? How do I know a) what they want? b) if they are satisfied?		
What kinds of problems or disturbances am I likely to encounter?		
If I need help, whom can I turn to?		
When and where are we dependent on others to fulfill our assignments?		

  b. The Work Assessment Questionnaire (Appendix A.4) is shown on an overhead projector, and the facilitator asks the participants to think about their job and which box they would check for each question based on their experience. (Explain with one or two examples how a concept such as variety or workload may be viewed in a negative or positive way by different people.)

  c. Participants receive a copy of the Work Assessment Questionnaire and complete it individually by checking the box that best describes their evaluation of their job.   After completing their survey, participants come up one by one and enter their results on the overhead transparency with the blank answer boxes. In order to avoid participants' comments on each others' responses, the overhead projector should be turned off at this point.

Table 12.3   Analysis of Internal Service Orientation

(for areas/departments with *no direct* customer contact)

QUESTION	ANSWER	COMMENTS Evaluation/ Experience + −
Who is the immediate recipient of our product or service?		
How do I know what I have to do? (Who are the people involved in the process?)		
How do I know whether the product or service is good or not? Who is likely to tell me? (What is expected of me?)		
What kinds of problems or disturbances am I likely to encounter?		
If I need help, whom can I turn to?		
When and where are we dependent on others to fulfill our assignments?		

d. When all answers have been entered, the facilitator turns on the projector and the group discusses the results. The main focuses of interest are clusters on the positive or negative side or clusters at the center. The facilitator lists key points of the discussion on the flip chart.

Phase 3

a. The facilitator explains that in order to get as detailed a picture of people's work situations as possible, other barriers to optimal performance need to be identified.
b. Ask participants to take a moment and think about restrictions or difficulties that they run into in their daily work, such as procedures, regulations, management directives, equipment problems, etc.
c. Using the brainstorming technique, the facilitator asks participants to share the problems as they see them and lists all answers on the flip chart. (Note: In brainstorming, there are no right or wrong answers; participants are not allowed to comment on each other's ideas at this point. The only questions permitted are those asking for clarification if it is not clear what the person means. The goal is to generate as many items as possible.)

Phase 4

a. The facilitator briefly reviews the main topics/issues and problems discussed in phases 1 and 3 and asks participants to select the most important issues that they would like to see addressed or improved.
b. The group discusses what direction and form possible improvements in these areas could take, who would need to be involved, and so forth. If appropriate, a set of recommendations to be shared with management (and the union, if applicable) is developed.

Phase 5

a. A procedure is agreed upon for how the participants will be informed about next steps, their involvement, action taken, and so forth.

b. The facilitator (possibly together with representatives from the group) discusses findings and action recommendations with management and the union.
c. Participants are informed about action plans agreed to by management, and their further involvement where appropriate is discussed.

Facilitator Tips

The success or failure of this group process depends largely on the facilitator's moderation skills. Pay attention to the following points:

- The introduction is crucial and must be carefully planned. Make sure participants understand why they are there, how the meeting will be conducted, what will happen as a result, and so on.
- Create a climate of trust in which participants feel free and willing to voice their opinions. Make sure there is enough time for participants to express frustrations and let off steam, if necessary, before going on to the next stage.
- Hold back with your opinions and interpretations. But make sure you understand what participants mean; ask follow-up questions for precise information and clarification.
- The goal is not to achieve consensus among participants. There is nothing wrong with conflicting opinions. But help the group to distinguish between "fact" and "subjective evaluation."
- Flip chart records will be of greatest value for further action if you write down quotes, ideas, and imagery used verbatim.

TOOL #5: CARD WEEK(S)

GOAL: Workers and managers jointly address questions of improving work organization and search for solutions for the "thousand daily hassles" that are never addressed.

TARGET: Managers at different levels and the people directly working for them (unit size: 5-15)

TIME: Negligible for employees (basically no work interruption). Required: 1-2 hours during one week for supervisors/managers.

MATERIALS NEEDED: 4X6 cards

FACILITATOR: Supervisor

PROCEDURE: Phase 1: Information meeting with all employees

Phase 2: Identification of problems: 4X6 card week

Phase 3: Working on problem solutions and feedback to all employees involved

Phase 1

Employees are informed about the goals and process of the 4X6 card week in the context of a regular department meeting. If such regular meetings are not already held, they should be established as a regular feature in the context of the 4X6 card week.

The following aspects are important to consider when planning the information meeting:

1. The 4X6 card week should be announced one to two weeks in advance. This allows employees to prepare themselves and to think about the daily hassles bothering them.
2. The supervisor has to clarify the limits of what can be changed, especially with respect to changes requiring major capital outlay/investments. Otherwise, unrealistic expectations may be created which, if not met, can easily lead to resignation and disinterest.
3. The supervisor has to assess wether employees believe the situation can be changed. If the prevailing mood is one of resignation, the card week may have little chance of succeeding. In this case, management may first have to prove that it is serious about its willingness to solve problems. This may require using a well-known problem as an example, asking people to suggest improvements and following through on solving the problem.

Phase 2

The actual execution of the 4X6 card week requires publicity and advertising: Though the focus is on daily hassles that ought to be addressed as they occur, daily routines and pressures leave them unresolved. That is why they ought to become the "action focus" now and again.

Employees are encouraged to list all the problems that concern them now or that have bothered them for a while. The focus of the problem collection is on the daily hassles people have to contend with. However, no limitations should be set for the types of problems to be identified.

For each problem a 4X6 card is used. The card lists a brief description of the problem, the job affected by this problem and, if possible, suggestions for how the problem might be solved.

After the most pressing problems are listed, additional problems might be identified by focusing on various specific work aspects on each day of the card week. For example, ergonomics, time pressures, job disruptions, and so on.

Phase 3

The supervisor groups the cards according to topic areas. Problems are also categorized according to whether
- they can be solved quickly and easily
- the required solution is obvious but may cost money
- additional information is required from the employees affected or from other sources
- they fall into somebody else's area of responsibility and thus need to be passed on
- they require a meeting with a group of employees, etc.

This process is to be followed by specifically addressing the problems and starting the implementation of suggestions for resolving them as quickly as possible. It is extremely important that visible steps to solve problems are taken immediately, even though they may focus on small problems only. If these problems are not addressed, employees will quickly lose interest and willingness to participate.

Furthermore, all employees involved, not only the ones immediately affected by a problem, have to be kept informed about the problem-solving process on an ongoing basis.

It is not enough to solve problems. The people involved have to know about it!

If a reward system for suggestions already exists in the organization, this system must be used to reward employee input and suggestions.

NOTE

1. See Emery and Emery, *Participative Work Design*. Also Eberhard Ulich, "Subjektive Tätigkeitsanalyse als Voraussetzung autonomieorientierter Arbeitsgestaltung," in Felix Frei and Eberhard Ulich, eds., *Beiträge zur psychologischen Arbeitsanalyse* (Bern, Switzerland: Huber, 1981), pp. 327-347.

PART V

SPECIAL ISSUES

13. Union Participation in Work Design

In this book we have argued that people develop greater competence for effective thinking and acting through direct participation in redesigning work activities to expand opportunities for decision-making and problem-solving. We have also argued, however, that the process of participation in work redesign stimulates competence development only when it is reinforced. That means that if employees' contributions and efforts are either not used at all or used in ways that undermine their own interests, they will be unlikely to continue participating. In the United States, unions are the most common vehicle through which workers can acquire an "official" voice in decisions about their work.

The importance of employees' right to participate in industrial governance was central to the passage of the National Labor Relations Act (NRLA) in 1935, at the height of the last major era of industrial restructuring. For the first time in U.S. history, the legitimacy of potentially conflicting interests between labor and capital was accepted and a structure was created that would allow for the negotiation of each party's goals. The notion of "democracy in industry" provided the philosophical underpinning of the NLRA, which placed collective bargaining at the core of American industrial relations. As Senator Robert F. Wagner, the sponsor of what also became known as the Wagner Act, explained:

> The principles of my proposal were surprisingly simple. They were founded upon the accepted fact that one must have democracy in

industry as well as in government; that democracy in industry means fair participation by those who work in the decisions vitally affecting their lives and livelihood; and the workers in our great mass production industries can enjoy this participation only if allowed to organize and bargain collectively through representatives of their choosing.[1]

The right of employees to an independent voice in the decisions affecting their lives and livelihood has recently been reemphasized by such notable figures as former U.S. Secretary of Labor Ray Marshall as essential to creating high performance workplaces.

In the current debate about how to reestablish U.S. competitiveness, the collective bargaining system – or the existence of unions per se – is sometimes viewed as a key obstacle to improvements. This short-sighted perspective ignores the fact that the collective bargaining system did much more than create the basis for collectively negotiating of wages and benefits and establishing procedures to protect workers from arbitrary or abusive treatment. As has recently been pointed out, "By organizing the major companies in steel, auto, and other mass production industries, industrial unions successfully took wages out of competition ... and by raising the standard of living for a broad segment of society industrial unionism made possible the mass consumption on which a healthy mass production economy depended."[2]

Yet, while unions both contributed and benefited from the success of mass production industries, they now face the same realities as management in confronting global competition. As mass production structures, processes, and technologies become obsolete, so grows the pressure for change in the traditional industrial relations system. The call for flexible production supported by multiskilling, flexible job assignments, and worker participation in decision-making processes challenges the system of elaborate job classifications, rules, and procedures established by unions to protect their members against exploitation and abuse. Indeed, the Taylorist system embraced by management was used by unions to strengthen shop floor control and led to the establishment of parallel hierarchies within unions based on the separation of thinking and doing.[3] Many advocate the need for new union strategies and tactics in order to effectively represent employees' interests in the context of new forms of work organization.[4]

These calls for new strategies have created considerable debate and conflict within the U.S. labor movement at all levels. It is not our intent here to recommend to unions whether or how they should go about responding to pressures for change. To do so would violate the principles of "self-design." We do observe, however, that unions have traditionally been a major force for expanding workers' education and development opportunities and that they can play an important role in the process of designing work to promote learning and competence development. To do so will require, however, new proposals, new tactics, and new roles for unions.

A FRAMEWORK FOR ANALYZING EMPLOYEE PARTICIPATION IN UNIONIZED FIRMS

Participation refers to a process through which employees exercise influence on decisions affecting their work. Different types of participation processes can be distinguished, as can differing levels of influence over different types of issues or decisions. For example, participatory processes can be *formal,* through a system of rules that explicitly establishes decision-making structures, or *informal.* Influence can be exerted *directly* by employees entering personally into decision-making deliberations, or *indirectly* through representatives. The range or scope of decisions that employees are able to participate in can be *narrow*, confined to immediate job-related issues, or *broad,* encompassing the major business strategies of the firm.[5]

The most widespread form of employee participation in work design in the United States is an informal system of direct employee participation. This informal system (frequently invisible to the casual observer) can be found even in workplaces designed according to the most rigid application of the principles of scientific management discussed in Chapter 2. In fact, this informal system was the major discovery of the famous Hawthorne experiments of the 1930s.[6] In a 1974 comparison of five different systems of employee participation, American workers, especially those in smaller plants, rated their informal influence as highly as did workers in the Israeli kibbutz system, where workers directly elect their managers and the managerial function is rotated.[7]

Informal influence can be achieved through a "participative management style" where supervisors solicit and incorporate employees' ideas and suggestions. It can also develop through "shop floor bargaining" where employees and supervisors make deals outside the formal work rules that benefit both parties' needs. For example, a work group may agree to increase its output in order to help a supervisor meet production quotas in exchange for the opportunity to leave work early if the quota is met.[8] Informal systems of participation provide a certain level of influence which can in fact be extremely powerful at times. They do not, however, provide employees with a reliable means for positively contributing to improvements in products and processes that benefit either their own or the company's interests. Informal participatory systems tend to collapse with changes in personnel and during economic downturns, leaving employees with no means to represent their interests, as witnessed in the past decade.

Historically, the most common formal means for employees to participate in decisions about work design in the United States has been to form a union or association and then to engage in collective bargaining over the terms and conditions of employment. In this type of indirect participation, employees' interests are represented in the collective bargaining process by elected union representatives. National and state labor laws regulate the range and scope of issues that employees have the right to participate in deciding.

Within the collective bargaining relationship, labor and management typically employ two different types of negotiating strategies: distributive and integrative.[9] Distributive strategies are used when the issue being negotiated is perceived by the parties as zero sum, meaning that whatever one party gains the other party loses. Distributive strategies typically use adversarial tactics geared toward winning. Integrative strategies are used when issues are perceived as non-zero sum, meaning that bargaining can achieve an outcome that satisfies both parties' needs. Integrative strategies make use of collaborative or problem-solving techniques geared toward generating contractual provisions that meet the goals of both parties. Any particular labor-management relationship involves a mix of distributive and integrative strategies depending on the history of the relationship and the immediate context in which collective bargaining takes place.

Recently there has been much wider experimentation with systems of direct "quasi-formal" employee participation among U.S. companies.[10] The most common form is modeled on the Japanese quality circle system where work groups meet on a regular basis to discuss ways to improve the production process or the product. About half of U.S. companies appear to have adopted some form of direct employee participation in job-related decision-making. A much smaller number of firms are experimenting with systems of direct formal employee participation such as the sociotechnical system design described in Chapter 7. Only a tiny fraction of companies have experimented with direct formal employee participation in "strategic" or capital decisions at the highest level. Fewer than 1 percent of even those companies where employees are significant shareholders have nonmanagerial workers serving as employee representatives on the board of directors.[11] Few companies have structures comparable to the works councils found in Germany. The most extensive experiment in formal direct employee participation in the United States is found at Saturn (see Chapter 4) and required special dispensation from the National Labor Relations Board.

In comparison to other countries, U.S. labor laws are quite restrictive concerning the range and scope of issues over which employers are required to bargain.[12] The U.S. philosophy since the passage of the NLRA holds that it is management's right to manage the business and the union's job to make sure employees get fair treatment and a fair share of the proceeds.[13] Barred from direct structural influence on core business decisions, unions have focused largely on distributional issues such as the negotiation of wages and working conditions while seeking influence over other issues outside the collective bargaining process.

In the minds of many Americans, "collective bargaining" is synonymous with adversarial tactics such as strikes, slowdowns, boycotts, and lockouts. In reality, however, integrative-cooperative bargaining is as common in collective bargaining as distributive-adversarial bargaining, especially when the labor-management relationship is characterized by respect for the other party's legitimate institutional interests and premised on the principles of good faith negotiating.

In the last decade adversarial tactics have come under widespread attack and unions have been urged to adopt a more "cooperative" or "win/win" approach to labor-management relations. Such cooperative relations are frequently held to be superior to traditional collective bargaining. Not surprisingly, unions have regarded this development with suspicion, in part because the push for a less adversarial position, often complemented by proposals for direct employee participation programs, has usually come from management and not infrequently has been coupled with simultaneous threats of plant closings, outsourcing, workforce reduction, or other concessionary demands. In addition, many unions have come to learn that "quality of work life" (QWL) and employee involvement programs, introduced with the rhetoric of cooperation, trust, and working together, have rarely entailed real worker participation and influence over the organization of their work. Though aimed at improving management's access to workers' knowledge and suggestions for improving quality and productivity, these efforts frequently have remained uncoupled from a willingness to give up any real control. As a result, Banks and Metzgar note, "In many places, QWL-type programs have achieved significant success in changing attitudes in the way management wanted, but have not substantially affected productivity, quality, or costs. Where there has been success in these areas, it is because the knowledge and insights of workers have had a direct impact on changing the way that work is actually done."[14]

Unionism in other Western industrialized countries has been less adversarial at the firm or facility level, perhaps because unions have more formal influence at the industry and governmental policy level. Most European unions negotiate contracts on an industrywide basis, which strengthens their position. Their negotiation partners are usually a bargaining team from the employer association in a particular industry. In addition, union participation and consultation in managerial decision-making are required by law in Germany and in some Scandinavian countries. Works councils at the firm level in Germany, for example, though varying greatly in terms of the influence they exert, have codetermination rights regarding such issues as general working conditions, supervisory methods, and personnel policies connected with mergers, shutdowns, and adoption of new production methods.[15] Though technically independent from the union, works councils are often dominated or influenced by union activists, thus building a link between union policies and goals and firm-level concerns.

In these countries, public policy makes union decertification and avoidance much more difficult than in the United States, as has been widely demonstrated in the past decade. Thus, many major companies in European countries have chosen to work *with* rather than against their unions in taking on the challenges of global wage competition, changing markets, and new technologies (for an example, see the Volvo Uddevalla case in Chapter 4). Large industrial unions, such as the German and Swedish metalworkers, for example, have long defined negotiations on working conditions as including questions of plant restructuring, new forms of work organization, and training and skill development. In a proactive strategy, the IG Metall in Germany developed its own set of guidelines for work reorganization into work groups, emphasizing the utilization of the full range of workers' abilities and skills, self-regulation, continuous learning, voluntariness, and assuring union input in the process.

UNIONS' ROLE IN SKILL AND COMPETENCE DEVELOPMENT

Contrary to the negative image of trade unions in many circles in this country, there is growing evidence that strong unions can be the foundation for meaningful and effective worker participation efforts. An analysis of innovative practices at large unionized and nonunion firms reported more teamwork efforts at unionized companies, according to General Accounting Office 1984 data.[16] A study of 1,000 manufacturing plants using labor-management problem-solving teams suggested, furthermore, that unionized plants were significantly more efficient than nonunion plants.[17] As team-based work systems in unionized plants are a product of negotiation, "and emphasize quality of worklife goals of workers as well as the productivity goals of management, these programs tend to have greater legitimacy and are more likely to survive," according to Eaton and Voos. "Ironically," these authors conclude, "it is precisely because unionized workers can say no as a group that they can also collectively say yes."[18]

Training, skill, and competence development are an arena of growing importance in labor-management cooperation. Training programs jointly administered by unions and management already spend more than $300 million per year and represent the fastest growing segment in the nation's learning system.[19] Unions like the United Auto Workers, the Communication Workers of America, the United Steelworkers of America, the building trades unions, and many others have taken a proactive role both in initiating the redesign of jobs to demand more skill and in providing learning opportunities for their members to perform these jobs. This is particularly important at a time when well-paying but relatively low-skilled jobs in the manufacturing industry are rapidly disappearing and a growing part of future union membership will be in the service sector, involving many women, minorities, and immigrants. As Kochan and Wever have suggested, "Unions will have to broaden their constituencies by developing strategies that organize internal and external labor markets in the interest of more continuous and high-quality employment for both high and low-skilled service sector workers."[20]

There is evidence to support the argument that the part played by unions in skill formation in the new economy may be analogous to their role in influencing wage formation during the mass production era. Wolfgang Streeck argues that "unions should embrace skill formation as the centerpiece of a new, cooperative and productivist strategy, and at the same time insist on the unions' need for a strong independent power base giving them a capacity to impose rules and obligations on employers that these would not voluntarily obey or accept."[21] While the broad and changing technical, social, and problem-solving competences required for quality-based competition are best acquired through work-based learning, there is little evidence, at least in this country, that employers will take the lead to go beyond more narrowly defined technical training, in part because of short-term cost calculation and because it is not in their immediate interest to enhance employees' job mobility in an environment of increasing competition for skilled employees. An active, interventionist union strategy that negotiates work-based competence and skill development projects that are not overspecialized but produce broad and flexible skills thus will benefit not only the membership, but the economy as a whole.

Collective bargaining is the centerpiece of such a strategy. Including work-based competence development initiatives in the collective bargaining agreement gives them formal contractual status, increases the likelihood that the terms and provisions of the initiative will be implemented, and provides recourse to either party if the contractual provisions are not implemented as intended. In addition, the provision of contractually guaranteed funds protects competence development initiatives from the ups and downs of corporate budgeting decisions and the whims of public financial support. The best examples of this are the joint training funds negotiated between the UAW and General Motors, Ford, and Chrysler. Since 1982 these funds have provided auto workers with unprecedented opportunities for formal education and training as well as nonformal learning and competence development through participation in work redesign.[22] And the negotiated and jointly governed apprenticeship programs in the building and construction industry are now widely advocated as a means to develop a highly qualified workforce in other industries.

As the MIT Commission on Industrial Productivity pointed out, public policies in many other countries are geared toward promoting competence development. Legal, political, and economic pressures against worker layoffs in Sweden and Germany, for example, in addition to benefiting employees, have also caused major car manufacturers such as Volvo, Mercedes, and VW to focus on a product range that is quality- rather than price-competitive. Due to a well-functioning apprentice system and increased training efforts in recent years, largely imposed by trade unions and works councils, German car manufacturers have a large pool of excess skills, placing them in a unique position to respond flexibly to market and technology changes.[23] Somewhat paradoxically, it may be the *constraints* imposed on access to external labor markets that lead to a focus on internal competence development. By contrast, the strategy of many U.S. firms has been to turn to external "contingent" labor markets for workforce adjustments, a strategy made easy due to the absence of government regulations and weakened labor unions. While this may have benefited the corporate bottom line in the short term, the long-term costs of this strategy in terms of U.S. competitiveness, unemployment, and a falling standard of living are starting to become increasingly visible.

THE INEVITABILITY OF CONFLICT

Redesigning work to promote broader workforce competence will not be achieved without conflict. Issues of competence and qualification are not neutral in the American workplace. *Power,* and with it resources, is largely allocated to individuals based on occupational positions which are obtained (at least in theory) by formal qualifications. Members of highly skilled occupations, from physicians to electricians, jealously defend both the content and the competences of their occupation through long apprenticeships and elaborate systems of rules that determine who can enter the occupation and what level of competence must be demonstrated for mastery. Now new technologies and changing contexts are blurring the lines between occupations, reawakening old interoccupational conflicts, and generating some new ones. The lines between physicians' job content and that of nurses and other health care professionals, for example, are being redrawn, as are the lines between "skilled" and "unskilled" manufacturing jobs. Managers and supervisors have only partially, reluctantly, and begrudgingly relinquished aspects of their decision-making power to employees.

It is important to recognize that developing a more competent and highly qualified workforce, as important, worthwhile, and even necessary as it may be, is bound to involve conflict, since it can only succeed through changing the existing balance of power. The methods offered in this volume assume that the existing organization of work in most workplaces contains some interests that conflict, some that overlap, and some that may either overlap or conflict depending on specific policies and practices. Rather than presenting participation and cooperative problem-solving as *the solution* to conflicting interests, the approach proposed here is intended to promote an understanding of which issues pertaining to competence development through work redesign represent high degrees of overlapping interest among major stakeholders, and therefore lend themselves to cooperative strategies, and which are probably distributive in nature and best handled through other means – collective bargaining or external political action, for example.

One of the problems with unilateral management efforts to reorganize work in order to reduce rigid job classifications and introduce multiskilling has been the lack of a clear understanding of the goals of such strategies, along with a certain amount of confusion between means and ends. As many companies and unions have learned, the mere existence of some form of employee involvement groups does not necessarily lead to quality and productivity improvements if employee influence is restricted to a narrow range of immediate production problems and ignored when it raises concerns about more important issues. Similarly, simplistic approaches to combining job classifications and cross training, particularly in highly skilled occupations, may lead to the "jack of all trades, master of none" phenomenon with the potential of deterioration of competent task performance along with frustrated and dissatisfied workers.

Unions, on their part, have often resisted involvement in participatory projects or fought against any kind of flexibility in work assignments for fear that such attempts might erode member solidarity or threaten the union goals of job security. While such fears may be well founded, a number of unions have demonstrated how assuming a leadership role in advocating direct member participation and more flexible forms of work organization can actually benefit the membership and the union's goals and strength in the long run. Rather than excluding these issues from the collective bargaining process, some of the most successful employee participation projects have been those where the union in a proactive quid pro quo strategy negotiated the parameters of participation and work rule flexibility to move closer to the goal of workplace democracy and meaningful work activities. In some cases, there has been an implicit or explicit recognition of the need for such changes to protect the job security of union members. A case in point is the extensive worker participation program negotiated between District 100 of the International Association of Machinists and Eastern Airlines during the period 1983-1985. Ironically, it was management's resistance and lack of commitment to the process that led to the demise of one of the most promising worker participation programs in recent U.S. industrial relations history.[24]

Indeed, strategies of direct member participation in self-management and cooperative-integrative bargaining may well coexist with adversarial bargaining if "adversarial" means a recognition and acceptance of the presence of inherently conflicting interests between capital and labor. As one of the most successful unions in recent history, the German Metalworkers' Union, has proven, a highly active and cooperative role in the redesign of work organization, accompanied by demands for skill upgrading and broader competence development, is not irreconcilable with a tough position on securing future employment, as evidenced by the lengthy and successful strike in 1984 for a 38.5 hour work week.

(For a practical tool to assess overlapping and conflicting stakeholder interests in relationship to work design for competence development, see Chapter 12, Tool #1.)

NOTES

1. Quoted in Clyde W. Summers, "Industrial Democracy: America's Unfulfilled Promise," *Cleveland State Law Review* 29 (1979): 34.

2. John Hoerr, "What Should Unions Do?" *Harvard Business Review* (May-June 1991): 36.

3. See Thomas Rankin, *New Forms of Work Organization: The Challenge to North American Unions* (Toronto: University of Toronto Press, 1990), for an excellent discussion of how the structure and decision-making processes of North American unions mirror corporate structures and reflect the underlying principles of scientific management. See also Edward Cohen-Rosenthal and Cynthia Burton, *Mutual Gains* (New York: Praeger, 1987), chapter 4.

4. See, for example, Thomas A. Kochan, Harry C. Katz, and Robert B. McKersie, *The Transformation of American Industrial Relations* (New York: Basic Books, 1986); Rankin, *New Forms of Work Organization*; Charles Hecksher, *The New Unionism* (New York: Basic Books, 1988); Cooke, *Labor-Management Cooperation.*

5. See K. Walker, "Workers' Participation in Management: Problems, Practice and Prospects," *International Institute of Labour Studies Bulletin* 12 (1974), entire issues, for a useful typology of forms of employee participation. In this chapter we are discussing participation only in the management function. Other forms of employee participation such as participation in ownership through shareholding will not be discussed. See J.R. Blasi and D.L. Kruse, *The New Owners* (New York: Harper, 1991), for an excellent discussion of this form of participation. Employees are the top shareholders in nearly half of the 1,000 public corporations traded on stock exchanges. Blasi and Kruse predict that, by the year 2000, employee ownership will play a crucial role in takeover battles and proxy fights. In addition to direct stock ownership, employee pension funds will control 30 percent to 50 percent of the stock of many companies. Employee control of capital has the potential to significantly influence business strategy in the future. This in turn can be expected to influence many aspects of work design.

6. For a good discussion of the "forgotten lessons" regarding workers' participation contained in the Hawthorne experiments, see Paul Blumberg, *Industrial Democracy* (New York: Schocken, 1973), chapter 2.

7. A study by Tannenbaum and his colleagues compared a sample of different sized manufacturing plants in different industries in five countries. The participation systems compared were the Israeli kibbutz system, where workers elect managers and the managerial function is rotated; the (former) Yugoslav "Workers Self-Management System," where the workers' collective is the final decision-making body; family capitalism in Italy, where owners directly manage the enterprise; the Austrian system, where the government is the major shareholder in most large corporations which are legally structured as private corporations; and the American system of managerial capitalism. See A. Tannenbaum, B. Kavcic, M. Rosner, M. Vianello, and G. Wieser, *Hierarchy in Organizations* (San Francisco: Jossey-Bass, 1974).

8. For a detailed description of shop floor bargaining in an automobile factory, see Linda Kaboolian, "Shifting Gears: Auto Workers Assess the Transformation of Their Industry," doctoral dissertation. University of Michigan, Ann Arbor, 1990.

9. For a thorough discussion of these two different negotiating processes, see Richard Walton and Robert McKersie, *A Behavioral Theory of Labor Negotiations* (New York: McGraw-Hill, 1965).

10. By "formal" we refer to systems that are incorporated as an official and legally binding part of of the structure of decision-making in the firm. Thus a number of emerging direct employee participation programs, while more structured than an informal participative management style, are nevertheless informal systems since management retains the right to disband them at will. For example, systems of direct employee participation that are established as part of labor contracts are formal.

11. Blasi and Kruse, *New Owners*, p. 216.

12. The National Labor Relations Act, Section 8 (a) (5), states that "subjects at the *core of entrepreneurial control* are permissive bargaining subjects." In contrast to mandatory subjects, which imply a legal obligation by the other party to negotiate, "when either party wants to negotiate over permissive subjects, the other party has no legal obligation to negotiate over these subjects."

13. Cooke, *Labor-Management Cooperation*.

14. Andy Banks and Jack Metzgar, "Participating in Management," *Labor Research Review* 14 (Fall 1989): 15.

15. Business International S.A., *Industrial Democracy in Europe* (Geneva, 1974), p. 39.

16. Cited in Adrienne E. Eaton and Paula B. Voos, "Unions and Contemporary Innovations in Work Organization, Compensation, and Employee Participation," in L. Mishel and P.B. Voos, eds., *Unions and Economic Competitiveness* (New York: M.E. Sharpe, 1991).

17. Maryellen Kelley and Bennett Harrison, "Unions, Technology, and Labor-Management Cooperation," cited in Bryan Miller, "Not All It's Cracked Up to Be," *Across the Board* (November 1991): 24-28.

18. Adrienne E. Eaton and Pauls B. Voos, cited in Hoerr, "What Should Unions Do?," p. 38; see also Cooke, *Labor-Management Cooperation*.

19. Carnevale, *Put Quality to Work*, p. 15.

20. Thomas A. Kochan and Kirsten R. Wever, "American Unions and the Future of Worker Representation," in G. Strauss, D.G. Gallagher, and J. Fiorito, eds., "The State of the Unions." *Industrial Relations Research Association Series* (1991): 372.

21. Wolfgang Streeck, "The New Industrial Relations: A Strategic Role for Unions in Vocational Training?," paper (Madison: University of Wisconsin, December 1990), p. 3.

22. For an overview of joint union-management education and training programs, see Louis A. Ferman, Michelle Hoyman, Joel Cutcher-Gershenfeld, and Ernest J. Savoie, eds., *Joint Training Programs: A Union-Management Approach to Preparing Workers for the Future* (Ithaca: ILR Press, 1991).

23. Wolfgang Streeck, "Industrial Relations and Industrial Change: The Restructuring of the World Automobile Industry in the 1970s and 1980s," *Economic and Industrial Democracy* 8 (1987): 437-462.

24. Banks and Metzgar, "Participating in Management."

14.   The Changing Role of Supervisors

The traditional functions of the master craftsman demanded a broad spectrum of both occupational and social expertise. His role encompassed the design and planning of the product, the organization of the actual production process, the guidance of journeymen, and the teaching of apprentices.

The Fordist system of mass production, based on the separation of planning and execution functions, emphasized the control function of supervisors and created a set of job demands with inherent tensions and potential conflicts (see Figure 14.1).

The problems and tensions inherent in this position might be exacerbated by the establishment of a worker participation process or work reorganization into semi-autonomous work teams. If work teams are formed, supervisors often raise concerns, reflected in typical statements such as these:

"I don't have a problem with work teams, but ...
- I've gotten my people involved before,
- the authority of the supervisor must not be questioned,
- the work still has to be done,
- the work team has to be able to deliver,
- it shouldn't take too much time,
- the supervisor must not lose control of things,
- it must not create more work for the supervisor,
- we can't raise unrealistic expectations,
- the workers must not neglect their other tasks because of the group,

- the work teams cannot be involved in investment decisions,
- the teams have to be in line with the overall departmental and organizational plan,
- it can't lead to endless discussions of decisions that have already been made."

These concerns are rooted in the supervisors' sandwich situation in which

- they are overwhelmed by the pressure for a smooth production flow,
- they sometimes see the workers as a part of production only,
- they experience themselves as just a cog in the wheel,
- they are hardly ever trained in group process and problem-solving skills.

Figure 14.1   Inherent Tensions in the Role of Supervisors

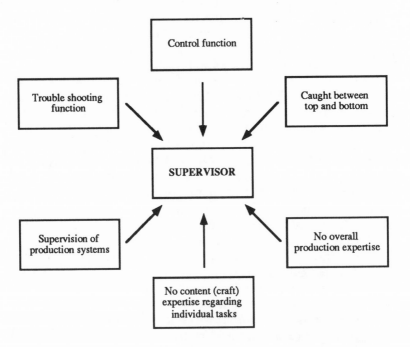

Supervisors, as lower or middle level managers, find themselves in a multiple role conflict, with competing pressures and often little recognition and support (see Figure 14.2).

Figure 14.2   Role Conflict of the Middle Manager
                   (Sandwich Position)

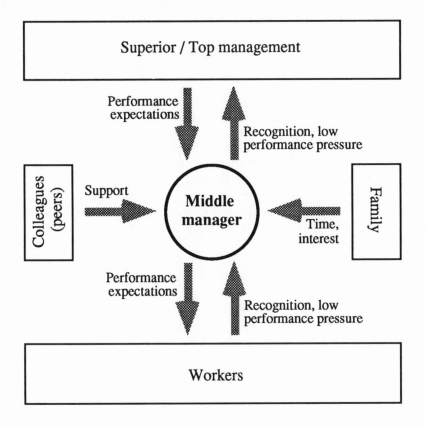

While supervisors may rarely show open resistance to bottom-up
worker participation projects, they are rightfully concerned about
the effect of such changes on themselves. A study of the responses of 139 supervisors in eight plants to employee involvement programs such as quality circles, Quality of Work Life
(QWL) programs, and semi-autonomous work teams surfaced
three major areas of concern:
- Job Security: The popular notion that supervisors may become redundant as a result of employee participation wor-
  ries supervisors, too. If left unclarified, this concern may
  understandably lead to resistance or a "hands-off" attitude
  on the part of supervisors.
- Job Definition: Any real work reorganization project will
  change the supervisory role and responsibilities. Unless the

new tasks are well defined and complemented by the necessary training and support, supervisors may choose to fall
back into old, more comfortable behavior patterns.
- Work Overload: Additional work for supervisors may be
generated in implementing and coordinating employee participation projects. If supervisors feel unfairly burdened
with additional responsibilities, enthusiasm is likely to be
low.[1]

In spite of these very legitimate concerns, organizations often
lack a coordinated strategy to get supervisors actively involved in
the change process. Instead, it is assumed that resistance to
change is normal and is likely to disappear over time. It has been
argued throughout this book that, in order for work reorganization projects to be successful, the employees affected have to be
involved in the design and implementation of the change process;
this also holds true for supervisors. Klein suggests that a proactive supervisor involvement strategy would have to contain the
following elements:

- Supervisory involvement in the design and implementation
of worker participation projects and a say in how decisions
made affect their job.
- Support-based training that clarifies how employee involvement differs from other programs. Such training
preferably includes ongoing consultation and feedback with
higher level management and possibly consultants. A participatory management style must start at the top, and
higher level management needs to role model the sharing of
decisions with middle and lower level management.
- Responsibility with authority based on the understanding
that the perceived loss of power is real when employees
take over many day-to-day decisions. A redefinition of the
supervisory role must include the transfer of the appropriate
authority to go along with new responsibilities and should
address necessary changes in the support, performance
evaluation, and reward system.
- Supervisory networks based on mechanisms for information exchange and discussion among peers can help the
more skeptical individual to see the value of employee participation.[2]

If these elements are included in a broader change strategy,
the frequent assumption that a gain for the workers must mean a
loss for supervisors becomes unjustified. Work redesign is not a
zero-sum game. The benefits for one group need not be to the

detriment of another group. This is evident if we contrast the role of supervisors in group-based work organization based on sociotechnical systems principles with their role in a traditional system (see also Chapter 7). In a traditional work system the supervisor is expected to control the task execution for each individual job, particularly if the jobs and work tasks are linked so that the scope of activities and decision latitude of individual workers are very limited. Detailed job descriptions and task instructions support the execution of the supervisory function.

The left side of Figure 14.3 shows the relationship between workers, tasks, and the supervisor in the traditional work organization structure.[3] The supervisor controls workers A, B, and C in assigning them the execution of tasks X, Y, and Z. The coordination resulting from the separation of each work task becomes an additional supervisory function.

Figure 14.3   Supervisor's Task in Different Systems

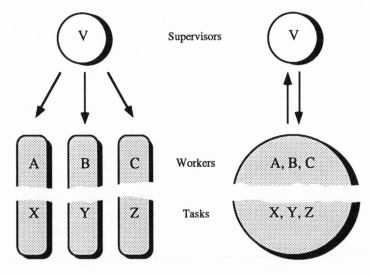

Supervisors

Workers

Tasks

Fragmented work organization: Work organization in sociotechnical systems:
individual tasks are assigned to each worker   groups are responsible for a range of different tasks

The right side of Figure 14.3 illustrates the relationships between workers, tasks, and the supervisor in a sociotechnical system. A group of workers, A, B, and C, are in charge of executing tasks X, Y, and Z, as a relatively independent but interrelated set of work activities. Group members decide who will work on which specific task. In addition to taking on coordination activities, the group also handles disruptions, variances, and production problems. In this context supervisors become the link between self-regulated work groups and between these groups and the larger organization. They manage the variances between the system's internal demands and the demands of the organizational environment (boundary regulation/management).

In addition to this function, the supervisor's role in this system consists of four key elements: group leadership, competence development, control of variance and disruptions, and system development.[4]

GROUP LEADERSHIP

Instead of direct instruction and control, supervisors play a mediator or facilitator role in helping the work group solve production problems or conflicts within the group. They provide constructive (learning-oriented) feedback about deviations from production goals and objectives. This leadership role involves assisting the group in defining their primary work activity and in setting realistic goals in the context of existing resources and constraints.

COMPETENCE DEVELOPMENT

Supervisors support and promote individual competence development, leading to increased work group flexibility and multiskilling. The "collective competence" fosters the group's ability to regulate variances and disruptions with increasing independence and to solve unusual or more complex problems.

CONTROL OF VARIANCE AND DISRUPTIONS

Supervisors assist the workers in handling variances and disruptions. For example, they are involved in planning and balancing the production volume and thus provide the conditions that support an optimal workflow within the department. Or, they offer expert or technical knowledge if production problems occur so as to assure that problems and disruptions can be addressed within the work group without negatively affecting other production units.

SUPPORT AND IMPLEMENTATION OF TECHNICAL AND ORGANIZATIONAL INNOVATIONS (SYSTEM DEVELOPMENT)

Particularly in the context of high quality, production knowledge is essential. The supervisor will therefore become an increasingly important link between production and more technical research and development units. Reintegrating the planning function of the craft tradition into the supervisor's role makes the supervisory function the connecting link between engineers and workers. The supervisor thus becomes a key figure for the development of a successful participation process in technological innovations. (For an example of changing supervisory roles in a work redesign process, see Chapter 8.)

If the necessary training and support are provided to help supervisors take on and accomplish these tasks successfully, then
- Participatory job design for employee competence development need not be a threat to supervisors.
- Resistance to change is less a function of the individual involved than of the way in which the organization manages change.
- A successful change process can create the potential for a true leadership position for supervisors, with new and challenging responsibilities and more interesting and rewarding tasks.

NOTES

1. Janice Klein, "Why Supervisors Resist Employee Involvement," *Harvard Business Review* (September/October 1984): 89.
2. Ibid., pp. 92-93.
3. Emery and Emery, *Participative Design: Work and Community Life*.
4. Alioth, "Selbststeuerungskonzepte." pp. 1823-1833.

15.   Compensation Practices in the New Manufacturing Environment

Ken Mericle

The broad changes occurring in the U.S. economy, especially manufacturing, are generating substantial pressure on existing compensation practices. New management strategies such as just-in-time (JIT) manufacturing and total quality management (TQM), the comprehensive application of computer technology in computer integrated manufacturing (CIM) systems, and new forms of worker involvement are all part of a new style of production. This new system is highly interdependent and is focused on a smooth and flexible flow of quality product (or services) through the production system.

Many if not most U.S. companies are well into implementation of the above measures before attempting to bring existing personnel and labor relations practices in line with the logic of the new system. Compensation practices present a particularly challenging dilemma. On the one hand, the existing compensation system frequently generates behaviors that are inconsistent with or even counterproductive to the goals of the new production system. On the other hand, the centrality of compensation in the concerns of most workers, modern theories of management notwithstanding, and the vested interests, both individual and collective, in the status quo mean that compensation systems are very difficult to change and new systems very difficult to implement successfully.

Modern management seeks a compensation system that promotes flexibility in task assignment; concerns for quality, delivery reliability, cost control, and general customer satisfaction; acceptance of new technology; acceptance of group process and involvement in group activity; commitment to continuous improvement; and so forth.   Classic Taylorism promotes narrow task specialization within fragmented job structures and hierarchical pay structures.   It also establishes production standards for individuals or groups and enforces the standards by linking them to pay (incentive systems) or discipline (measured day work). These Taylorist pay practices are frequently in direct conflict with management's new goals.

In spite of this incompatibility it is not easy to abandon Taylorism.   Unions have succeeded in negotiating protective pay practices, regulation of workloads, elaborate structures of job control based on seniority rights, and many other significant protections, all based on the premise of Taylorism.   To abandon Taylorism is to abandon a whole system of contractual rights and tangible protections that the labor movement has been constructing since the turn of the century.   Even when union leaders reach the conclusion that change is inevitable and that it is time to accept the new systems, and begin the difficult task of redefining their members' interests, there are no guarantees that their members will arrive at the same conclusion.   This is particularly true in the area of compensation policy.

FORCES DRIVING CHANGE

In the new manufacturing environment several factors combine to create new imperatives for compensation policy.   The new management strategies based on JIT and TQM have resulted in a reconceptualization of productivity and a rethinking of the relationship between productivity and quality.   The new social relations of production emphasize group problem-solving with a serious attempt to extend worker concerns beyond the context of their immediate job and to tap the knowledge and creativity of workers in addressing broad organizational concerns.   In the case of autonomous work groups – or what the authors of this book call work design for competence development – jobs may be broadened, technology reorganized, and responsibility and accountability internalized within the group. The new technology involves automated systems that are potentially both more highly integrated and more flexible. Computer systems that are vastly more powerful, more user friendly, more easily integrated, and less costly will result in the introduction of automated systems in lower volume, less standardized environments.

Competitive pressures from more advanced countries and more advanced organizations and the dynamics of the customer-supplier relationship will eventually force most companies to adopt part or all of these changes. The focus of change (management strategies, social relations of production or technology) and the rate of change will vary from organization to organization and from industry to industry depending on position within the international economy, basic technology (process, mass production, batch production, etc.), and a host of other factors. The new practices will focus more and more attention on production costs, quality, and rapid response to changing markets. As the new production system becomes entrenched, interest in new and more compatible systems of compensation will grow.

REQUIREMENTS OF NEW MANAGEMENT SYSTEMS

Both the meaning of productivity and the means of attaining higher productivity levels change in the context of just-in-time manufacturing and total quality management. Under Taylorism the main focus of productivity enhancing efforts is direct labor, and the main approach is micro analysis of individual direct labor jobs. Industrial engineers simplify by breaking jobs down into elements or even micro motions, eliminating unnecessary motions, resequencing for efficiency, and redesigning the layout, tools, and even product, all with the goal of minimizing the amount of necessary direct labor time for the operation. As simplification progresses, the complexity of remaining tasks is reduced, and it becomes easier and easier to imagine mechanized or automated systems capable of performing the operation. The details of this process and its impact on individual jobs and the general nature of work in capitalist societies have been thoroughly analyzed by Braverman and others.[1]

The pay systems that accompany and reinforce this process of work simplification are linked to another fundamental aspect of Taylorism, the establishment of production standards through a systematic process of work measurement (time study, standard data, predetermined motion-time systems). Once the operation has been simplified, the amount of time required for the operation is estimated, and a production standard is established. There is a direct linkage between pay and productivity in individual incentive systems where pay is tied directly to pieces produced. In measured daywork systems the operator earns an hourly wage, but is held accountable for the production quota and may be subject to discipline if it is not attained.

It is very important to examine the *implicit assumptions* underlying this Taylorist approach to maximizing productivity. Perhaps most fundamental is the assumption that efficiency of the production system is maximized when the individual efficiencies of its constituent operations are maximized. In other words, the factory will run most efficiently when all direct labor operations have been simplified, measured, and placed on standard. A second implicit assumption of classic Taylorism is that the problem of quality attainment is trivial. Through standardization and simplification of the operation a very high level of task specialization is attained. Performance of the specialized tasks requires neither complex thought nor complex manual skill, and hence the potential for error is minimized. In this environment management can concentrate on maximizing production and deal with quality after the fact as a secondary problem of production.

Both of these assumptions do not hold up very well in the modern manufacturing environment. JIT proponents directly challenge the maximization assumption implicit in Taylorism. The essence of their criticism is that maximizing production at individual operations, rather than maximizing system efficiency, creates a multitude of inefficiencies that are the direct consequences of the micro maximization strategy.[2] Some of the most important of these inefficiencies include excess inventories, excess space requirement, excess material handling, complex production control, and poor product quality (delays before detection, damage in handling, lack of accountability, obsolescence, etc.). All of these inefficiencies are the consequences of producing more at individual operations than the production system itself can effectively absorb. Indiscriminate micro maximization generates system inefficiency.

The JIT response concentrates on a macro or systems approach to productivity maximization in which the smooth flow of product through the system with minimum inventory buildup at all levels is emphasized. The productivity problem is totally transformed under this formulation. Instead of a narrow focus on minimizing direct labor time for a given level of output, the systems approach minimizes the combination of all inputs (direct, indirect, and management labor; material, work-in-process, and final goods inventory; space; machinery and equipment, etc.) *for a given level of output.* Apparent inefficiencies in the use of an individual input can be tolerated if the inefficiency is part of an overall strategy of input minimization and system maximization.

TQM expands on the JIT approach and challenges the second Taylorist assumption by locating quality in a central position in addressing the productivity issue. TQM suggests that maximizing productivity and maximizing quality are not conflicting, but rather complementary goals. By preventing quality problems ("build it right the first time") the maximum amount of *quality* output can be achieved for a given level of system inputs.

TQM emphasizes decentralization of responsibility for quality throughout the organization, and perhaps especially to those who add value directly to the product. It stresses a preventive approach to quality management through techniques like statistical process control. It raises the goal of continuous improvement of the production system through group efforts at problem identification and problem-solving utilizing simple applied statistics and group process techniques.

The philosophy and procedures of TQM make the same general demands on compensation systems as does the JIT approach to manufacturing. In fact, TQM and JIT are really part of a single management strategy in the sense that JIT is impossible if quality is not assured as inventory is eliminated. It is hard to imagine JIT without the comprehensive approach to quality suggested by TQM; likewise, it is hard to imagine implementation of TQM without inventory reduction and other changes suggested by JIT.

The implications of this combined management strategy for compensation policy are readily apparent. The following principles flow directly from the internal logic of JIT/TQM:

1. The compensation system should generate identification with and concern for *system* efficiency.
2. The compensation system should generate identification with and concern for quality goals.
3. The compensation system should promote effective group behavior.
4. The compensation system should encourage competence development related to system productivity, quality, and group behavior goals.

Production-driven pay systems like individual incentive and measured day work do not score high when measured against these standards. This is especially true when jobs are very narrowly defined, and highly specialized job classifications proliferate in a hierarchical pay structure. These practices promote production whether the product can be absorbed by the system or not. They frequently discourage concern for quality. If workers are paid to inspect every fifth piece they produce, one way they can beat the standard and increase incentive earnings is to perform the inspection as infrequently as is consistent with not getting caught. If they can produce more in less time by utilizing more material, they may disregard material yield in favor of minimizing the expenditure of their time. Likewise, a method that produces higher quality levels may be sacrificed for a method that maximizes output.

These pay systems reinforce individualistic and very narrowly focused concerns in the workplace. The emphasis on individual production discourages concern for the effectiveness of others in the system and for the efficiency of the system as a whole. The narrowness of the scope of many jobs limits the capacity of many job holders to see the connections between their tasks and those of others in the system.

It is possible to identity compensation practices that are consistent with JIT/TQM requirements and new forms of work organization as discussed in previous chapters One nearly universal goal seems to be to restructure the jobs into fewer, broader classifications in a flatter pay structure. This approach can be conveniently illustrated by examining what typically happens in the conversion from functional to cell manufacturing. Cell manufacturing is a typical mode used to implement JIT/TQM in batch production, metal fabrication operations. Under cell manufacturing the machinery and equipment required to manufacture a part (higher volume) or a family of closely related parts (lower volume) are grouped into a cell. In a machining cell this might involve grouping, turning, milling, drilling, and boring equipment together in the cell. Where previously this equipment might have been located in functional departments – lathes and screw machines in a turning department, milling machines in the milling area, for example – it is now grouped in a confined area, and parts flow from operation to operation with minimal inventory stocks, handling, storage, and so on.

The job of cell operator is quite different from the individual machine operator classifications. It is both enlarged (horizontal expansion), in that the cell operator is now responsible for operating different types of equipment, and enriched (vertical expansion), in that new tasks such as statistical process control, preventive maintenance, additional setup or pre-setup activities, and planning and control functions are typically added to the job. If volume justifies multioperator cell design, all operators typically have the same classification and are expected to be able to perform and regularly rotate through all tasks.

Not all JIT/TQM applications involve as radical a physical restructuring of the basic technology as occurs in cell manufacturing. Indeed, process and assembly industries already involve the kind of product-centered manufacturing process that cell manufacturing is designed to achieve. Nevertheless, even in applications where changes in the organization of physical technology are relatively minimal, employers still seem to favor fewer, broader job classifications in flatter pay structures.

The JIT/TQM approach, along with new forms of group-based work organization, is also generating considerable interest among employers in indirect group incentive systems such as productivity gainsharing and profit sharing. These systems reward group behavior and in theory provide a financial incentive to bring individual behaviors in line with group goals. They should generate interest in the performance of the organization as a whole and thereby support the systems approach to productivity inherent in JIT/TQM. They also should help sustain interest in group processes and group problem-solving. Under gainsharing, bonuses are based only on quality product which is shipped to and accepted by the customer. No payment is made for internal scrap or external returns. Thus gainsharing provides a direct incentive to pay attention to quality. Some gainsharing programs are being structured to provide direct rewards for performance linked to specific JIT/TQM concerns, such as delivery reliability, customer satisfaction, quality, yield, and other targets for which data series are available.

The final direction suggested by JIT/TQM relates to competence development required by upgraded jobs (see Chapter 3). It is possible that pay-for-knowledge plans will be adapted to provide incentive for skill and competence development. At present most pay-for-knowledge systems covering production workers are really pay-for-flexibility systems; that is, they reward workers for learning additional jobs or positions within broad work groups and for being willing to rotate through these positions, thus increasing flexibility in staffing. Pay-for-knowledge systems, which compensate for increased general knowledge that might be required by enriched jobs, are far less common.

REQUIREMENTS OF NEW SOCIAL RELATIONS OF PRODUCTION

JIT, TQM, and forms of work organization aimed at ongoing competence development are premised on a high level of mobilization of workers within the production process both in terms of individual involvement and group participation. TQM relies heavily on the quality circle model of problem solving groups that meet on a regular basis to identify and solve quality problems and to generate a process of continuous improvement. The same structure has been used to address cost, productivity, and quality of worklife concerns.

JIT suggests a more job or work group centered approach to worker involvement. Again, cell manufacturing provides a useful model. Workers could play a major role in designing cells, including applying the group technology principle in defining product groups, selecting the necessary equipment, planning the layout of the cell, applying the ergonomic design principles, and so on. Once set up, teams or self-managed work groups could be responsible for planning, coordination, and execution of cell functions.

Of course it is also possible to treat all design as exclusively an engineering function and to operate cells under the umbrella of conventional supervisory structures. However, both the rhetoric and the internal logic of JIT/TQM suggest that the system works best with high levels of worker input and commitment, as discussed in previous chapters. Furthermore, the design of the system itself requires higher levels of cooperation. JIT, through the elimination of inventory and the linkage of manufacturing operations, increases the level of interdependency within the production system and also its vulnerability to disruption. One of the operating principles of JIT is to design the system to expose problems and force their solution. Another operating principle is to anticipate problems and solve them in advance, before they have the opportunity to disrupt. This is the principle that instructs preventive maintenance, setup reduction, and statistical process control programs. All of this works better when workers are involved and committed to making the system work. One way of looking at quality circles, team concept models, and semi-autonomous work groups (see Chapter 7) is as a form of "preventive" labor relations designed to anticipate and solve human problems before they are transformed into production problems.

Compensation practices obviously can play a role in fostering group consciousness and effective group behavior. They can also play a role in facilitating group formation. Unions have begun to demand direct rewards for participation in cooperative efforts. This usually results in union-initiated proposals to implement profit sharing or, more commonly, some form of productivity gainsharing. Companies frequently become interested in these same bonus systems because they are viewed as a means of promoting employee involvement.

REQUIREMENTS OF NEW TECHNOLOGY

New management systems and the new social relations of production can be introduced in a low-tech or high-tech environment. For example, low-tech manufacturing cells with autonomous work groups can be created simply by moving existing manually controlled equipment into a cell configuration. On the other hand, a high-tech cell consisting of robots interfacing with computerized numerical control (CNC) machine tools, automated gauging equipment with computerized statistical process control (SPC) and feedback loops to the machine tools, and mechanized or automated material handling could be designed for the same application. Flexible manufacturing systems with automated product changeover procedures (tool change, fixture change, etc.) represent a further step in the technological evolution. The point at which a company enters this technological continuum will depend on availability of investment funds and technical expertise. Many firms opt for the low-tech solution and gradually upgrade.

Several developments suggest that automated systems will become increasingly viable in low volume applications. Computers are faster and have more user memory and more mass storage. Programs are more user friendly, more flexible, and more multifunctional. Integration within local area networks and with modems is more feasible. Hardware components interface more readily: microcomputers with mainframes, programmable logic controllers with computers, computers with video. The costs of all previously mentioned developments continue to fall. All of this means that flexible, integrated systems are increasingly pos-

sible, practical, reliable, and financially feasible. While computer integrated manufacturing may still be very expensive and
technically complex, there can be no doubt about its growing
potential.

As automation penetrates the workplace the concept of direct
labor has less and less relevance. Remaining workers are "trouble shooters," "system monitors," or "technical facilitators" as
opposed to operators. The relationship between expenditure of
their labor time and increase in the value-added of a given product is less and less direct. In automated systems it is often very
difficult, if not impossible, to measure jobs and set meaningful
production standards. In this environment pay systems based on
measurement of direct labor are less and less relevant. Maximizing system up-time is a far more important goal than minimizing
the labor time required for individual manufacturing operations.

Once again the implications for compensation policy are quite
clear. Measured daywork and individual incentive systems make
little sense when manufacturing tasks cannot be broken down
into measurable operations. A systems approach to manufacturing suggests a systems approach to compensation – that is, compensation practices that support the smooth and continuous operation of the system. This probably means reducing distinctions
between manual and white-collar workers, in particular elevating
manual workers to salaried status. As mentioned previously, incentive systems, if they are necessary, should be indirect and
broadly based, covering at least the work group and possibly the
entire operation. Some type of gainsharing emphasizing up-time
objectives seems most appropriate.

BARRIERS TO CHANGE

Thus far I have argued that new management systems, new
social relations of production, and new technology all suggest
that Taylorist, hierarchical, production-driven pay systems are
obsolete. Management's acceptance of this conclusion seems apparent in their demands for fewer classifications, truncated pay
structures, and termination of individual incentive pay systems.
Although some unions have initiated demands for these changes,
this movement is almost entirely management-initiated and it has
occurred suddenly and proliferated rapidly. Prior to 1980 profit
sharing was largely limited to a few retirement plans designed as
substitutes for regular pension plans; productivity gainsharing

was a marginal and rather obscure practice which by and large had not penetrated mainstream corporate America; pay-for-knowledge had not been invented; and the movement for simplified job and pay structures had barely begun.

If the old pay systems are truly obsolete, any attempts by unions to prolong the lives of these systems will probably result in a slower and less complete implementation of the new approach to manufacturing. It is difficult for a local union to know with any certainty how much cooperation is necessary to preserve high-wage jobs. Noncooperation and delay can be an effective part of any union strategy to shape these programs and insure an orderly transition to any new system. A clear understanding of the new system, a clear set of union objectives, and an action plan for implementing them are all integral to any union transition strategy. All of this takes time and frequently does not happen at all unless the union is capable of exerting direct pressure on the employer. In the long run this kind of conflict and bargaining contributes positively to successful implementation by providing workers with an effective voice in the design of the systems and in the redesign of labor relations practices like compensation policy. It can also be an important aspect of building commitment to the new systems that emerge.

The union is caught in a very difficult dilemma. The pressure to modernize can be intense. Many countries have more advanced practices than the United States; some countries have both more advanced practices and lower compensation costs. The extent of international competition varies greatly from industry to industry and product to product, but very few segments of manufacturing are unaffected. Customer-supplier relationships represent another source of pressure. One feature of the new system that is proliferating very rapidly is supplier certification programs. Major corporate customers dictate to their small and less powerful suppliers the conditions that must be met to be certified and remain a supplier. Generally these conditions include proof of quality, more responsive delivery schedules, lower prices and, less frequently, evidence of employee involvement groups or teams. As more firms within an industry adopt the new system, pressures intensify on those remaining to follow suit. If the union does not cooperate, the consequences may be immediate in the form of job loss, as in the example of a lost supply contract or the discontinuation of uncompetitive product areas, or more long-term, as in the gradual erosion of labor standards.

On the other hand, change can be very costly and extremely risky, especially in dealing with compensation systems. For one thing, union members develop powerful vested interests in existing pay systems. A piece worker who earns 160 percent of base rate and exceeds the plant average by 30 percent is not likely to support attempts to eliminate the incentive system. The paper maker on a paper machine who may have been required to accumulate seniority in other positions on the crew for twenty-five years before attaining the top classification and pay level is unlikely to support proposals for flattened wage structures and rotating work teams. A full-time job evaluation or time study steward, although well aware of the problems with these procedures, is unlikely to respond positively to developments that deemphasize their importance. A bargaining committee member is unlikely to support any of the above changes if the adversely affected are among the active and politically influential members of the local. This list of examples could easily be extended. The point is that many unions have learned to live with Taylorism.

Two aspects of union success that relate directly to compensation systems are contractual procedures that protect income and the seniority provisions that constitute a system of job control. Both are based on the premise of a Taylorist pay system and job structure. Examples of income protection language include (1) required procedures for setting fair production standards; (2) limitations on the employer's right to change existing standards; (3) provisions covering payment for work performed under nonstandard conditions and for off-standard work; (4) temporary transfer language; and (5) the right to reevaluate jobs when duties have been added. Examples of job control language include (1) required procedures for preparing job descriptions and evaluating jobs; (2) negotiated classifications and wage rates; (3) posting and bidding procedures; (4) use of seniority as the dominant principle for evaluating job bidding; and (5) seniority rules for determining who will do work outside of the classification. Not all contracts have these provisions; not all rights are easy to enforce, and many unions have seen an erosion of this type of language during the decade of the 1980s. Nevertheless, much of the language remains, and it continues to offer tangible benefits and protections to many workers.

The new pay systems nearly always threaten these benefits and protections. Consider the position of a local union bargaining committee that is asked to support structural changes in the organization of production and accept major changes in compensation practices. In previous negotiations the committee has probably been forced to accept concessions on wage levels and protective language. Employment levels are probably much lower than they were five or even ten years ago. The committee has probably not been involved in the design of the new production system. The system has probably been presented to them in pieces with no attempt to explain how it fits together, what its goals are, and why it is necessary. The new compensation system is complex and involves unfamiliar concepts. Management may be unwilling to provide information necessary to evaluate the new system properly. The membership is divided: some feel that changes are necessary to protect the remaining jobs; others feel that the changes are unnecessary or unworkable and are designed to weaken the union; no one wants to make any personal sacrifices. Under these circumstances a cautious, slow, and skeptical approach is the only rational response, even when management is loudly proclaiming that the wolf is at the door.

PRODUCTIVITY GAINSHARING

The basic concept of productivity gainsharing is simple; it is the execution that is complex.[3] In brief, productivity gainsharing is a variable compensation system that pays a bonus based on increases in productivity as measured against a collective productivity standard for the organization as a whole (or some substantial part of the organization).

The first step in designing a gainsharing formula is to determine *how productivity will be measured*. Productivity is a relationship between what goes into the production process (inputs) and what comes out (outputs). In the classic gainsharing plans like Scanlon, Modified Scanlon, Rucker, and Improshare this relationship is expressed as the ratio of inputs divided by outputs.

Each of the classic approaches differs in how inputs and outputs are measured. In Scanlon the ratio is payroll cost divided by sales value of production. In Modified Scanlon plans the input base is expanded to include other production expenses such as materials, disposable utilities, maintenance expense, depreciation, and so on, while the measure of outputs is the same. In Rucker plans the input is the same as the original Scanlon plans – payroll – but the measure of output is changed to value added. Improshare departs from all of the above and measures inputs as actual hours worked and outputs in direct labor standard hours.[4]

Many companies are now foregoing these traditional gainsharing approaches in favor of designing their own "customized" formulas; however, these customized plans are almost always variations of the traditional approaches.

Two basic distinctions are important in understanding the differences between the traditional plans. Scanlon, Modified Scanlon, and Rucker measure inputs and outputs in dollars and are referred to as monetary plans. By contrast, under Improshare both inputs and outputs are counted and evaluated without the intervention of prices; this and similar plans are referred to as physical plans. Thus the first key distinction is monetary versus physical plans.

The second distinction relates only to the input component of the productivity ratio. Scanlon, Rucker, and Improshare are based on measuring only labor inputs (payroll in the first two cases; hours worked in the latter). By contrast Modified Scanlon plans include labor and additional factors in defining inputs for purposes of measuring productivity. Thus the second key distinction is "labor only" versus multifactor plans.

Some customized plans mix the physical and monetary approaches in the same productivity ratio. An example of such an approach would be $ of Payroll:Tons of Paper, a ratio that measures inputs in monetary terms and outputs in physical terms. The matrix in Figure 15.1 illustrates these different combinations and the gainsharing plans that fit in each cell.

The choice of the productivity ratio is probably the most important decision in designing a gainsharing plan. The ratio will determine the level of risk assumed by plan participants. Physical productivity can be influenced by how hard, how smart, and how carefully people work. Hence the physical plans tend to be more responsive to the collective creativity and effort of the labor force. Monetary productivity is affected both by physical usage of inputs relative to outputs and by price movements of the inputs and outputs. If input prices are rising while product prices are flat or falling, the bonus potential of the plan will fall. Hence monetary plans involve a higher level of assumed risk because price movements are beyond the control of plan participants. Likewise, labor-only plans are less risky than multifactor plans because labor is a more controllable input than are the other factors typically included in the multifactor plans. Risk is also higher because prices of all input factors affect bonus potential.

The flip side of the risk coin is the *potential size of the target and bonus*. The multifactor plans provide a large target: bonus dollars can be earned on any factor where expense can be reduced for a given level of output. The extent of risk depends on price volatility, the extent to which participants exert real control over the various inputs, and the extent to which workers contribute and management implements.

Figure 15.1   Classification of Gainsharing Plans

Measurement of Productivity

		Physical	Monetary	Mixed
Range of	**Labor Only**	Improshare	Scanlon Rucker	Customized *Payroll* *Unit of Production*
Inputs	**Multi-factor**		Modified Scanlon (Multicost)	Customized *Production Cost* *Unit of Production*

Multifactor, monetary plans are often favored by management because they correlate more closely with profitability. Labor costs typically fall in a range of 15-40 percent of sales value of production, and in capital-intensive manufacturing can be much lower. If the ratio is low, success in improving productivity will have a small impact on total costs and gross profit. By contrast, some multifactor plans include input factors representing up to 80 percent of sales value of production. Under such plans, increased productivity as measured by the plan will almost assuredly be accompanied by increased profitability. It is not surprising that plant managers who are themselves evaluated on the basis of bottom-line results typically find the multifactor approach appealing.

If the organization is suffering from serious financial difficulties, the monetary, multifactor plans may be most appropriate because of their focus on a broad segment of production costs. Corporations live or die by their results in the monetary world. Physical productivity is an important goal, but it is a means to an end, and the end is profit. If profits are truly threatened, everyone is probably better off with a plan that is as closely linked to profitability as possible. However, one danger with the broadly cast multifactor plans is that, because of the inclusion of uncontrollable factors, they become so complex and so difficult to influence that workers feel powerless to produce positive results and lose interest in the plan. Frequently there is an inverse relationship between the inclusivity of the productivity ratio and the inherent capacity of the plan to motivate participants. For this reason it is essential under multifactor plans to provide the participants with detailed information about plan performance broken down by individual input factors, and with ongoing interpretation of the data. It is also essential to have well-established participation groups to provide a mechanism by which workers can influence performance and process results.

The *choice of productivity ratios* will also determine the complexity of measurement and the ease of monitoring plan results. Scanlon plans are simple because they are based on broad and easily tracked accounting categories: payroll and sales value of production. Scanlon is also easy to explain. By contrast, under Improshare measurement is highly complex, and monitoring requires an understanding of industrial engineering and cost accounting concepts. Multifactor plans require an understanding of accounting concepts and computerized accounting systems.

Each approach to measuring productivity has its advantages and disadvantages. None is universally superior. The tradeoffs between different approaches are subtle and complex. The choice of a ratio should be made only after the basic concepts are well understood, the specific circumstances of the company have been thoroughly analyzed, a clear set of goals has been articulated, and historical data and future projections have been exhaustively analyzed.

The union can not make intelligent decisions about gainsharing unless these conditions have been met. This means that the union must be involved from the very beginning in the process of education and design. It may mean special training for the union in industrial engineering, cost accounting, general accounting, or some other specialized field. It also means that the union must articulate the goals of its members in regard to gainsharing, and their goals must be included in the objectives of the plan. Finally, it means that the union must have access to the numbers, to computers, and to technical assistance if required. Anything short of fully meeting these conditions means that the union will not be participating as an equal in the joint design process.

Many companies have no intentions of involving the union in this manner. They make unilateral decisions, or decisions with an outside consultant, and impose the plan on a take it or leave it basis. Sometimes companies pay lip service to jointness but are unwilling to provide the educational resources, or data, or to incorporate union goals. Both of these approaches are likely to generate suspicion, ill will, and perhaps even open opposition on the part of the union. Plans that originate in this way are unlikely to be successful. Gainsharing represents a new culture and, as described earlier in the chapter, is likely to be part of a much broader and potentially more threatening set of changes in the organization. It is unlikely that the culture can be changed and the broader program successfully implemented if the union is hostile and uncooperative. To be successful the company really has no alternative to true jointness; it can do it right the first time or do it again six months or two years or six years later. Many companies learned this painful lesson in attempting to implement employee involvement groups without fully involving the union. Other companies are still in the process of learning it.

In addition to determining the productivity ratio, many other important decisions must be made in designing a gainsharing program. Who will be included in the plan – the bargaining unit only, the bargaining unit plus first line supervisors, wall-to-wall? What time period provides a fair basis for the initial measurement of productivity and the establishment of a base period ratio? What calculations will be made to determine the size of the gain? How will the gain be split between the company and the bonus pool for the workers? Will the calculations be made on a weekly, monthly, quarterly, semiannual, or annual basis? Will a portion of the gain be set aside in a reserve fund? Will bonus payments be based on a weekly or monthly moving average to smooth peaks and valleys? What principle will be used to distribute individual shares from the bonus pool? What mechanisms will be provided to inform employees of results and give them opportunities to participate actively in improving productivity? What procedures will be used to adjust the plan if basic underlying conditions change? How will disputes be resolved? What additional goals – quality, delivery reliability, customer satisfaction, and so on – should be included along with productivity improvement? How should these goals be measured and related to the productivity formula? These are complex issues, and the positions taken will have a large impact on the bonus potential and viability of the gainsharing plan.

Gainsharing is a promising concept in the new manufacturing environment. It can help to broaden workers' outlooks and focus their attention on getting quality products out the door and into the hands of the customer. It can help promote competence development and flexibility, cooperation and effective group behavior. It can result in cost reduction. It can also fail to achieve any of these goals. To be successful, gainsharing plans must provide a fair bonus opportunity; workers must be given the means to participate effectively, and they must believe that they have the power to influence plan outcomes. These conditions are most likely to be met if the plan goals and features have been jointly designed by the union and management and if the union plays an active role in implementing and monitoring the plan.

PROFIT SHARING

Profit sharing is a variable compensation system that pays a bonus based on profitability of the organization as a whole or a profit center within the organization. Many profit sharing formulas have a threshold level of profits which must be reached before any share of profits is diverted to the bonus pool. The threshold may be linked to a profit rate (4 percent return on sales; 10 percent return on equity) or it may simply be an absolute dollar volume of profits ("10 percent of all operating profits beyond $10 million will be set aside for distribution to employees").

Most of the issues in designing a profit sharing plan parallel those in gainsharing. There are several issues related to the definition and measurement of profits: (1) Is the formula based on gross, operating, pretax, or net profit? (2) Are the standard accounting definitions of profit redefined to exclude certain categories of expense or revenue? (3) Are any expense or revenue categories subject to special rules for purposes of calculating profits under the profit sharing plan (transfer pricing, depreciation, allocation of corporate expenses, etc.)? (4) Is the formula based on profit rates (return on sales, return on assets, return on equity) or absolute dollar amounts of profit? The issues related to eligibility, bonus distribution, and conflict resolution are the same as those under gainsharing.

The greatest difference between profit sharing and gainsharing lies in the area of employee involvement. Profitability is affected by far more factors outside of the influence of employees than is productivity. As a consequence it is much more difficult for workers to see the relationship between their individual efforts and the profit performance that is determining the size of the bonus. Profit sharing may result in workers paying more attention to the performance of the company. They may begin to read company financial statements and analysis by the business press, but profit sharing is unlikely to become a powerful motivator of individual behavior in the workplace. To the extent that the plan covers smaller numbers of people, as in single profit center plans, and is based on measures of profit that are higher on the income statement, such as gross and possibly operating profit, workers may develop a greater sense of control and the plan may be a more powerful motivator; but even plans with these features are likely to require that substantial attention be paid to structuring employee involvement.

This means that negotiating profit sharing should not end with the formula. Workers need to understand all of the changes that are occurring in the organization, and they need structures that allow them real influence in shaping the changes. If this is accomplished, profit sharing becomes a kind of barometer of how well the system is adapting and performing – a scorecard that generates interest in collective efforts and final outcomes.

PAY-FOR-KNOWLEDGE

Pay-for-knowledge systems violate two widely applied principles in wage setting in the United States. The first principle, central to the concept of job evaluation, is that *the job is evaluated, not the job holder* – that is, the evaluation and the pay level are determined by the duties and requirements of the job, not the characteristics of the individual. Someone may bring impressive educational credentials, twenty years of experience, and exceptional manual skills to a job, but unless the *job* requires the education, experience, and skill, the individual will not be compensated accordingly. Pay-for-knowledge backs away from this principle by tying compensation not to what the person does but to what he or she is capable of doing.

In the case of production jobs, pay-for-knowledge usually means an incremental wage supplement that is earned after the individual is trained in and qualifies for an additional set of jobs beyond some core set of tasks. The typical situation might require everyone to know five positions in a rotating crew. Upon qualifying for an additional five positions the individual would receive a pay-for-knowledge supplement, typically in the 15 to 40 cent per hour range. There may be additional supplements for learning a third or even fourth group of five jobs, but the systems are generally capped at some point.

Pay-for-knowledge differs from typical seniority provisions on temporary transfer in that once individuals qualify, they earn the supplement(s) whether they are working in their core tasks or in the peripheral activities. In other words, *individuals are paid for what they know.* This approach violates the second principle of equal pay for equal work. The main advantage of pay-for-knowledge is that it provides a direct financial incentive to learn new skills and to be flexible in accepting job assignments.

In the skilled trades, pay-for-knowledge typically means extra money for establishing minimal qualifications in crafts outside that in which the individual originally apprenticed. A journeyman electrician may receive some training and be required to pass an examination in welding. Once qualified, the electricians receive the supplement whether they are required to weld or not. Controversy with these systems centers on jurisdictional, safety, and deskilling concerns.

The general concerns of unions about pay-for-knowledge include fear of favoritism (who is given the opportunity to learn new jobs/crafts?), qualification/disqualification (who decides when an individual is qualified/what procedures are used to disqualify individuals whose skills have lapsed?), and equity (why should workers doing the same job receive different wage rates?).

Pay-for-knowledge plans are most likely to succeed in situations where the principles of payment based on job content and equal pay for equal work are least firmly established. Where these principles are widely accepted, different strategies for

achieving flexibility and skill broadening may be more successful.

CONCLUSION

The new compensations systems are best understood as part of
a new style of manufacturing. The new production system is
spreading rapidly due to powerful competitive pressures. It provides companies with a new approach to improving productivity,
controlling costs, and enhancing profitability. Unions typically
have been exposed to this system piecemeal and have had difficulty understanding the relationship between the various components of the system. Its internal logic, goals, and potential impact
have also remained obscure. This lack of clarity about the underlying production system and its relationship to compensation
practices has meant that existing pay practices have been difficult
to change and new practices have been difficult to design and
implement effectively. Unions need to adopt a strategic approach
in analyzing their interests and responding to both the new production and compensation systems. Companies that are truly interested in successfully implementing these systems must be willing to share power with unions in a genuinely joint process.

NOTES

1. Harry Braverman, *Labor and Monopoly Capital: The Degradation of
Work in the Twentieth Century* (New York: Monthly Review Press, 1974).
Braverman's book gave rise to an enormous body of work by others that de-
veloped and elaborated its themes.

2. There are many good books that stress the systems approach inherent in
JIT. See, for example, Richard T. Lubben, *Just-in-Time Manufacturing: An
Aggressive Manufacturing Strategy* (New York: McGraw-Hill, 1988), and Ya-
suhiro Monden, *Toyota Production System: Practical Approach to Production
Management* (Norcross, Ga.: Industrial Engineering and Management Press,
1983).

3. The upsurge of interest in gainsharing in the 1980s has generated a
number of new books on the subject. Some of these include Brian Graham-
Moore and Timothy Ross, *Gainsharing: Plans for Improving Performance*
(Washington, D.C.: BNA Books, 1990); Brian Graham-Moore and Timothy

Ross, *Productivity Gainsharing: How Employee Incentive Programs Can Improve Business Performance* (Englewood Cliffs, N.J.: Prentice-Hall, 1983); Institute of Industrial Engineers, *Gainsharing: A Collection of Papers* (Norcross, Ga.: Industrial Engineering and Management Press, 1983).

4. Mitchell Fein, the inventor of Improshare, has written extensively on the subject. A good introduction is his short book, *Improshare: An Alternative to Traditional Managing* (Hinsdale, N.J.: Mitchell Fein, 1981).

APPENDIXES

A.1. Interest Matrix

Organizational goals (interests) / Employee goals (interests)	market/competition			Workforce availability (adequate numbers and level of competence)	labor market		Stabilization of social environment/social progress
	Adaptation to changing market demands	Competitiveness (price, quality, quantity)	Cost minimization; profitability	Workforce availability (adequate numbers and level of competence)	Support of consumer purchasing power	Avoidance of external re-gulations (tariffs, restrictions)	Stabilization of social environment/social progress
Job security							
Fair, increasing wages							
Preservation of health and continued ability to work							
Competence preservation and further development							
Participation in organiza-tional decision-making							
Decreased separation of planning/execution functions							
Cooperation and meaningful social relationships at work							
Socially accepted/valued activity							
Profitability not at the expense of society							
Meaningful activity							
Task variety and discretion/ decision latitude							
Avoidance of unnecessary work stress							
Positive prospects for promotion/mobility							
Identification with the organization							

... related to:

Interest Matrix (continued)

... related to the organization itself

Employee goals (interests) \ Organizational goals (interests)	Optimal utilization of resources	Performance demands and increase	Minimization of conflicts	Organization specific competence development	Avoidance of training requirements (demands)	Transmission (communication) of values and norms	Protection of organizational dominance and power	Organizational attractiveness (retaining core staff)	Prevention of labor solidarity
Job security									
Fair, increasing wages									
Preservation of ability to work									
Preservation and further development of competence									
Participation in organizational decision-making									
Reduction of separation of planning/execution functions									
Adequate social relationships									
Socially accepted/valued activity									
Profitability not at the expense of society									
Meaningful activity									
Task variety and discretion									
Avoidance of unnecessary work stress									
Positive future prospects									
Identification with the organization									

A.2. Subjective Task Analysis Questionnaire[1]

For the various tasks in your department assign a value from 0 to 10 to each task for each of the characteristics listed below. (0=lowest value; 10=highest value)

	Task 1	Task 2	Task 3	...	Task n
Elbow Room/ Decision latitude					
Variety					
Learning Opportunities					
Mutual Support / Respect					
Meaningful Contribution					
Future Prospects					
TOTAL					

A.3. Subjective Job Assessment Questionnaire[2]

	Not at all true	Some-what untrue	Neither true nor untrue	Some-what true	Very true
1. My job requires the use of a variety of re-sources (tools, docu-ments, etc.).	1	2	3	4	5
2. People stick together in this department.	1	2	3	4	5
3. I am responsible for the tools and equip-ment I use on my job.	1	2	3	4	5
4. My job requires thor-ough training.	1	2	3	4	5
5. My job allows me to determine the pace of my work.	1	2	3	4	5
6. My supervisor ac-knowledges my ef-forts.	1	2	3	4	5
7. I can do what I do best in this job.	1	2	3	4	5
8. How my job is to be done is exactly pre-scribed.	1	2	3	4	5

	Not at all true	Some- what untrue	Neither true nor untrue	Some- what true	Very true
9. What I've learned in this job I can always use again somewhere else.	1	2	3	4	5
10. I usually have to hurry to get my job done.	1	2	3	4	5
11. My job lets me know how well I've done it.	1	2	3	4	5
12. My job provides op- portunities to move ahead.	1	2	3	4	5
13. My job requires inde- pendent decision- making.	1	2	3	4	5
14. My job allows me to talk with co-workers while I work.	1	2	3	4	5
15. If I don't do my job right, my co-workers would suffer.	1	2	3	4	5
16. I have to do things for which I don't really have the necessary knowledge and preparation.	1	2	3	4	5
17. I have so much to do that I feel like I'm in over my head.	1	2	3	4	5

		Not at all true	Some-what untrue	Neither true nor untrue	Some-what true	Very true
18.	My job allows me to move around.	1	2	3	4	5
19.	The workers support each other in this department.	1	2	3	4	5
20.	My job requires that I have to be able to react fast.	1	2	3	4	5
21.	My job requires close cooperation with other people in the organization.	1	2	3	4	5
22.	I know how work is organized in this department.	1	2	3	4	5
23.	I know how my job fits into the bigger picture.	1	2	3	4	5
24.	Sometimes my job seems too difficult.	1	2	3	4	5
25.	I know what co-workers are doing in their jobs.	1	2	3	4	5
26.	This job gives me responsibilities.	1	2	3	4	5

	Not at all true	Some-what untrue	Neither true nor untrue	Some-what true	Very true
27. My job allows me to learn new things.	1	2	3	4	5
28. My supervisor criticizes people in the presence of others.	1	2	3	4	5
29. So much is happening on my job that I can hardly manage.	1	2	3	4	5
30. I feel closely watched and controlled on my job.	1	2	3	4	5
31. I know what my job is all about.	1	2	3	4	5
32. My job is important for things to run smoothly in this department.	1	2	3	4	5
33. My job offers a lot of variety.	1	2	3	4	5
34. My supervisor is supportive of and interested in people's work.	1	2	3	4	5
35. I can use all my skills and abilities in my job.	1	2	3	4	5

	Not at all true	Some-what untrue	Neither true nor untrue	Some-what true	Very true
36. If needed, I get help from my co-workers.	1	2	3	4	5
37. My job is demanding.	1	2	3	4	5
38. I can see what happens with the product of my job.	1	2	3	4	5
39. My job gives me the feeling that I've really accomplished something.	1	2	3	4	5
40. My job involves tasks that are too complicated.	1	2	3	4	5
41. Making mistakes on my job could be costly.	1	2	3	4	5
42. My job allows me to decide myself how I want to do it.	1	2	3	4	5
43. My job requires co-ordination with co-workers.	1	2	3	4	5
44. My job requires that I do too many things at once.	1	2	3	4	5

	Not at all true	Some-what untrue	Neither true nor untrue	Some-what true	Very true
45. Workers here also know what other de-partments do.	1	2	3	4	5
46. My job allows me to show what I've learned.	1	2	3	4	5
47. My job is boring.	1	2	3	4	5
48. My job can only be done well in coopera-tion with co-workers.	1	2	3	4	5
49. How I do my job af-fects the health and safety of co-workers.	1	2	3	4	5
50. My job requires that I do the same thing over and over again.	1	2	3	4	5

ANALYSIS OF SUBJECTIVE JOB ASSESSMENT QUESTIONNAIRE

For the analysis of the Subjective Job Assessment Question-naire the items should be grouped according to the list below. If this questionnaire is completed by a small work group, analysis can be done by adding the number of employees checking each box and thus identifying the areas with the lowest scores, which might need to be the focus of change. (Note: The score for the items marked with an asterisk needs to be reversed! Also: For high scores in area 6, work pressures, obviously also represent negative findings and need to be reversed.)

If this type of analysis is to encompass a larger group of em-ployees in different departments, it is useful to use a statistical computer program package for analyzing the data.

1.   SCOPE OF ACTION/DECISION LATITUDE

1.1. Autonomy
   5)   My job allows me to determine the pace of my work
   8)   How my job is to be done is exactly prescribed*
   18)   My job allows me to move around
   30)   I feel closely watched and controlled on my job*
   42)   My job allows me to decide how I want to do it

1.2. Variability
   1)   My job requires the use of a variety of resources (e.g., tools, documents, etc.)
   33)   My job offers a lot of variety
   47)   My job is boring*
   50)   My job requires that I do the same thing over and over again*

2.   UNDERSTANDABILITY/TRANSPARENCY

2.1. Understandability of Task
   11)   My job lets me know how well I've done overall
   23)   I know how my job fits into the bigger picture
   31)   I know what my job is all about
   38)   I can see what happens with the product of my job
   39)   My job gives me the feeling that I've really accom-plished something

2.2. Social Transparency
    22)   I know how work is organized in this department
    25)   I know what my co-workers are doing in their jobs
    45)   Workers here also know what other departments do

3.   RESPONSIBILITY

3.1. Responsibility for a Shared Goal (status)
    15)   If I don't do my job right, my co-workers would suffer
    26)   This job gives me responsibilities
    32)   My job is important for things to run smoothly in this department

3.2. Responsibility for Materials and Other People
    3)   I am responsible for the tools and equipment I use on my job
    41)   Making mistakes on my job could be costly
    49)   How I do my job affects the health and safety of co-workers

4.   QUALIFICATION

4.1. Job Demands (qualitative)
    4)   My job requires thorough training
    13)   My job requires independent decision-making
    20)   My job requires that I have to be able to react fast
    37)   My job is demanding

4.2. Utilization
    7)   I can do what I do best in this job
    35)   I can use all my skills and abilities in my job
    46)   My job allows me to show what I've learned

4.3. Future Prospects (psychological)
    9)   What I've learned in this job I can always use again somewhere else
    12)   My job provides opportunities to move ahead
    27)   My job allows me to learn new things

5.   SOCIAL STRUCTURE

5.1. Co-worker Support
2)   People stick together in this department
19)   The workers support each other in this department
36)   If needed, I get help from my co-workers

5.2. Cooperation (Interdependence)
21)   My job requires close cooperation with other people in the organization
43)   My job requires coordination with co-workers
48)   My job can only be done well in cooperation with co-workers

5.2. Supervisor Support and Respect
6)   My supervisor acknowledges my efforts
28)   My supervisor criticizes people in the presence of others*
34)   My supervisor is supportive of and interested in people's work

6.   WORK PRESSURES

6.1. Workload (quantitative overload)*
10)   I usually have to hurry to get my job done
17)   I have so much to do that I feel like I'm in over my head
29)   So much is happening on my job that I can hardly manage
44)   My job requires that I do too many things at once

6.2. Demands (qualitative overload)*
16)   I have to do things for which I don't really have the necessary knowledge and preparation
24)   Sometimes my job seems too difficult
40)   My job involves tasks that are too complicated

A.4. Work Assessment Questionnaire

How would you describe the following aspects of your current job?	++	+	+/-	-	--
Variety					
Freedom to plan my own work					
Possibility of checking my own work					
Work pace					
Prerequisites for doing the job well					
Ability to use my knowledge and skills					
Opportunity to learn new things					
Difficulty of work					
Working environment (noise, lighting, temperature, ventilation)					
Working hours/schedule					
Workload (physical/mental)					
Respect and support from colleagues					

Support from and relation-ship with supervisor					
Appreciation of efforts / sense of achievement					
Opportunities for devel-opment / further education and training					
Clarity of work flow					
Access to information					
Importance of my work within the department as a whole					
Cooperation with other units					
Cooperation within my department					
Relationship between au-thority and responsibilities					
Other …					

A.5. Job Satisfaction Questionnaire[3]

This questionnaire addresses a variety of job characteristics that can influence people's satisfaction with the work they do. Please check the appropriate box for each item, indicating how important these aspects are for your job satisfaction.

	not at all important	somewhat important	quite important	very important
Task variety				
Being able to determine when I do what				
Low time pressure				
Being able to use my knowledge and skills				
Being able to learn new things				
Challenging work				
Good work environment (noise, temperature, cleanliness)				
Work schedule/working hours				
Low physical effort				
Low psychological stress				

Good relationships with co-workers				
Good relationships with supervisors				
Recognition by my peers				
Society respects my work				
Promotion prospects				
Good wages and benefits				
Job security				
Good union representation				
Vacation time				
Other aspects (please specify)				

Please indicate below how satisfied you are at this point with the following aspects of your job.

	very dis-satisfied	somewhat dissatis-fied	somewhat satisfied	very satisfied
Task variety				
Being able to determine when I do what				
Low time pressure				
Being able to use my knowledge and skills				
Being able to learn new things				
Challenging work				
Good work environment (noise, temperature, cleanliness)				
Work schedule/working hours				
Low physical effort				
Low psychological stress				
Good relationships with co-workers				

Good relationships with supervisors				
Recognition by my peers				
Society respects my work				
Promotion prospects				
Good wages and benefits				
Job security				
Good union representation				
Vacation time				
Other aspects (please specify)				

NOTES

1. Emery and Emery, *Participative Design: Work and Community.* Also: Eberhard Ulich, "Subjektive Tätigkeitsanalyse als Voraussetzung autonomie-orientierter Arbeitsgestaltung," in Felix Frei and Eberhard Ulich (eds.), *Beiträge zur psychologischen Arbeitsanalyse* (Bern, Switzerland: Huber, 1981), pp. 327-347.

2. Ivars Udris and Andreas Alioth, "Fragebogen zur Subjektiven Arbeitsanalyse," in E. Martin, I. Udris, U. Ackermann, and K. Oegerli, *Monotonie in der Industrie* (Bern, Switzerland: Huber, 1980), pp. 61-68; 204-207.

3. Luzian Ruch and Norbert Troy, *Textverarbeitung im Sekretariat* (Zürich, Switzerland: Verlag der Fachvereine, 1986).

Author Index

Subject Index

ability, 22
absenteeism, 50, 100
Alcatel STR, 175-189
American Revolution, 41
American Society of Mechanical
Engineers (ASME), 44
American working class, 41
apprentice system, 269
assembly line, 46
attribution fallacy, 128
automated systems, 291-292; flexible manufacturing systems, 67
automobile industry, 80-112
autonomous or self-managed work
groups, 162, 290
autonomy, 10, 20, 192

bargaining: unit, 299; adversarial,
271; and adversarial tactics,
264; cooperative-integrative,
271
barriers, 152, 195; to optimal performance, 250
behavior, 20, 23, 29, 32, 364 128-
131
beliefs, 19
Bethlehem Steel, 45
bonus systems, 291
bottom-up, 193; assessment, 219

boundary maintenance, 160
brainstorming technique, 253
British coal mining industry, 53
business policy, 207

capitalism: family, 43; finance, 43;
industrial, 42; managerial, 43
card week, 255
career models, 200
cause-effect thinking, 129
cell manufacturing, 67, 71, 288,
290
centralization, 64; centralized
structure, 192
change process, 6, 34, 125
Chrysler, 268
codetermination, 266
collective activity, 164
collective bargaining, 261-265,
268; agreement, 201; process,
271
collective productivity standard,
295
collective resource approach, 55
collective responsibility, 198
communication, 30, 124, 125, 139,
165; barriers, 188

About the Authors

FELIX FREI is co-owner and Director of AOC, Zurich, an international consulting firm working with companies and labor unions on leadership, organization redesign, and competence development projects. He is a former research scientist at the Institute for Work and Organizational Psychology of the Swiss Federal Institute of Technology in Zurich, and directed a research project on competence development through work activity sponsored by the "Humanization of Worklife" fund of the German Department of Research and Technology. He has contributed numerous books and articles to the German work psychology literature.

MARGRIT HUGENTOBLER is Adjunct Research Scientist at the Institute of Labor and Industrial Relations and the School of Public Health at the University of Michigan. Her work is concerned with the improvement of work environments through participatory approaches to work design, occupational health and safety, and workplace stress. She currently lives in Switzerland where she works at the Swiss Federal Institute of Technology in Zurich. She has co-authored articles which have appeared in such journals as *Health Education Quarterly*, *Labor Studies Journal*, *Journal of Occupational Medicine*, and *Journal of Applied Behavioral Science*.

SUSAN SCHURMAN is Director of the Labor Extension Center at the Institute of Management and Labor Relations at Rutgers University. Both her research and practice focus on how to redesign work to improve the outcomes for both employers and employees. She has co-authored many articles and book chapters in U.S. and international publications in the fields of employee participation, workplace health, and occupational stress.

WERNER DUELL is the Executive Director and co-owner of AOC Berlin, and was previously a member of the research team at the Institute for Work and Organizational Psychology of the Swiss Federal Institute of Technology in Zurich. His practice as a consultant focuses on work design and organization development. His research addresses the utilization of industrial robots in Switzerland and the impact of computer-based control systems on work activities. Jointly with Felix Frei, Werner Duell authored the original "Leitfaden für qualifizierende Arbeitsgestaltung" on which this volume is based.

ANDREAS ALIOTH is co-owner and Director of AOC, Zurich. He was a fellow at the Institute for Work and Organizational Psychology of the Swiss Federal Institute of Technology in Zurich and is currently teaching business administration at the University of St. Gallen. His research and practice focus on leadership, organization development, and the implementation of alternative work design. From 1982-1989 he directed the Swiss national research program: Work Life: Humanization and Technological Change. He is the editor of the publication series "Working World."